THAT TIME WE *Kissed* UNDER THE *Mistletoe*

JULIE CHRISTIANSON

This one's for Auntie Karen, who makes Christmas a little more special each year.

And for Uncle Kurt, who taught us all to believe in second-chance love.
(I adore you both!)

Chapter One

Sara

I've been at my family's new lake house for less than an hour, and a dozen smoke detectors are already wailing. Or maybe it only *sounds* like a dozen smoke detectors. After all, I'm in the middle of the Adirondacks. In December. The snow-covered mountains, towering pine trees, and frozen lake *could* be causing an echo. Then there's the fact that I'm hungry, which—let's face it— makes everything worse.

Either way, what could possibly be burning?

I swear I was only preheating the oven.

Oh, Sara. Curse you and your obsession with fresh-baked brownies.

Thanks to my goal of single-handedly supporting Betty Crocker—not to mention avoiding a certain lifelong resident of Abieville—I'd made a pit stop at a market outside of town before I even got here. Along with enough grocery staples to help me survive my current mission, I bought a box of chocolate fudge brownie mix.

What can I say? I'm a big fan of fudge.

That is, when my ears aren't exploding.

As smoke snakes across the freshly painted kitchen, I snatch the fire extinguisher from the pantry and haul open the oven door. Clouds of gray smoke billow out like an appliance tornado. Unfortunately the burst of oxygen only riles up the flames. Coughing and choking, I try to engage the fire extinguisher, but nothing happens.

"Nooooo!"

The thing should be brand new, but it must be defective. Which is *so* not convenient. My parents bought this house six months ago and renovated every inch of it, hoping to turn the home into a high-end rental property. So burning the whole place down right before Christmas would be a less-than-holly-jolly glitch to everyone's holiday.

Grabbing the stainless steel bowl I'd planned to use to mix the batter, I quickly fill it at the sink, then I spin around and toss the water directly into the flames. Unfortunately, half the liquid doesn't reach the oven, and the other half just seems to anger the fire gods.

Still, I refuse to give up without a fight. So I refill and toss another bowlful of water at the fire. Then a third. Half blinded by waves of smoke, I listen as steam sizzles and pops in the blackness. That, at least, sounds promising.

Stepping forward—gasping and waving—I peer at my results. The flames seem to be out, so at least the immediate emergency is over. But there's a mystery pile of ... something ... still smoldering inside.

Wait ... are those ... dish towels? And cloth napkins? Place-mats? Yep. And they're all printed with Santa's reindeer. Make that Santa's *very charred* reindeer. Which means this is the full set of matching kitchen linens I gave my mother last Christmas.

So how did they end up in the oven here?

I suddenly flash back to my mom telling me she was sending some of our "extra" home goods off with the movers so future guests could enjoy them in Abieville. She explained people vacationing in the Adirondacks would expect rustic appointments, not Waterford and Limoges. And apparently deer placemats equal rustic.

So in this moment, I've learned a few important things:

1. Moving companies sometimes stick stuff in ridiculous places.
2. Impulse brownies come with unexpected risks.
3. Katherine Hathaway thinks my Christmas gift is ... "extra."

I guess I shouldn't be *too* surprised. My parents love me a lot —almost *too* much sometimes—but they're also sticklers for appearance and tradition. Our family traces its roots back to the Mayflower, and their appreciation for pedigree knows no limits. So while this particular set of linens came from a luxury store, the pattern is definitely on the kitschy side.

Not exactly repping that Hathaway life.

So long, New York City penthouse.

Hello, small-town Abieville.

My family started coming here the summer I was fourteen. That's when a client of my father's offered up his vacation house as a thank-you for some long-shot settlement outside of court. The location was perfect: far enough from the city that it felt like a getaway for my mom and me, but close enough for my dad to visit us on weekends.

We all stopped coming to the lake after I went off to college, but when the owner passed away last spring, my parents bought the place, hoping to get it listed on Platinum Stays.

For the record, Platinum Stays is an exclusive vacation rental site that requires an evaluation of potential listings before they'll give their seal of approval. Unfortunately, the scheduled home visit fell just days before our family's annual fundraising gala on Christmas Eve.

A.K.A. my birthday.

The Hathaway Gala raises tons of money each year, which we always donate to Children's Village. The cause is almost as important to my parents as I am, so we all agreed my mom couldn't possibly leave the city in the final days of planning. That's why I volunteered to come to Abieville to handle the home evaluation myself. What can I say? I'm a team player who also thrives on pleasing my parents. And all I had to do was meet with an evaluator from Platinum Stays.

And oh, yeah, *not* burn down the house.

So far, I'm doing a less-than-stellar job on my first goal. Which makes me a little worried about my second goal: avoiding Three.

Not the number three.

I'm talking about Three Fuller.

The man.

Three's actual name is Bradford Fuller, in case you're wondering why any parent would saddle their offspring with a digit for a first name. Mrs. Fuller didn't. What she *did* do is join all her sisters in using their maiden name—Bradford—for their sons. And since all the male cousins are also named Bradford, each baby got a nickname handed to him at birth.

Mac. Ford. Three. Brady. You get the picture.

Three *the man* broke my heart ten years ago, right here in Abieville. On Main Street, to be specific. And I already have a hard enough time not thinking about Three now, which is awfully annoying after a decade.

My best friend, Bristol, warned me being in this town again might rev the engine of my Three-thinking. So I promised her I'd keep away from him at all costs. But I can't focus on keeping away from anyone while this kitchen's full of smoke.

Maybe I should try the extinguisher one more time just to be absolutely positive the fire's out. With a bit more effort and a lot of luck, my mom and dad might never have to hear about this. Which would be good for me, not to mention good for whoever temporarily stored my mom's rustic reindeer in the oven.

My hands are still a little shaky, but I pick up the fire extinguisher again. No dice. This thing is definitely busted. After taking a couple of deep breaths to calm my nerves, I peer through the dark haze at the stainless steel oven that betrayed me. And that's when the side door into the kitchen flies open with a bang behind my back.

For the record, this door leads out to a lakefront surrounded by acres and acres of tall, snow-heaped pine trees. I've stayed here enough summers to know this property has plenty of space for murder.

If I screamed no one would hear me.

A gust of icy winter air raises goose bumps on my neck, and I spin around to face my intruder. I can barely see through the smoke, just enough to make out a pair of broad shoulders filling the doorway. The intruder appears to be dressed all in black. The hoodie over his head is drawn tight like a robber's mask. Without thinking, I rush forward and heave the fire extinguisher at his head.

"Get out!" I howl as the metal thunks off of the robber's skull, and he goes down hard. "I'm calling the police!" Yanking my phone from my pocket, I'm about to call 911, when I hear the front door slam open across the house.

Seriously?

When did Abieville become a village of people busting down doors?

From the entryway a deep voice calls out, "Hey! Everyone all right in here?"

"Help!" I shriek. "I'm probably being robbed." Then I realize whoever's in the doorway could be a robber too. "I've got a fire extinguisher," I shout, "and I'm not afraid to use it!"

Sure the extinguisher is broken, but the front-door robber doesn't know that. So I sneak along the wall, tip-toeing toward the dining room, prepared to make my escape into the backyard. And that's when two men dressed in sweats and beanies burst around the corner from the entryway.

"Don't come any closer!" I chuck my phone at the taller one in front, but it bounces off his big body, clattering to the floor.

"Whoa, lady. Are you nuts?" asks the smaller of the two men. As both their gazes follow the trajectory of my phone from the ground upward, I catch my first glimpse of the taller one's face. Then I have to gulp to keep from throwing up.

Because the tall stranger is none other than Three's cousin, Ford Lansing.

Welp. This is awkward.

"Ack! Sorry, Ford," I manage to choke out. "I thought you might be trying to rob me."

When Ford hears me say his name, he does a double take, squinting down at me. "Sara Hathaway?" His eyes slowly widen. Like teacup-saucer wide. "I haven't seen you in—what's it been— ten years? What are *you* doing here?"

"Oh, you know. Just putting out a fire." I chuckle nervously, nodding to indicate the kitchen behind us. Meanwhile my cheeks flame up hotter than the reindeer I just roasted. Not only is Ford a firefighter, but I'm sure he's heard all about how Three broke my heart.

I met Three and his cousins my first summer in Abievlle. We all hit it off, but there was a special spark between Three and me. We quickly became a thing—just a sweet, innocent romance. At least that's what I told my parents. But by the end of August, I had to face facts: I'd grown real feelings for Three.

Every summer after, we spent as many waking minutes together as we could, and we spent the rest of the school year longing for June again. By the time college rolled around, I was blindly in love. And by that I mean I'd fooled myself into believing Three loved me back.

So on our last night together, I offered him my whole heart along with my commitment to a long-distance relationship. That's when Three Fuller dumped me, and my first love went up in flames.

Now that I just scorched a bunch of oven mitts in an actual

oven? Ford's probably going to think I'm even more pathetic than I was a decade ago. As evidence of my theory, his face wrenches into a frown. "No, I mean what are you doing back in Abieville?" he asks. "I figured you'd be lawyering it up in the city by now."

"Oh. That." More nervous chuckles from me. Then, to make matters worse, I begin to babble. "I actually spent a few years after undergrad working internships, building up my resume before law school. But I *should be* offered a position at my dad's firm soon. And I'm here now because my parents bought this house to turn into a rental property. Except they want it listed on some exclusive site that requires an evaluation first. Platinum Stays. My mom calls it the Rolls Royce of vacation rental sites."

A wave of hysterical laughter bursts from me.

Why, Sara? Why?

There's zero chance Ford Lansing cares about my parents or their soot-filled lake house. Not to mention some exclusive new vacation rental site. Still, my adrenaline's pumping too hard for me to stop now. "Anyway, Platinum Stays scheduled the home evaluation for December 21st," I ramble on.

"Tomorrow?"

I nod. "Which is super-inconvenient since my parents have this big fundraiser thing they do every year on the 24th. Actually, it's a full-on gala. And Christmas Eve is also my birthday. So yeah. It's a lot for them to juggle. Heh heh heh." I flash a desperate smile at Ford and the other guy, who's now staring at me like I've lost my mind.

Yes, sir. I do not disagree with you.

"So"—my shoulders slowly creep up—"I offered to come to Abieville for a few days to handle the process for my parents. And when I stopped for groceries, I got some brownie mix. You know. To make brownies." I pause for a breath, but I'm pretty much having an out-of-body experience, hovering above an iceberg of awkwardness in the dining room. "Unfortunately, some movers with bad ideas stuck my mom's reindeer placemats in the oven, and I accidentally set them on fire. I was just putting out the flames when this intruder broke in! See?"

I grab Ford by the elbow, dragging him into the kitchen and over to the hooded man sprawled face down on the floor. "So I defended myself with a fire extinguisher."

"Yeah, you did." Ford shakes his head, squatting to check out the body. When he rolls the limp stranger over, the man's face is covered in blood and hoodie. I squeeze my eyes shut.

"I'm too freaked out to look," I moan. "Is he dead?"

"Nah." Ford grunts. "But he's no intruder either. That's my cousin, Three."

Great smoldering reindeers.

My second goal just went up in smoke.

Chapter Two

Three

As I start to regain consciousness, I have no idea where I am or what just happened to me. The only thing my brain's computing is an absolute monster of a headache. From what I can tell, a trio of blurry shapes are crowded over my body. I start to lift my head, but all I see are stars. When my already-foggy vision tunnels into a woozy blackness with fresh zaps of light, I try to sit all the way up like that might help the situation.

Newsflash: it doesn't.

"Take it easy now, Three," says the medium-sized blur. I can't quite place the voice, but I'm pretty sure I know the guy. "Let's do this slow." As he helps me into a seated position, something warm trickles along the nape of my neck. Smells like copper.

Must be blood.

Where am I?

"Ouch," I grunt. Pain shoots through my skull, making me wince.

"You *are* alive!" squeaks a woman with a high-pitched voice. Let's call her Little Blur. She's a brunette I think, based on my fuzzy view. I shake my head to clear the fog, but that only makes the dizziness worse.

"People who are un-alive can't sit up," I mumble.

"Zombies sit up," she blurts. "I mean ... not to argue with you. But."

I wince again. "I'm not a zombie."

"Are you sure?" A snort comes out of the extra-large blur with the extra-deep voice. "By the end of last night's poker game, you looked a lot like the undead."

I shift my crossed eyes over to the bulky shape. Even with my vision blurred, I recognize that voice. Ford.

Right.

Now I remember where I am.

My cousin and I had been out for an early evening jog around the lake with Kenny Monroe.

The medium blur.

"I get up at the crack of dawn to teach high school kids all week," I grumble. "Of course I'm tired by Friday night. Plus winning all your money is exhausting." I make a half-hearted effort to stand, but Ford lays a hand on my shoulder to stop me.

"Stay down until we get you checked out," he commands.

Running a hand around my scalp, I assess the surface damage myself. From what I can gather by feel alone, I've got a goose egg on my forehead big enough for its own zip code. There's also a gash at the base of my skull I probably got on my way down.

That's where the blood's coming from.

The midsized blur—Kenny—bends down to examine my lumpy head.

"Hey, Ken," I groan pressing my eyes shut again, fighting a thick wave of nausea. To keep from puking, I dip my head, chin to collarbone.

"Looks like you got nailed pretty good," Kenny says. He's a paramedic. Ends up on calls with Ford all the time. "You probably got a concussion."

"I didn't *get* anything." I lift my chin. "Somebody *gave* it to me." From off to the side, a voice yelps. This is the woman. The one who beaned me.

Little blur.

Before landing the blow to my head, she whirled around so quickly, I didn't even get a look at her. I just went down. Now I swallow hard. Open one eye. Settle my gaze on the petite brunette. Then I almost hurl for real. Because I'm the guy who once convinced Sara Hathaway I wanted to end things between us. That my feelings were never as deep as hers.

Lies.

It was for her own good, though. At least that's what I told myself ten years ago, and I still stand by the decision. But what on earth is *she* doing back in Abieville now?

In this exact house?

"You hit me," I groan, gulping down a swell of acid in my throat. If Sara remembers the last time we were together, she probably thinks she had a pretty good reason to deck me.

"I did." Her cheeks flush pink now, like the cotton candy we used to get at the 4th of July carnival. When she starts chewing her lip, I swear I can taste the sugar mixed with her cherry Chapstick.

Ford huffs out a breath, leans against the counter. "Good thing you've got such a thick skull. And a little blood never killed anyone." My cousin's one of only two people who knows what really went down with Sara and me. The other one's my sister. I tell Nella everything, too.

Well. *Almost* everything.

"I could've killed you," Sara blurts. "What were you thinking, breaking into a house without knocking?" There's a thread of panic in her question, and she pushes a strand of long black hair behind her ear. Then she blinks at me. Lake-dark eyes. Enormous lashes. She's even more beautiful than she was a decade ago. When I open my mouth to speak, no words come.

So Ford answers for me.

"Kenny, Three, and I were jogging along the lake," he says.

"We thought we smelled smoke. Then we heard the detectors go off. Three's way faster than us, so he sprinted ahead."

Sara's eyes are all black pupils and smoke-gray irises. "You were trying to help?" She keeps her gaze locked on mine. "I'm so sorry."

Her voice is soft now, and a twinge of sympathy for her pings behind my ribs. But I refuse to let my defenses down. Being around the Hathaways always made me feel less than. Unworthy and adrift. So Sara's a slippery slope I can't afford to get my heart anywhere near.

Not again.

"I thought some faulty wiring might've started a fire," I mutter, finally forcing myself to speak. "Everyone in town knows this place is being renovated. I didn't want the empty house to burn down, so I tried the back door. It was unlocked. I assumed the contractors left it that way, so I came in." I cringe a little as my head throbs in two different places. "I had no idea anyone was staying here." I furrow my brow, peering up at Sara. "Why *are* you staying here?"

She takes a beat. Works her jaw. "My parents bought this place after Mr. Peabody died. They're the ones renovating it."

Whoa.

My insides churn.

This is bad news. The *worst.*

The Hathaways only ever used this house as a summer getaway. Once they stopped coming, I assumed I'd never have to see them or Sara again. But now her parents are going to live on Abie Lake permanently? She'll be visiting all the time. I'll never be able to escape her.

This town is way too small.

"Huh." Ford scratches his temple. "I'm kinda surprised the Abieville gossip mill didn't know your folks were the ones moving here." He snaps a glance at me. "Aunt Elaine and Betty Slater are usually on top of intel like this. Did you have any idea?"

I scowl at him. "Obviously not."

"Well, this is just an investment property," Sara hurries to say. "And my dad's always discreet when it comes to finances. He hired a third-party management company to handle the purchase and remodel, so our name probably isn't on any of the paperwork." She glances around the smoky kitchen, wrinkling her nose. "For the record, I tried putting out the fire, but the extinguisher malfunctioned."

Ford bends down to pick up the abandoned fire extinguisher. "Did you try pulling the pin?"

She blinks at him. "The what?"

"The pin." He shakes his head, and a crooked smirk creeps across his face. "It's kinda hard to get a fire extinguisher to function with the pin still engaged."

"Well. I. Uh." Her throat starts to blotch. "I did not know that."

"Don't feel too bad," he says. "You aren't the first person that's happened to in this town. Natalie Slater—our cousin Brady's wife—she did the same thing a few summers back."

"The day of Kasey and Beau's wedding," Kenny chimes in. "That was a whole thing."

Sara's brow lifts. "Brady's married to Natalie now? And Kasey married Beau? Wow."

"Yeah." Instead of elaborating, Ford sets the extinguisher down where I'm still slumped on the floor. When he straightens, I follow his gaze to the smoldering oven.

"So how did the fire start, anyway?" I ask.

"I was baking brownies," she says, a tiny shrug hitching her shoulders.

"These appear to be well done," Ford snarks, peeking inside the oven. "Personally, I prefer my baked goods a little more on the gooey side."

A small laugh slips out of Sara now, and I'm transported back to those long summer days we spent together. Boating on the lake. Swimming at the beach. Strolling down Main Street with ice cream cones. She'd stop to lick the drips off of her wrist, and all I'd want to do is taste her sweet lips.

Every single time.

"All jokes aside," Kenny says, reaching down to me, "we need to get you off the floor, man." He and Ford help me stagger into a chair. Then Kenny takes my pulse. Stares into my eyes. Moves his finger back and forth while I'm supposed to track it. "You gotta be checked out at the hospital," he says. "I'll call a rig. Take you to Northampton Medical."

"No ambulance." I grimace. "I can slap a Band-Aid on that cut and call it a day."

"You lost consciousness," Kenny says. "Plus you're nauseated. Blurred vision. Could be serious."

I wave his comments away. "I got at least one concussion playing football in high school."

"All the more reason to get your head checked," Ford points out.

"I don't need the doctor to tell me I should take it easy for a day or two."

"Sorry, but self-diagnosis is a no-go," Kenny persists. "You could be more injured than you realize."

"Fine," I mutter under my breath. "But save the emergency vehicles for people who really need them. I can drive myself to the ER."

"NO WAY!" Ford shakes his head, like he's scolding me. "Driving after a head injury is totally unsafe. The fact that you're even suggesting it proves you're at least a little bit off."

I blink up at him, chagrined.

What if Ford is right? My brain could be swelling right now, influencing my decision-making. And even on non-brain-injury days, I'm prone to bad choices.

Like falling for Sara Hathaway in the first place.

"Besides." Ford shrugs. "We were running around the lake, so you don't have a car here, remember? None of us does."

"I do," Sara says softly. "I drove a rental out from the city."

She leans over me, and a whisper of her perfume slams my brain even harder than that fire extinguisher. "This is all my fault," she adds, her voice a little breathless. "I can take Three to the hospital."

I cringe. "Absolutely not."

Ford darts his gaze at me, a flash of amusement in his eyes, then he turns to Kenny. "Guess you better call the rig, then."

"Don't." I clench my jaw, sending more pain spiraling through my cranium.

"We're kinda out of other options," Kenny insists.

"So what do you say, man?" Ford asks. His mouth slips sideways. "Life-saving vehicle, or Sara?"

Oof. *What's the bigger emergency?*

I heave out a groan. "I pick Option C."

Chapter Three

Sara

Newsflash, there is no Option C.

But ultimately Ford came up with a compromise: I'd drop all the men off at Ford's. Then Ford and Three would drop Kenny off at his house. Then Ford could drive Three up to Northampton to drop Three off at the ER.

Yes, that's a whole lot of dropping. But I'm used to that in Abieville.

Especially Three dropping me.

The good news? I didn't actually have to drive Three to the hospital. Unnecessary time alone with him is the last thing I need. Plus Bristol would kill me if she found out I volunteered to do it.

So you're probably wondering why I decided to brave the snowy roads and follow Ford's car all the way to Northampton anyway. The answer is guilt, plain and simple. Seeing Three all fogged-up and disoriented on the kitchen floor had me kind of queasy. He looked so vulnerable and blurry-eyed and shaggy-haired. And I was to blame for any potential injury he might've sustained.

Am to blame, I mean.

So I just had to make sure I didn't mortally wound Three. One quick trip to the ER, and I'd be back to isolating myself at the lake house until Christmas Eve.

Fa la la la la, la la la la.

Joy to the world.

That's what I hum to myself on the drive to Northampton. All the houses on the way are decked out with lights across the rooftops and wreaths on the front doors. Most of the windows have electric candles glowing in them. They don't do that in the city, and I kinda love that about this place.

The hospital's waiting room is pretty holiday-centric too, which is a welcome change from the completely undecorated lake house. After all, my parents weren't expecting anyone to be staying there until the new year.

So I'm in the waiting room now ... waiting ... waiting... as a lively version of "We Need a Little Christmas" leaks through overhead speakers. There's an artificial tree in the corner loaded with twinkle lights and glittery ornaments. Poinsettias surround the check-in window, where a hulk of a man in blue scrubs sits sorting files.

Despite the holiday decor, he looks about as happy to be here on a Saturday as I am. Across from me a white-haired lady is knitting a scarf that looks long enough to stretch to the North Pole. When the song reaches the part about slicing up the fruitcake, my stomach growls. Loudly.

Oof.

I really wanted those brownies.

Craning my neck down the hallway off the lobby, I hope to spot a vending machine in case I'm stuck here for much longer. Maybe there are some down by the restrooms. I could go for a Snickers bar. Or some Goldfish crackers. Cheetos. Anything to keep me from gnawing on my fingernails if things get desperate.

After fifteen more minutes, I try asking the hulk for any

update on Three, but hospital employees aren't allowed to share information with me since I'm not family.

Thanks a lot, HIPAA.

Okay, I didn't actually mean that. I know privacy is a good thing. I'm just hungry. Plus a little guilty. And also worried. But that's all.

I just have to hope the doctors determine Three is okay. Soon. Then I can get back to staying as far away from the man as I can for as long as we both shall live.

While the minutes drag on, though, my insides start to turn into sailor knots of concern. Did I really injure Three that badly? I feel like I've been here for the better part of a week, although it's probably only been an hour. Tapping my foot, I will my brain to stop replaying old memories of Three and me on a loop.

Good memories.

Three and me on his uncle's boat, cruising Abie Lake at sunset.

Three and me building castles on the sand at the Beachfront Inn.

Three and me at Abie Park with a band covering songs from the early 2000s. I'd packed us a picnic that afternoon, and he'd brought along cornhole and a Frisbee. Ford was there too, cracking jokes, singing along.

We used to be friends, Ford and I. Still, being friends with Three's cousins shouldn't matter. I don't *want* to want Three anymore. I handed him my whole heart, and he threw all four chambers of it back in my face. So recalling the good times with him is dangerous. And focusing on *the end* of us doesn't make these guilt pangs feel any better, either.

When I flash back to him telling me he was never "looking for something serious" a giant, gaping pit opens up inside me. So now I'm worried and hungry *and* pit-y.

Bristol's voice suddenly sounds in my head. *Why on earth do you still care about this guy?*

What I need is a distraction.

Turning to the plexiglass display of medical pamphlets beside my chair, I grab the one in the first slot. Some casual reading should do the trick. Maybe I'll learn about something useful— like all the vitamins and supplements in Betty Crocker fudge brownies. Except the pamphlet in my hand is titled "You and Your Erectile Dysfunction."

No thank you very much, sir.

I quickly stick the pamphlet back into its slot, but the next one, unfortunately, spells out advice for "Living with Hepatitis B."

Yikes. What's going on here in Northampton?

Shoving that one back too, I snatch up the third pamphlet. The words "Perimenopause and Me" are stamped above a middle-aged woman grinning at the camera like menopause will be the absolute best thing that's ever happened to her. But before I can ditch this last pamphlet, a low voice rumbles above my head.

"Sara. You're still here?" I glance up and there's Ford, looming over me and my perimenopause pamphlet. Are the man's running shoes made of marshmallows? How come I didn't hear him coming?

"Oh, hello, Ford." I scramble to push the evidence into my purse. Who knows? Maybe he didn't notice the subject matter.

He arches a brow. High. "Studying up on what to expect in your golden years?"

Yep. He totally noticed.

"Never hurts to be prepared," I stammer, ignoring the heat in my cheeks. "How's Three?"

Ford's brow dips, and he runs a hand over his chin. "Well, the blast from that fire extinguisher really did a number on him. Then he hit his head on the way down. Took a few stitches. The doc says he's definitely concussed."

"Ugh." I chew my lip, and the knots in my abdomen cinch up even tighter than they already were. "I'm so sorry."

Ford glances over his shoulder at the door to the exam rooms. "The nurse is getting a wheelchair for Three now. He should be out soon."

"Wheelchair?" I wince. "Oh no. He can't even walk?"

"He probably could, but the meds have him kinda loopy. Either way, it's hospital policy for patients to be wheeled to the curb."

"He's going to be okay, though?" I'm keeping my tone hopeful, like I might be able to manifest future positivity by speaking it out into the universe. If Three is, in fact, all right, Ford can take him home, and I can get on with my life.

My very Three-avoidant life.

"He's gonna be all right." Ford bobs his head. "He just needs to be watched closely for the next few days."

I let out a small sigh of relief. Three's got plenty of family in Abieville to keep an eye on him, which means my job here is done. I'm so relieved, in fact, my stomach growls again.

Loudly.

Ford's brow hikes back up again. "Impressive, Hathaway."

"Don't mind me." I cringe, pressing a hand to my middle. "Just your garden-variety alien invasion in my gut."

Ford shrugs. "Happens."

"I guess so. But that's probably my signal to head out." I glance at the door to the exam rooms and rise from my seat. Under the circumstances, I'm probably the last person Three will want to see again, and I *definitely* don't want to see *him* again. More importantly, I don't want Ford or Three or anyone else in Abieville to think his proximity bothers me so much.

Because it *shouldn't* bother me so much. It *doesn't* bother me.

Much.

Still, a lump gathers in my throat, and I swallow hard against it. "Would you just apologize to Three for me one more time?" I ask. "Please?"

Ford stuffs his hands in his pockets. "Sure thing."

My legs suddenly feel heavy as lead. "So." I shift my weight. "Do you think Three will just stay at his parents' house?"

Ford's jaw tenses. "Probably not."

"With his sister then?"

"Doubt it," he says grimly.

I blink. "But he and Nella used to be so close." In fact, the way Three cared about his sister was one of the things I loved most about him. A man who's good to his family is more attractive to me than just about anything else. And Three was already stupidly attractive even when he was nowhere near the other Fullers.

"Oh, they're still close." Ford scratches the scruff at his chin. "The thing is, our whole family's supposed to spend the next two weeks on a cruise from California to Hawaii. All the aunts, uncles, cousins."

My heart plummets as I realize Three probably won't be cleared to travel with a concussion. "Oh, no."

"Oh, yes." Ford looks down at the floor, scuffs his shoe along the carpet. "We're all booked on the red eye to LAX tonight. Then tomorrow, we're boarding a ship in the Port of Los Angeles. Even our grandmother's going."

I suck in a breath. "Big Mama?" The last time I saw her, she was a rickety wisp of a thing with puffy white hair and a dry sense of humor. She must be in her nineties by now. "She was always so nice to me. I'm just so glad she's still ..." My voice trails off.

"Yeah. She's *still*." Ford lifts his gaze. "That's why we all wanted to take this cruise with her while we could." His eyes cloud over. "Everyone's planning to carpool to the airport in a couple hours. Three's folks have never even been on a plane, so there's no way he's gonna let them or Nella miss this trip."

Before I can ask who'll take care of Three, the door from the hallway opens and a perky nurse wheels Three into the waiting room. He's got a bandage stretching from the nape of his neck up and around the top of his skull with auburn spikes poking out around the edges.

"Hello, kidsss," he slurs at us. Then he looks up at the nurse with a sleepy grin. "Hello, Hairy."

"Close." She offers him a patient smile. "But my name is *Mary*, remember?"

"I like you, Hairy," he murmurs.

"Oof." Ford rakes his fingers through his hair. "How long's he gonna be like this?"

Mary inclines her head and lowers her voice. "Every case is different," she says. "And Mr. Fuller could seem better, then regress. Either way, you'll likely see signs of impairment for another day or two."

"Or *Three*," he crows, pumping a fist in the air. "That'sss my name!"

"You're right, Mr. Fuller," Mary tells him before addressing us again. "The doctor wants to see him back for a checkup on Tuesday, and I have his discharge papers and instructions for aftercare here." She holds up a packet of papers. "As for this first night, whoever's in charge will need to keep a close watch, and wake him up every few hours for a cognition check."

"Cognition check?" I wrinkle my nose.

"It's not difficult," she says. "He just needs someone to ask him a few simple questions like his name. The date. If he knows where he is. The paperwork has some suggestions. If he can answer correctly, that's a good sign his brain is healing, not regressing."

Three looks up at me and lifts his finger, like he's pointing at the ceiling. "I can't go on the airplane!"

"I know," I groan. "Ford was just telling me you're supposed to take a cruise for Christmas."

"Ahh. Cruise, ssschmooze." Three's lips twitch. "Hey, that rhymesss."

Mary's gaze bounces between Three, Ford, and me. "So who am I releasing Mr. Fuller to?"

"No one, sssnow-one," Three cackles. "Ford can drop me off at home on the way to the airport."

Mary bends down, speaking gently to Three. "Mr. Fuller, you absolutely cannot stay home alone tonight."

"*Home Alone!*" A goofy smile breaks across his face. "That's my favorite Christmas movie!"

Ford reaches for the packet. "I'll take those papers." When Mary hands the stack over, he addresses Three. "We can watch *Home Alone* as soon as we get back to your place." Ford grasps the back of Three's wheelchair. "Then after the doc checks you out on Tuesday, you and I can fly out to meet everyone in Hawaii."

"Hold on," Mary says, her face slipping into a regretful wince. "Even if Mr. Fuller has a positive checkup, he is concussed. I'm afraid he won't be cleared for airplane travel for at least a couple of weeks."

"But that's the length of your cruise," I blurt, like I'm the only one in the room capable of doing simple math.

Mary's eyes go extra soft. "I'm so sorry."

"Not your fault," Ford tells her, and a thousand guilt-knives stab my brain.

Gee. Whose fault is it, I wonder?

"No worries." Ford claps Three on the shoulder. "I'll just skip this trip."

"Pffft." Three waves his hand away, pushing a bubbly raspberry through his lips. "You finally got time off work, and you never get to travel. You need a vacation more than anybody ... *buddy.*" At this, he lets out an amused snort.

Ford bobs his head. "It's no big deal."

"LISSSTEN to me!" Three aims a pout at his cousin. "I'm NOT taking you away from the family at Chrissstmasss." Under his breath, he repeats "Christmas" then bursts into a fresh round of laughter.

"Okay." Ford's brow creases. "What about one of the other guys from school? All you teachers are off for winter break. Could Nicky or Josh stay with you?"

"They're headed to Vermont to sssski." Three shakes his head then winces, which kind of makes my skull hurt too. "I would've gone too," he adds, "except for our umm... our..." He scrunches up his face. "Thingy."

I blink down at him. "You mean the cruise?"

Three barks out a laugh, his eyes in a squint. "Heh heh heh. Yeah. That. Cruissse."

"What about Kenny?" I whisper to Ford.

"Nah." Ford smirks. "His wife just had a baby, and they already had four kids. They're frazzled enough with a newborn plus the older ones. I can't ask him to pitch in for something this big so close to the holidays."

"NO KENNY!" Three barks. "BOOO!" Ford and I glance at each other, and my insides swirl like a washing machine on the agitation cycle. I never meant for any of this to happen, but it's all my fault just the same. If only I hadn't tried baking those brownies ...

Stupid Betty Crocker.

Stupid kitschy reindeer.

My heart's in my throat now, and I start gnawing at my bottom lip. When I convinced my parents to let me handle things in Abieville, I did everything I could to minimize the risk of bumping into Three. That's why I stopped at a grocery store outside of town. It's why I took the long way to the lake, circumventing Main Street. I told myself it was just until Christmas Eve. And by the time I got out the mixing bowl and set the oven to preheat, I was positive I could avoid Three Fuller the entire time I was here.

Instead, I clocked him with a fire extinguisher. Now I'm basically ruining a Christmas vacation for multiple members of his family.

Unless ...

"I hate to push the issue," Mary says gently, "but my shift is ending soon, and before the hospital can release Mr. Fuller, someone has to commit to his care. So, who's taking him home, folks?"

"I'll do it!" I choke.

Ford's eyes pop wide. "You will?"

"Sure," I manage to squeak.

After all, being stuck with Three for a few days can't be worse than perimenopause.

Chapter Four

Three

Wait. What planet am I on?

Did Sara Hathaway seriously just offer to go home with me?

For the next three days?

A voice in my head puts up a silent protest as I squint up at Sara. "Nope thanksss. You ... umm... not ... you... ... no. Nope thankssss." Except I must be using my actual mouth and stammering out loud, because Ford just looked down at me.

"*Nope* thanks?" He bites back a laugh. "Did you just say 'nope thanks?'"

"Yesss," I slur. "That idea isss ... not excellent." That last word comes out more like egg-sssell-ent. And what I actually mean is that Sara Hathaway staying with me is a monumentally *terrible* idea. When I try to scowl to emphasize the terribleness, fresh pain shoots through my skull. Then I see stars and grunt like a baby piglet.

Ugh.

Good thing I'm not trying to attract anyone right now.

Especially Sara Hathaway.

"Her offer is actually very nice," Ford says, glancing at her. "Thanks, Sara."

She shrugs. "No big deal."

But it is a big deal. It's the biggest deal. I can't be around her. I'll ... I'll ... "Nooo," I moan.

"Come on, Three." Sara splays her hands. "You're only in this situation because of me." She takes a beat. "Well, me and Betty Crocker."

I pull down my brow. Ouch. "I have no idea what that meansss."

"It means I'm the only viable option you've got for this job."

"Hey, *I* have a job." I puff out a laugh. "A good job. An *important* job." This fact is completely unrelated to the situation, but for some reason, I feel like I need to tell Sara I'm gainfully employed. Maybe that's because the Hathaways never thought I'd amount to anything.

Maybe I didn't think I would either.

"Of course you have a job," Sara says.

"I can't remember what I do right now, though." I lift a hand to rub my throbbing skull. Everything entering my brain seems to be sifting through a layer of cheesecloth.

"You're a high school history teacher," Ford says. "Remember?" He's talking at me slowly and loudly, like he's communicating with a brick wall.

"Duh." I harrumph. Except no, I didn't remember. But I don't want anyone to realize how messed up I am, or Sara might not give up on this idea of staying with me. "I have a few brain cellsss left. Like ... three. Like my name again." I hear snickering, then realize it's me.

I'm the one snickering.

That's when Nurse Hairy hands over a couple of plastic bottles to Sara. "Mr. Fuller's pain meds are pretty strong." She rattles the pills. "You'll have to monitor his follow-up doses for those and for the antibiotics. He won't be able to keep track of them himself. Also, he shouldn't do any driving. No signing legal documents. No operating heavy machinery."

A snort slips out of me. "What about *light* machinery?"

Oh, man.

That's probably the dumbest joke I've ever told. I really *am* all kinds of loopy right now. So yeah, I guess I can't stay by myself, but I also don't want Ford's trip to be ruined on my account. Same goes for the rest of my extended family which—let's face it —is half the town. All my single friends who aren't related to me are in Vermont. And I haven't dated a woman seriously enough to stay with her since—well—let's just say it's been a long time.

My only real choice is ...

I lift my gaze to Sara.

She's staring down at me with her big eyes all wide open, and a wave of something unsteady crashes over me. Leftover heartache? Concussion fog? Either way, I can't let Sara think she affects me.

She doesn't affect me.

"You're ssso pretty," I murmur.

Oops.

Sara throws a hand up to her throat. "Oh!"

I crinkle my face, grimacing up at Ford. "What did I just say? Am I talking out loud? Did I—"

"We better get you home," Ford interrupts. "I have time before I need to go the airport." He turns to Sara. "I'll wait with Three over at his place while you grab whatever you need to stay there with him for the next few days."

"But—"

"I'll send you the address," Ford adds. "His place is just a couple blocks off Main Street."

"It's just that ... " Sara's cheeks and throat begin to flush. Pink. Soft. Shiny. "Someone's coming to evaluate my parents' property tomorrow morning," she says. "So if Three can't be left alone at his place, he'll have to stay at the lake house with me."

"Wait." I pause, fumbling the right words. "What about my ... thing?"

Sara's brow lifts. "What thing?"

"Umm." I shift my jaw. "My ... thing. With the clothesss in it."

Ford drags a hand over his face. "Your suitcase. I guess I can bring that over to the Hathaways' house."

"But I'm packed all wrong," I tell him. "For *not* cold weather." I lift a hand to count what I'm missing for the snow. "I need sweatssss. Beaniessss. Sockssss. Long underwear."

Great. Of all the clothing items to start listing, I had to throw in underwear.

"I'll repack for you," Ford says, with a smirk. "You don't sound like you're in any condition to make wardrobe decisions anyway."

"That'sss real sssswell of you, cuzzz, but—"

Ford cuts me off. "If I can't stick around and help out while you're healing, the least I can do is swap out some stuff in a suitcase for you. It'll make me feel better when I'm on that cruise ship indulging in the unlimited drink package."

"Okey dokey." I rub my forehead, realizing I'm fresh out of arguments. "Sounds like a plan, Ssstan," I slur. And now I kind of want to crawl under this wheelchair and hide for the rest of my life.

Not only did I bring up my underwear, but I've apparently become a man who says things like *real swell, okey dokey,* and *sounds like a plan, Stan.*

"I'll just swing by your place to get your things," Ford says, "then I'll meet you and Sara over at the lake house." Ford looks at Sara. "Work for you?"

She swallows hard and chirps, "Totally works!" But then she glances at me, with her teeth clenched like this isn't working for her even a little bit. As she pushes the wheelchair toward the exit, my head starts swimming and spinning and aching. This is so not good. Sara is definitely wishing she wasn't stuck taking care of me.

Yeah. You and me both, kid.

Too bad we don't really have any other choice.

But it's just for a few days, right? Then this can all be over. For both of us.

I open my mouth to say this to Sara and puke all over myself.

Terrible plan, Stan.

Chapter Five

Sara

Thirteen Years Ago: June

As I write this, I'm on the porch with Abie Lake behind me, and my dad's just gone back to the city for the week. My mom's always a little sad when he leaves us on Sundays, so she's taking a nap. Which means now is probably as good a time as any to confess something. But not out loud. Only in my journal:

They were right.

If I told them, they'd just say I told you so, which I would kind of deserve. As you know, I fought them both tooth and nail about wasting my precious summer staying at some lame house in a town this small, but I'm willing to admit I was wrong. After spending an entire year stuck at a boring all-girls school—where good old Principal Manheim was literally the only guy—this place is actually kind of amazing.

Last night, I went to a beach bonfire and met a group of kids who live here year-round. One of them is named Three, which is totally weird. But also, he's totally cute and insanely nice.

Stupid me, I didn't realize it might get cold on the lake after the sun went down, so I showed up wearing only a sundress and sandals. And sure, I could've wrapped up in the blanket I brought, but I was using it to sit on the sand. So Three offered me his sweatshirt.

Don't quote me, but I think I might like it here at this lake house after all ... I might even want to come back next summer.

Chapter Six

Sara

As Three and I hobble through the front door, I have one arm wrapped around his washboard abs, and he's got his body slung over my shoulder. I can tell he's trying not to put his full weight on me, but the guy's pretty heavy anyway. Luckily, Nurse Mary gave him a spare pair of clean scrubs, so we managed a little vomit triage back at the hospital. But the rest of his clothes are either smoky or they smell like antiseptic soap. Nevertheless, I'm determined to handle whatever he throws at me.

Unless it's a fire extinguisher.

Speaking of which.

I glance across the dining room through the archway into the newly remodeled kitchen, and my stomach twists at how close I came to torching this place. It's a one-hundred-year-old farmhouse, sitting on two acres of lakefront property. There are three bedrooms, two baths, and a den-slash-office-slash-library. The original hardwood floors have been refinished. All the moldings, bead board, and chair rails sport fresh coats of paint or stain. The covered porch is quaint and cozy with cushioned Adirondack chairs and hurricane lamps. Everything's perfect, just waiting for Platinum Home's stamp of approval.

And I almost burned it all down.

I give the still-smoky air a good long sniff as Three and I lurch together past the coffee table. "Sorry this place stinks like burnt reindeer napkins," I say, gently extricating myself from him.

Three lowers himself onto the couch. "I like barbecues."

His statement doesn't make total sense to me, but then again, neither did mine. At least he isn't slurring nearly as much as he was earlier. Maybe the pain meds are starting to wear off. Still, neither one of us needs a reminder of what got us into this mess in the first place.

I nod toward the kitchen. "I'll get everything cleaned up and back to normal while you're in a bath."

"Bath?" He pulls a face. "I'm really more of a shower guy."

"Unfortunately, you're not supposed to get your stitches wet."

He blinks up at me. "Stitches?"

"On the back of your head."

"Huh." He reaches up and touches the bandage. "I don't remember getting stitches."

"Exactly." I cross my arms. "That's why I'm in charge."

He tips his chin. "I'm pretty sure I could shower without getting my head wet."

"Maybe so. But Mary said you're still at risk of dizzy spells." I widen my stance to defend my decision. "If you fall in the shower, not only could you injure yourself even more, but I'd have to haul your naked body out and—"

"Got it!" Three throws a hand up. "No naked hauling."

I toss him a crooked smile. Hopefully this cooperation will continue, and Three will never have to know how much I dread being near him. On the other hand, I don't want to get along with him too well, either. That will only make saying goodbye harder. And I've already done hard goodbyes when it comes to Three.

"Do you want to call your parents to let them know what's going on?" I ask. "Or your sister?"

Your girlfriend?

My insides heave, even as the thought crosses my mind. Of course Three could be in a relationship. I mean, just look at the man. He's gotten even more gorgeous over the past decade. And I'll bet any current woman of his dreams never gave him a concussion while trying to bake brownies.

"My brain's too foggy to talk to anyone." Three winces, running a hand along the top of his skull. "My mom will figure out something's wrong and insist on staying home to play nursemaid. I really don't want her to miss out on the cruise. My dad either. Or Nella. They all deserve this vacation."

My shoulders creep up, like guilt is making them float. "Your family's going to find out what happened eventually."

"Hopefully not before they board the plane." He slips his phone from his pocket. "By then it will be too late." He squints down at the screen, shaking his head. "Could you text them for me? I can't focus right now."

"I guess," I say, but my throat goes dry. "I really hate lying, though."

"Same." His teeth clench, then he shifts his jaw back and forth. "Just ... Sara ... Please?" He gazes up at me, his eyes wide and pleading. Like two baby bluebirds in a nest begging for a worm.

Wait. Does that make me the worm?

Yep. A worm who got us into this mess.

"All right." I sigh, taking his phone and dropping down beside him. "Who should I text first?"

"We have a family group thread," he says. "Search for Original Fuller House."

"Fuller house?" I eye him sideways. "Like the TV show?"

"Nella was obsessed with the Tanners when we were kids." He lets out a puff of a laugh, and I almost smile too. But when I open the thread, the evidence of the closeness between Three and his family only sharpens the knife of my guilty conscience.

"What do you want me to say?" I ask, despite the lump in my throat.

"Hey ... fam," he begins to dictate. "Before I get too far into winter break mode ... I'm going to ... no, I want to ... no, I *think* I should finish up my progress reports." He's speaking slowly, like he's dealing with a head injury. Which he is. "Go with that last option," he says. "The thinking one. That's honest enough, right? I mean, I *could* be thinking about finishing my progress reports. Just talking about finishing my progress reports means my brain's thinking about them."

"You're right." I nod when I've caught up. "Go on. I'm ready for more."

"I know you all want to get to the airport a couple hours before the flight," he continues, "so ... Kenny can just drop me off when I'm done." Three pauses again. "That's something else that *could* happen too. Kenny's totally capable of taking me to the airport. So yeah. We're still not lying. Technically."

"Sure." These are basically semantics sidestepping the whole truth, but if that makes Three feel better, I guess he'll be easier to be around until the doctor clears him to be alone. Hopefully on Tuesday. Today's Saturday, so I just have to get through a couple more days. I can do that. Probably.

"Are you done?" I ask, glancing at him.

"No. Add this." He holds up a finger. "Don't wait for me when you get through security. Just head straight to the gate. I'll see you soon."

At this I can't help frowning. "You'll see them *soon*?"

"Soon is relative." He lets out a little snort. "And so are they. *MY* relatives, I mean. Except they're not mean. They're nice."

Soooo, okay. Three may not be slurring anymore, but he's definitely still ... groggy. Under the circumstances, though, I suppose I should just be grateful. He could be super-sad. Or super-angry with me. He is missing Christmas with his family after all.

"Okay." I hit send. "Done."

Three slumps back against the couch. "Thank you, Sara." My name falls out of his lips all soft and slow and drowsy.

"No big deal," I say, but my cheeks heat up. I shouldn't let him affect me like this. No, I *can't* let him affect me. I barely survived the rift in my soul ten years ago. And yes, we're older now, but I'm wiser too. If I'm going to get out of this situation with my emotions intact, I'll need to keep my wits about me.

You'll need to keep a close watch on him overnight, the nurse's voice echoes in my head.

Yeah. Thanks a lot, Hairy.

"Here." I push Three's phone back into his hands, and hop up from the couch. "Just sit tight while I get your bath ready. Ford should be here soon with your suitcase." Three nods like a compliant kid, then he lets his eyes slip shut. With the bandage wrapped around him, he looks so innocent. Almost fragile. Which is ironic considering how broken he made me feel the last time we were together.

"Sara?" he murmurs, with his lids still closed.

"What?"

"I like it *really* hot."

Gah! My throat constricts, and I gag a little on my spit. "Excuse me?"

"The water," he says. "I like it really hot. Hot enough to turn my skin red."

His voice is deep and dreamy, and there go my cheeks again. Oh man. My heart might not stay in one piece through the rest of the night, let alone a few more days.

Chapter Seven

Three

So yeah, I might've told Sara I'm a shower guy, but this bath she set up for me is pretty much heaven on earth. Or in this case, heaven in Abieville.

A wireless speaker on the back of the toilet is playing some kind of soothing classical music. Small tea lights flicker along the edge of the vanity. The water's topped with pine-scented bubbles, so I slide under until I'm up to my chest, letting the heat soak through to my bones.

Not five minutes later, a knock sounds on the door. "You alive in there?" Sara asks, on the other side.

"So far, so good," I answer, but her voice sends memories of us flooding through my brain. I guess that's the side effect of these pain meds slowly filtering out of my bloodstream. The clearer my head gets, the more I'm freed up to replay images from the past.

Like Sara at a bonfire in my oversized sweatshirt, the bottom hanging almost to her knees.

Sara sipping my super-sized Coke, her lips leaving a ring of cherry Chapstick on the straw.

Sara on my lap while I steered my uncle's boat around the lake. She'd lean back against me, her long hair blowing across my face, the sweet scent of her suntan lotion filling my lungs. She was young, but already so true to herself. Confident enough to wear her heart on her sleeve. Back then, she saw the good in everyone. She saw the good in *me*.

But that brand of innocence—the total certainty you can and will conquer anything—comes only once in a lifetime. And wishing for its return is probably more dangerous than taking a fire extinguisher to the head.

Inhaling a deep pine-scented breath, I try to stop the tide of memories from washing over me, but I can't get them fully erased before Sara's back and tapping on the door again.

"Still doing all right?" she asks. "You haven't slipped under the water or anything?"

"Nope. Still breathing actual air."

There's a beat of silence. Then she says, "Sorry if I'm being annoying." Her voice is softer now. "I just want to be sure you're safe, since you're only in there because of me."

"You're fine." I tack on a sharp exhale, but the truth is, I kind of like that she's concerned about my welfare. Whether her worry stems from guilt or genuine emotion, I haven't had anyone looking after me—besides me—for the past ten years.

Not that my family and I aren't tight. In fact, some people think the Original Fullers are disgustingly supportive of one another. But when you let your roots spread in the same small town where you were raised, you also risk feeling like you're living at home forever.

So as soon as I graduated high school, I moved out and rented my own place. Took on multiple jobs to pay my way. Only came home on Sundays for dinner. At the time, I had independence, but that was only masking what I *didn't* have: confidence. Faith in myself. Faith that anyone outside my family might believe in me.

I had no grand plan or any idea who or what I wanted to be.

Meanwhile Sara had her professional goals on lock since

kindergarten. She was going to follow her father's path. Undergrad at Stanford then law school at Columbia, with a couple years of prestigious internships in between. Her future was big law in the city. Mine was small-town, USA.

Hathaway vs. Fuller.

So I told myself I was just making things easier on Sara, letting her off the hook by ending things first. But the man in me now recognizes I was mostly protecting my own ego.

Truth is, I still am.

Back then, she didn't understand why I pushed her away. And to this day, I don't think she has any idea how I truly felt about her. Which is the way it should be. The way things have to remain. Our futures are still at odds. I'm a hometown teacher, she's a New York attorney. No use denying that or hoping for something different.

By the time the bathwater's grown lukewarm, I've resigned myself to the fact that my being here with Sara for the next few days won't change anything between us.

It *can't* change anything.

Years ago, I let my emotions dictate my behavior for way too long before I had to accept reality. And reality's crashing in on me again. Sara's only here in town for a short time, then she'll be back to her full-time life, probably working at Hathaway Cooke. What I have to do now is resist any attraction I still feel for her until the doc clears me from her watch. Then I can go back to my house. Alone. And this houseful of memories will once again be a part of my past.

Sara and I won't have to see each other again.

Stepping out of the tub, dripping water on the bathmat, I grab a towel from the basket to dry off. Too bad all I have to put on are hospital scrubs or my old clothes which still smell a little like smoke and—

Knock, knock, knock.

"Yes, I'm still alive and awake," I call through the door.

"Good to know, but I have a delivery for you this time."

"Hold on." I wrap the towel around my waist and pull open the door to find Sara standing there clutching an over-stuffed duffle bag. Her eyes dip to my bare torso, then she garbles something that sounds like, "ACK!" When she tries shoving the bag at my body waiting for me to grab it, I glance down at the towel I'm clutching.

"If I let go of this ..." I begin, my voice trailing off.

"Don't let go!" Sara drops the bag and leaps backward, crashing into the wall of the hallway.

"Are you okay?" I ask, dipping my head.

"I'm great," she squeaks. "Totally great!" But Sara doesn't *seem* totally great. She's coughing and pounding on her chest. Not to mention her throat's getting blotchy. Still, a part of me likes that her gaze lingered on my abs. That she's affected by me after all these years. I'm not proud of this part. It's just the truth.

And also dangerous.

"No suitcase?" I ask.

Sara starts to sputter, nodding at the bag at my feet. "Ford said ... he thinks ... he told me to tell you this should be plenty for the next few days." He's probably right. And he's also probably trying to remind me this whole situation is only temporary.

Message received, cousin.

"Is Ford still here?" I crane my neck over Sara's shoulder.

She shakes her head. "He had to get to the airport. But he wanted me to tell you Merry Christmas, and he's sorry for bailing on you. I told him none of this is his fault."

"You're right." I bob my head. "It's not."

"Anyway." Sara takes a small step back down the hall, like a getaway in slow motion. "You're due for another dose of pain meds and antibiotics soon."

I pull down my brow, still clutching the towel at my waist. "To be honest, I kinda like feeling a little more clear-headed." *Not to mention more in control of my reactions to you.*

"I get that, but there are anti-inflammatories in the medication. Mary said that's important for at least the first twenty-four hours."

"Fine." My shoulders slump. "Guess I can't argue with Hairy."

At this, Sara's lip twitches. "I'm also supposed to check your stitches and reapply your antibiotic ointment. So I'll just be in the kitchen when you're—when you—" She swallows, her eyes dipping to my bare torso again—"get dressed." She spins on a heel, fleeing across the house, but not before I notice her throat's still blotchy.

I shut the bathroom door, and without waiting for permission, I peel off the gauzy bandage and tape. The last thing I need is Sara touching me more than absolutely necessary. She'd probably be all gentle and soft and good-smelling. So she's not getting anywhere near my head if I can help it.

Luckily my forehead's just bulging and bruised, and the stitches are tender but there's no evidence of fresh blood. Not too bad, all things considered. Using the towel, I rake at my hair— damp with sweat—until the auburn strands are spiked up. I could use a fresh trim sometime soon. Right now, though, I just need to get dressed so I can handle my own re-bandaging and medication.

Inside the duffle bag on top of a pile of clothes, I find a pair of gray joggers, a soft white T-shirt, and my favorite hoodie.

Bless you, Ford Lansing.

I've been told the sky-blue fabric of the sweatshirt really brings out the color of my eyes. But I bury that thought as soon as it pops up. Impressing Sara Hathaway—with my eyes or abs or anything else—is *not* on my agenda.

Still, she is the one controlling the meds and supplies for my stitches. So once I'm fully dressed, I head off to find her in the kitchen. She's wiping the walls around the oven, her black hair piled in a loose knot on top of her head. A few stray tendrils drape down over the nape of her neck, and my gut twists.

I remember my lips pressed there, the taste of her skin like a ghost from ten years ago. But I'm not about to start drooling over the woman like some kind of lovesick creeper. Because *of course* I'm not lovesick. Or a creeper. I'm just some guy who's stuck with his ex for the next few days due to circumstances beyond his control.

Still, watching her now reminds me of her work ethic and determination. Even when we were young, she had such big dreams. She made me want to discover who *I* was. Losing Sara was the first step toward finding myself. Now I can't help being drawn to the idea of testing out what I've learned.

"Hi."

"Oh!" She startles and twirls around. The dirty rag drops from her hand.

"Didn't mean to scare you." I duck my head in the most nonthreatening way I can muster. "I kinda thought you were expecting me."

"I was. I mean, I'm not scared. I was just ... really focused on cleaning." She stoops to pick up the rag, and when she stands again, she barely makes eye contact with me.

"Need any help?"

"No." Her mouth goes crooked, and she finally meets my gaze. "Or maybe I should say, 'nope thanks.'"

"Hey." I force out a laugh. "You're mocking a guy with a concussion."

"Still too soon?"

"*Forever* too soon," I say.

"Fair enough." She takes a moment to examine my head. "You took off the bandage yourself."

"Yep." I turn so she can see the back of my skull.

"Looks ... not so bad. I just need to put some fresh —"

"I can do it," I interrupt.

"But—"

"I'll be fine before the next dose of pain meds gets me all loopy again."

Sara narrows her eyes, but ultimately she fishes around in Mary's bag of supplies for the tube of ointment and a clean bandage. Then she monitors me closely while I wash my hands, dab on a layer of antibiotics, and affix the new bandage.

"See?" I splay my hands when I'm done. "Perfectly capable."

She presses her lips together. "At least let me get you something to eat. I've got some chicken soup I can heat up."

"What?" I arch a brow. "No brownies?"

She takes a beat, then her lips curve up. "Forever too soon."

"Fair enough." I stuff my hands in the pockets of my joggers. "Anyway, I'm not hungry. Just tired."

"In that case, I've got the guest room set up for you. But first ... hold on." She moves around the kitchen filling a glass of water and retrieving my meds. Then she watches as I swallow the tablets. I stick out my tongue to prove I did.

"For the record, I'm not trying to hover or treat you like a kid or anything," she says. "But I *am* supposed to write down and keep track of what you take and when."

"In other words, you're stuck being my mom?"

"Eww." She grimaces.

I run a hand over my head. "Please forget I said that."

"Agreed." A spot of pink warms her cheeks. "Forever too soon."

We're both quiet for a moment, shifting our weight. When Sara starts to chew her lip, she doesn't look like anyone remotely related to me. She looks like a woman I want to wrap my arms around and comfort. Which means it's time to put some distance between us.

"Guess I'll just call it a night," I say.

"Okay." She nods. "Sorry I'll have to keep checking on you while you sleep."

Yeah. You and me both.

I head back down the hallway past the bathroom to the guest room. Along one wall is a large antique dresser. A plush armchair sits in the opposite corner. A pair of mahogany nightstands flank a king-sized sleigh bed. The down comforter and duvet is a rich forest green. Piles of soft throw pillows and a quilt complete the lush bedding. The space feels cozy. Comfortable but elevated. Not bad for a rental property.

A Hathaway property.

After climbing into bed, I check my phone. There are a couple of missed texts from Nella and Ford, plus one voicemail from my mother. She's probably scolding me for cutting my arrival so close to our departure time. So I decide not to listen to her message.

Her disappointment will only make my heart hurt worse than it already does. So I skip to the texts from my sister, sent separately from the Original Fuller House thread.

> SMELLA
>
> We got through security and bought some plane snacks in the gift shop. Mom and Dad can't get over how expensive things are at the airport. In fact this may be the first and last time they ever fly anywhere.
>
> They bought one package of Peanut M&Ms to split between the four of us. LOL! You'd better get here soon and save me, Free.

Free is what Nella started calling me when she was little and couldn't pronounce the Th- in Three. It's way nicer than what I called her. My sister *is* way nicer than I am. In fact, she's way nicer than almost anyone.

> SMELLA
>
> FREE! We're at the gate now. Where are you? Ford's great and all, but I need my sibling buffer!

Oof. My insides twist, thinking about my sister waiting for me, with no idea I'm not coming. Unfortunately, the texts from Ford don't make me feel any better.

FORD

> Hey, cuz. We're about to board the plane. So far, I've managed to convince everyone you were just running late, but the jig will be up soon.

> You want me to tell your folks what actually happened? They can't hate me forever, right? After all, it's almost Christmas.

> On that note, I'm buying you a pooka shell necklace as soon as we get to Hawaii. Just call me Santa Claus. Love you, man.

At this my jaw goes tight.

My whole extended family might be a little nuts, but for the next two weeks, I'm going to miss their bone-crushing hugs, not to mention their particular brand of holiday chaos. Everyone was so ready to break from our usual traditions this year. We'd been dreaming of a tropical Christmas instead of a white one. Palm trees rather than noble firs. Umbrella drinks in place of eggnog. Flowered leis, not Santa hats.

I can only hope my parents and Nella will be too busy making once-in-a-lifetime memories to feel my absence too badly. Meanwhile, I'll be stuck here in a house that's not decorated for any kind of holiday—traditional or otherwise—with a woman who's only here with me out of guilt.

Speaking of guilt, it's time I text Ford back and let him off the hook.

ME

> I'm going to fill my family in on what's happening since you're all getting on the plane now, and it will be too late for them to change course. Thanks for taking one for the team until now. Go have a blast for both of us. Love you too, man.

I hit send, then tackle the harder task: texting the Original

Fuller House thread to tell them the truth. And I need to do that before the next round of pain meds kicks in.

One ripped-off Band-Aid coming up.

ME

> Hey, fam. I have some news, part of which you may have already figured out. First of all, please believe me when I tell you I'm totally safe, but I won't be flying to LA with you or taking the Christmas cruise.

> I had a bit of an accident earlier today that resulted in a concussion. Don't worry about me. I'm in good hands. I'm just not allowed to fly per doctor's orders. And I didn't want any of you to miss out on the holiday fun. So promise to have the best time ever, and I'll celebrate with you in the New Year. Until then, mele kalikimaka.

> PS: In case anyone's thinking about catching a return flight when you land at LAX, don't. I'm not at home, and you won't be able to find me where I'm staying.

> PSS: Don't be mad at Ford for temporarily covering for me. He's the best. I'm the jerk. That is all.

> Love you all times Three. (See what I did there?) Aloha.

As I hit send on the final text, I start to feel a bit of pain-med wooziness descend upon my brain again. That's bad enough. But to be honest, knowing Sara Hathaway will be watching over me in bed all night is also taking an unhealthy toll on my heart rate.

So I power off my phone, flip it face down on the nightstand, and climb under the quilt. If I wait to see who, what, when, or where someone in my family is replying to me, I'll never get any sleep.

Chapter Eight

Sara

The first time I check on Three, I find him lying on his side, head pressed into a soft down pillow. I click the nightstand lamp on, then jostle his shoulder—gently to begin with—then a bit more forcefully when he doesn't show signs of stirring.

"Three. Time to wake up." Even through the cotton of his T-shirt, his body feels warm. And I'm not intentionally gawking at the swell of his biceps, but the lamplight's illuminating his muscles, and it's awfully hard not to peek.

He's got one leg thrown free from the quilt, hooked around the top of it, so it's a good thing he's wearing fitted joggers. I remember Three's calves when he was just barely nineteen. I can only imagine his bare full-on man-calves now.

When a low hum sounds in the back of his throat, my pulse picks up, and I start to wonder what he's dreaming about. I, myself, spent the last two hours reliving past memories while cleaning up present smoke damage. For all I know, Three could be doing the exact same thing.

Dreaming about our past, I mean, not cleaning up smoky walls.

Stop it, Sara. This is not a romantic moment. This is a medical situation you *caused.*

"Come on, Three." I shake him again. His face looks so sweet and peaceful, I really hate to wake him. Then again, the man did cause me plenty of pain at one point in my life. Maybe I don't *have* to be quite so gentle with him now.

When I give him one more jiggle, he drags his leg back under the quilt and lets out a long groan. "I'm so sorry," he mumbles. The words are rusty with sleep, and I glance around the room, as if there might be someone else in here for him to be apologizing too.

He couldn't possibly have read my mind, could he?

"What did you say?"

"So sorry," he moans again.

I swallow hard, pushing aside the twinge in my stomach. Honestly, I would've given anything for this kind of apology from Three a decade ago. But the last thing I want is for him to think I'm still hurting over our breakup now.

"Three!" I whisper-hiss.

"Don't tell her," he mutters.

"Tell who what?" More jostling from me.

"Soooo tired," he grumbles, squeezing his lids shut even more tightly.

"Oh, no you don't," I protest. "You're not allowed to fall back to sleep yet. This is a cognitive test, and you haven't answered any questions."

"Candy canes," he murmurs. "Cruise ship. Carols. Christmas."

"Yes. It's almost Christmas," I say. "But do you know where you are?"

He blows out a long breath, eyes still squeezed shut. "Home alone."

"You're *not* alone, Three." I glance around the room. "Or home. Do you remember where you are?"

"Hmmm." He groans. "Lake house. With ... with ... Sara."

"That's right." I nod, even though he can't see me. "Good."

"Yes, she does. She smells *so* good."

Gah!

Did he just say that? My already-pounding heart kicks into overdrive, until I remind myself the man is clearly under the influence of pain meds. And half of what's coming out of his mouth sounds delirious. Which is exactly why I'm supposed to be doing a cognitive check in the first place. But I'm still not even sure he's conscious. So I have to push the issue. Literally.

"Three!" I shove his arm until his lids finally crack open just a sliver.

"Oh. Hey. Hi," he croaks.

"Hi. Can you open your eyes all the way and look at me? Please?"

Three moans, but he does as I tell him, propping himself up on an elbow. Of course my gaze automatically drifts to his straining biceps again. It's like my pupils are magnets and his arms are made of steel. But I'm supposed to be nursing Three back to health, not ogling him.

No matter how good he thinks I smell.

"Do you know your name?" I ask, dragging my focus to the planes of his face. That was one of the questions on Mary's checklist. If Three gets the answers right, I can get out of this room.

The sooner the better.

"Hmmm," he hums again, and I avoid looking at the press of his lips. "Yes."

Technically, that's an answer. But is it a conscious one? I have to clarify. "What *is* your name?" I ask again.

"Bradford." He blinks. "Bradford Fuller. From the Original Fuller House."

I sigh with relief. "Yes. You got it." He sinks back onto the pillows, slowly shutting his eyes again. "Get some more rest now."

I click off the lamp, and rise from the bed, preparing to slip out of the room. "I'll be back to check on you again in another couple hours."

Three mutters, "No, don't."

I freeze. "No don't, what?"

"Don't. Stay."

"Right." I squint at him in the dark. Is he serious? "I just said I'm going."

"No. Please. Don't go. Stay."

Oh no. This is a problem. What I *need* to do is get far away from Three and his mumbled apologies, not to mention his claims that I smell good. This is what my common sense is telling me. Then again, Three asked me to stay.

He wants you, Sara.

And the bottom line is I'm the one who did this to him. The least I could do is honor his request not to be left alone. So as much as I don't want to, I grab a spare blanket from the closet and curl up in the armchair across the room. Then I stare at him in the darkness, waiting for my pulse to return to its normal pace.

Guess what?

My stupid pulse doesn't comply.

He looks so sweet and innocent. Not like the guy who once crushed my heart. Maybe he's changed ... Maybe he's—No. That's risky thinking. What I need is a reminder of why I can never let myself soften toward Three again. So I slip out my phone knowing just who can harden me up, so to speak.

My best friend, Bristol.

We lived together all through college, then afterward she moved to the Bay Area for an art apprenticeship. She's a serial dater and social butterfly. Basically, everything I'm not. But she loves me anyway, and she's had my back since day one in the dorms.

ME

If you're around and you get this, I need to tell you something, but I also need you to promise you won't say I told you so ...

It may be the middle of the night here, but she's in California, so I'd bet my future salary at Hathaway Cooke that Bristol Kane is awake. Within two minutes, I have my answer.

BRISTOL

I would never say I told you so. Well. Okay, maybe I would, but I won't on this occasion.

See. I *knew* my girl would be up.

ME

You can't tell my mom either. This is absolutely Top-Secret Intel.

BRISTOL

I don't exactly make a habit of texting your mother.

But this is me opening up the vault. Everything you share will remain TSI. What's going on?

ME

Well, I tried my best, for a few hours at least, but then I sort of ran into Three in Abieville. And by "ran into" I mean I knocked him out with a fire extinguisher.

BRISTOL

????

ME

> I was at the house by myself, and I thought some intruder was breaking in, so I hit him with a fire extinguisher. The intruder turned out to be Three. Now he's got stitches plus a concussion, and he's my responsibility for the next few days.

BRISTOL

> Not gonna lie, my friend. This sounds like the plot of a romcom. Did you get into the eggnog early or something?

I snap a picture of Three and send it to Bristol, cringing as the flash goes off. Luckily he doesn't stir, but the light illuminates his slumbering face not to mention his bare biceps and forearms. Yes, I'm sending a shot of him without his permission, but a picture is worth a thousand texts. Not to mention he still owes me for the heartbreak on Main Street.

The text bubbles ripple as Bristol composes a response. Then they disappear. Then they ripple again. So I jump in to acknowledge I realize how insane this situation is.

ME

> I know. It's bad.

BRISTOL

> Do you, Sara? Do you really know? Or are you forgetting how you spent freshman year holed up in the dorms like some kind of mole-person? You practically made not-dating-in-college an Olympic event. I almost requested a new roommate, remember?

I gulp.

ME

> Maybe?

Fabulous, Sara.

Talk about a vague reply.

BRISTOL

I told you not to go back to Abieville. But you said you'd be able to steer clear of Three. And now the man is half naked, sleeping ten feet away from you.

ME

He's fully clothed.

BRISTOL

That is so not the point. I don't want my best friend becoming one of those zombies on The Walking Dead again. You need to pawn Three and his bandaged head off on someone else immediately.

ME

Everyone's either out of town for the holidays or busy with their own families. And this is all my fault, so I'm pretty much on the hook.

BRISTOL

If you ask me, he deserves to be knocked out. I never even met the guy, but I saw what he did to my best friend. Who is awesome. Who is you. So I kind of wish I was there to rip him a new one.

ME

To be fair, that was ten years ago. He's a teacher now. Seems to maybe have grown up a little.

BRISTOL

DUDE. Don't let his hotness sway you. Do you remember how he spent four summers making you fall for him, acting like the perfect guy, and then once he had you drooling in the palm of his hands, he said he didn't feel like that about you? HE IS THAT GUY.

ME

You think he's hot?

BRISTOL

Ugh. I think he's the worst. STOP.

ME

Thank you. This is exactly the kick in the butt I needed. So can you do me a favor, and check in to remind me of all this over the next few days? Please? Just an occasional text to boost my immunity, kind of like a Three Fuller vaccination.

BRISTOL

You bet I will. Consider yourself FRESHLY INOCULATED. Now quit staring at that human virus and go to sleep.

ME

Thank you, Doctor Kane. You're the best.

Two hours later, when I wake Three for another check, he sits up without any extra jostling or prodding. Then he answers all my questions, more clearly than he did the first time.

"You're doing great," I say softly, but I'm talking more to myself than to him.

"I'd be doing better, if you stopped quizzing me," he mumbles.

Now *that* sounds like the old Three.

This is a good sign that his concussion isn't getting any worse, which is the best-case scenario. Because the sooner Three is better, the sooner the doctor will clear him to be alone, and the sooner I can move on from this momentary blip on my radar.

For now, though, I return to the armchair, and dream about a cruise ship being sunk by an army of giant candy canes.

Chapter Nine

Sara

The next morning, I'm in the kitchen slicing up French bread, when I hear a throat clearing behind me. Even with a pan of eggs and butter on the stove, I still catch the scent of pine-scented bubble bath mixed with Old Spice. I take a deep breath and turn around.

Freshly inoculated, Sara.

"You're up," I manage. "Obviously."

Over a plain white T-shirt, Three is wearing a hoodie the exact same blue of his eyes. And in case I hadn't clocked it before, the man fills out a pair of sweatpants better than any history teacher I've ever had. His hair is rumpled and wild above the angry lump from the fire extinguisher, and his eyes are hooded. Almost shy. "Thanks for looking out for me last night," he says. His voice is full of drowsy gravel.

"Just doing my job. No big deal."

He tips his head to indicate the stove. "And now you're whipping up breakfast too?"

I set down the knife to avoid getting distracted by the deliciousness of post-sleep Three. A girl could end up slicing off her finger. "It's just eggs and toast." I shrug, popping two slices of bread in the toaster. "I had to eat. So, again, no big deal."

I'm trying to let him know—and to remind myself—I'm not doing anything special for Three Fuller. Nothing different than what I'd already be doing for me, anyway.

He pulls a stool from under the island, and slides onto it. "Well, eggs and toast is more than anyone else ever makes for me, so..."

His voice trails off, and my pulse ticks up. Three must not have a significant other after all. At least not one who takes care of him. Or maybe he does have someone special, and she just doesn't like to cook.

Or maybe you should stop thinking about Three's relationship status.

"How are you feeling?" I ask, changing the subject to anything but Three being in love with some other woman.

"Still pretty foggy, but at least a little clearer than last night."

"You did seem pretty out of it." I fill a glass of water at the sink, and hand it over along with his morning dose of meds. "Do you want anything for the pain?"

He washes the medicine down, wincing. "To be honest, a lot of yesterday is a big blur to me, so I'm gonna stick to antibiotics. I don't think pain meds and I are meant to be friends."

"Yeah." I nod. "That's kinda how I feel about brownies now."

"Right." He pushes out a laugh, as I pour him a cup of coffee. Then I arrange the sugar bowl, creamer, and a spoon on the island in front of him. He picks up the steaming mug. "Mmm. Smells good."

My cheeks heat up as I flash back to last night, although I'm sure he has no memory of his groggy ramblings about how good I smell. Three takes a sip without adding anything to it, then lifts his gaze to mine. "Tastes good too."

My heart skips a beat. But I quickly school my face into a

mask of *nothing-to-see-here-folks.* "It's just coffee," I say before turning to collect butter and jam from the fridge.

Ugh.

Why do I feel so out of control of my body and brain? Yes, Three's an insanely attractive man. But I've been down the hot-guy road before—with this hot guy, specifically—so I know better than to put much stock in physical attributes. In fact, the few men I dated in college and law school looked vastly different from one another, and we took our time getting to know each other as friends first. I appreciated their sense of humor, their kindness, their intelligence.

I definitely didn't focus on their abs.

But the truth is, I have years of history of attraction to Three. A history that *does* involve abs, and also his humor and intelligence. Not to mention he was the kindest man I knew.

Until he wasn't.

So I guess I can't be too surprised that I slipped back so easily into admiring him on the surface, because I've already experienced his depths. I just have to make sure to keep things shallow for the next few days.

"Just so you know," he says, "I did text my family last night before I went to bed. I figured it was too late for them to pivot at that point, so I told them the truth. Well. *Most* of the truth. I didn't specify how or why this whole thing happened." He touches his skull, cringing. "I can't remember much anyway."

A wave of relief washes over me, although I probably shouldn't care whether or not the Fullers think this situation is my fault. It's not like I was the one who broke Three's heart. Still, I can't help wondering if he was protecting me, or if he had other reasons for not wanting them to know we're together.

"I'll bet they're pretty upset," I say, setting the butter and jam on the island. Then I fill my own coffee mug, along with a generous serving of cream.

"Probably." Three drops his brow. "I haven't looked at my phone yet. The cruise line warned us the Wi-Fi onboard is spotty, so texts and calls could be unreliable. In another couple hours, they should be at sea, so I'm waiting until then to check my messages."

I tip my chin. "But they won't be able to contact you at that point."

"Exactly." He bobs his head. "I'm afraid hearing their actual voices might be too hard. I don't want to get all sappy and beg them to come home and be with me for Christmas." He huffs out a small, sad laugh. "I'm just glad they all get to be together," he adds. "The rest of my family, I mean. Even if I can't be with them."

I blink at him, swallowing against the lump in my throat. "That's very generous of you."

"Yeah." The syllable comes out gruff. "I try to be generous."

And sometimes you even succeed, I think. *Unless you count that one summer ...*

Three averts his gaze, staring down at his coffee, so I take the opportunity to fork some eggs onto a couple of plates and snag the bread from the toaster. Then I come around the island with our food and slip onto the stool beside him.

Seated like this, we don't have to look at each other while we eat, which is probably a good thing. Eye contact with Three can be dangerous.

Ask me how I know.

I dig into my breakfast, alternating between bites of toast and eggs, and sips of coffee. Three does the same, working on his food without speaking either. We're about halfway through when I can't stand the silence anymore. "So you're off work for two weeks for winter break, huh?"

From my peripheral vision, I catch him nodding. "That's one of the reasons we planned the cruise for Christmas," he says. "It's the only time of year I have two weeks off in a row. Thanksgiving's only one week. Same with spring break."

I continue to eye him sideways. "Don't teachers get summers off?"

"Yeah." Another nod. "But I run the summer school program for the school district. And I lead guided fishing tours at The Beachfront Inn on weekends. My cousin, Olivia, works there with her fiancé now. I kinda like helping her and Hudson out. And I really like the extra money."

I add an extra dash of salt and pepper to my remaining eggs. "You don't need a special administrative degree for that?"

He squints at me. "To lead fishing tours?"

I puff out a laugh. "To run summer school."

"Nah." Three selects a piece of toast from the stack. "There aren't a ton of takers in a town this small. A teaching credential is plenty."

"Hmm." I shovel a forkful of peppery eggs in my mouth.

"I also oversee swim lessons at Abie Lake once the weather's warm enough." Three spreads a thick layer of jam on his toast. "And I still pick up a lifeguard shift every once in a while."

My memory digs up a visual of Three in his lifeguard tank top and board shorts. I start to gag on my eggs. "That's a lot of jobs," I manage to rasp, once I stop choking.

"I'm the girls basketball coach, too."

"Wow." I clear my throat and gulp but my eyes are watering now. "I guess you've gotten"—blink, blink—"pretty ambitious over the years."

Three chews his toast, and I note the bob of his Adam's apple when he gulps. "For the record, I never lacked ambition," he says. "Some kids just need a little more time before they find their direction."

"You're right. I'm sorry." I shove more eggs in my mouth, trying not to choke again.

"That first year after graduation, Nella talked me into taking some college classes online." He swipes a few toast crumbs off the counter onto his plate. "To be honest, I was just trying to act like an adult. Fake it till you make it, you know? So I studied a little bit of everything, but I really ended up loving the history courses. I got hooked. Applied to Albany U to complete my undergrad, and the rest is ... well ..."

My eyebrow quirks. "History?"

"Oh, man." He flashes me a look. "That is ... that was ... just such a horrible pun. Like practically criminal. You may be called upon to defend yourself in court someday."

A smile tugs at my lips. "That's what I'm here for. Horrible puns, hot baths, and barely palatable breakfasts."

"Well, your eggs are pretty good." He tilts his head. "But I thought you were here because you almost killed me with a fire extinguisher."

Ugh. My stomach lurches at the reminder that this whole situation is my fault, so I turn my head before Three can see my smile fade. "Do you want more eggs? Toast? Anything?"

"No thanks." He wrinkles his nose. "Usually I inhale my food like I'm trying to set a world record, but I don't have much of an appetite."

"Maybe that's a side effect of the concussion. Or the meds." I slip my phone from the pocket of my pajamas. "You want me to look up lack of appetite as a symptom?"

"No need." He drops his fork onto the plate and pushes it away. "I'm sure I'll be eating you out of house and home soon enough."

I set my phone down on the island. "Well, hopefully you'll get the all-clear at your checkup on Tuesday."

"Yeah." He balls his napkin up and tosses it on his plate. "And by then, the home evaluation will be done, and you can head back to the city for Christmas." He stops short of noting that he'll still be stuck here in Abieville while his entire family and most of his friends are gone for the holidays. But the truth hovers in the space between us.

"Well." I avert my gaze, and slide off the stool. "If you're not going to have more food, I guess I'll just get the dishes then."

I collect our plates, forks, and coffee cups, and stack everything in the sink so I can hand-wash them. I don't want anything in the dishwasher when the evaluator comes. My goal is perfection.

Minus the reindeer linens.

When I transfer the eggs into a storage container and wrap the toast up in foil, Three says, "You're actually saving those eggs and toast?"

"Of course." I shrug. "I don't like to waste anything if I don't have to."

I'm just sticking the food into the fridge, when my phone buzzes behind me. But it's on the island where I left it next to Three.

"Is that the evaluator texting?" I ask over my shoulder. "He's supposed to send me a confirmation for our meeting."

Three checks the screen. "Not the evaluator," he says. "Unless he's listed in your contacts as The Queen."

The Queen?

I slam the refrigerator shut and whirl around.

"I totally forgot about my mom."

Chapter Ten

Three

"Wait." I guffaw. "Your mom's The Queen?"

Sara flinches. "It's just a joke," she says. "Kind of."

I press out a laugh, even though my last memory of Katherine Hathaway is anything but funny.

"I was supposed to update her after I'd had a look around yesterday," Sara says. "She's been waiting for an eye-witness report, but I got distracted by all the brownie-baking and concussion-inflicting." Sara crosses the room, and I hand her the phone. She quickly scans the message and groans.

"Uh-oh." I frown. "What does The Queen have to say?"

Sara proceeds to read the text out loud in a dead-on impression of her mom: "Sara Jane, did you get eaten by bears? You promised to text me, but I haven't heard from you yet. Not following through on commitments isn't the Hathaway way. Bear interference is the only logical explanation."

"Oof." I offer Sara a grimace of sympathy. "She tossed in some middle-name action there. Not a great start, *Sara Jane*. But at least she's kidding around. That's better than her being straight-up mad at you, right?"

Sara cringes. "Tone is pretty hard to read over text, especially with my mom. So that could be less humor and more passive aggressiveness. Either way, I can't just message her now. I owe her an explanation over FaceTime."

Even as Sara says this, I flash back to the last conversation I overheard between Mr. and Mrs. Hathaway. That was a decade ago, and a part of me wishes they hadn't been in the living room with the front window open when I came to pick up Sara that day.

But they were.

"Hold on," I blurt. "Your parents can't know you're here with me." And now my insides feel like they're being crushed in a trash compactor.

"Huh?" Sara's whole face contorts in confusion. "Why do *you* care?"

Wow.

After all this time, I guess Sara still doesn't know how her mom and dad really felt about me, or how deeply I was already hurting by the time I hurt her. "I don't care personally," I say, adding a nonchalant shrug for extra proof. "But if you tell your mom you're taking care of me because of the concussion, you'll have to explain the whole oven debacle. And then your parents—"

"No, you're right." She throws a hand up to cut me off. "I don't need to relive that particular lapse in competence. And I definitely don't want my parents questioning my ability to handle things here." She pauses for a beat, chewing at her lip. "I guess I could just go with the partial truth like you did. I'll say I forgot to text her because everything here looks so great." Sara glances at the oven. "I'll just leave out the part where I had to scrape a full layer of smoke out of the kitchen to get it that way."

"On that note," I say, "I should probably go check my messages. I've put the pain off long enough. Time to face the I'm-not-going-on-the-cruise-with-you music."

"Oof." Sara grimaces. "Good luck with that."

"Thanks." I offer her a crisp salute. "And good luck back to you."

Her mouth takes on an angle like a ski slope. "Is it weird that I kind of feel like we're in this thing together now?"

"What thing?"

"The not-quite-telling-the-whole-truth-but-not-lying-either thing."

"I wouldn't call it weird," I say. "I'd call this self-preservation."

As I head off to the guest room, leaving Sara in the kitchen to FaceTime her mother, my guts begin to twist. Sure, I told Sara not to mention my name so she wouldn't have to admit her blunder with the oven. But if I'm being completely honest, I don't want her mom to find out I'm here and launch into a series of questions about what a nobody like me is doing with himself these days.

I can imagine Sara's answer, and Mrs. Hathaway being ... unsatisfied.

So you're saying he's still lifeguarding and teaching swim lessons after all these years?

That's hardly the Hathaway way.

I'd be willing to bet Sara's parents haven't reversed their negative opinions on my small-town gig life. Who cares if I'm happy in my work? That I've found a career I love? No matter what I accomplish in the classroom, my professional trajectory will never score me a penthouse like theirs.

Ten years ago, I had a hard enough time feeling worthy of Sara even before I discovered how the Hathaways truly felt. One whiff of fresh contempt could send me right down the I'm-not-worthy spiral they bought me season tickets to back then. So, yeah. No thank you.

In fact, that's a big fat *nope thanks*.

Plucking my phone from the charger, I drop onto the bed and settle back against the headboard to wait for my phone to power up. The apple pops onto the black screen first, then I'm prompted to enter my passcode. When my home screen opens, the first thing I see is my green messages app with red notifications in double digits.

All righty then. I'm about to see what chaos I've missed.

On the cousins text thread, I've received sympathetic and/or humorous messages from almost everyone. They've offered to order extra drinks for me (Brady), sing an extra karaoke song for me (Lettie), share extra TikTok videos with me (Olivia), meet extra women for me (Ford), eat extra dessert for me (Tess), win an extra round of trivia for me (Darby), take extra notes on the tour of the USS *Arizona* for me (Kasey) and book another cruise for everyone for next year (Mac).

Of course, the Original Fuller House thread has a flurry of confused texts from all three of my family members.

Then there are the voicemails. I swallow hard before I listen. And my throat only gets more clogged as I go.

From Smella: "Freebie, I must've fallen asleep on the red-eye, and now I'm having a nightmare you're not in the window seat next to me. When I wake up in California, I know you'll be there wearing your signature grin, and we'll go stuff our faces at the ship's all-you-can-eat buffet together. This is the only outcome I will accept under the circumstances, or else I might cry a little. And I know you don't want me to cry."

From Dad: "Son, your mother and I are very sorry to hear about your accident. We both noticed you didn't share any details about what happened, and the fact that you're staying somewhere we wouldn't be able to find you is ... well, that's strange. But it sounds like you're following medical advice, and you've got a good head on your shoulders, so I told your mother you'll be all right. Since you're still in town, maybe you could check that the pipes aren't freezing over at our place. I've never left home this time of year. Feels kinda strange to be away, not gonna lie."

From Mom: "Bradford Fuller, you do NOT get to leave a cryptic text message about being mysteriously injured, then tell us to have the best time ever on this cruise. I expect a phone call, an email, or follow-up text immediately. In fact, I'd like all of the above. And I don't give a fig about bad Wi-Fi. If NASA can send astronauts to the moon, this cruise line can get a message to your mother. Do NOT make me charter a jet or hire a private investigator to track you down before Christmas."

I grit my teeth and check the time. Everyone should be aboard the ship by now, so I might as well get my responses over with. I must've been pretty out of it yesterday to think I could get away with zero contact between me and my family for the next two weeks. So I try placing a call to my mom, but the connection fails. Next, I compose a text telling her I'm trying to get a call through to her, and that I promise to send an update soon.

The text doesn't go through.

Tossing the phone on the bed, I rake my hands through my hair, but just end up angering the bump on my forehead. "Man, I hate this," I mutter under my breath. Nothing about being stuck here with Sara Hathaway can come to any good. Forget Christmas. Forget a replacement cruise next year.

This entire situation sucks.

I've got to get out of this house. I need fresh air. An escape. I want to forget for just a moment that I'm a prisoner of this concussion. So I tug on a pair of cargo pants, my North Face jacket, a beanie, and some gloves. Then I head out of the guest room. Sara's still in the kitchen, and she's clearly talking to her mom.

Great.

At least one of us is.

"Believe me," Sara says on the tail end of a sigh. "I want all this over with as much as you do, Mom."

Whoa. I freeze at the edge of the hallway.

"No. Absolutely not," she protests. "You have no idea how much I wish I were home already."

A rope of frustration snakes around my gut, tightening itself until I can barely breathe. But I shouldn't be surprised Sara can't wait to leave Abieville. After our last summer together, her parents have had a full decade to get into her head. To change the woman I loved. She'll never want someone like me. She's been indoctrinated.

The Hathaway way.

Hot regret courses through my veins. I've gotta get out of here before I overhear even worse. Creeping toward the front door, I pass the open archway where I might be visible, so I crane my neck peeking into the kitchen hoping I won't get caught. Then, since I'm not looking where I'm going, I plow right into the console in the entryway.

Crap.

Chapter Eleven

Sara

"Crap!" Three blurts somewhere behind me.

Seconds later the front door opens, and his boots clomp onto the porch.

"What was that?" My mom's eyes widen, filling the phone screen. Her hair is perfectly coiffed, and she's wearing a winter-white cashmere sweater and matching slacks at nine in the morning.

Very Katherine Hathaway.

"I have no idea." I make a show of peeking over my shoulder even as the door clicks shut. Three better not be trying to go somewhere without me. But I need to deal with my mom without giving his presence away. "Probably a bear," I say.

My mother frowns. "That's not funny, Sara." She's in her standard perch on the Chesterfield sofa in the living room. The New York City skyline jags behind her through the sliding glass door to the balcony.

"You're actually just hearing the TV in the other room," I tell her. "I got Netflix, Hulu, and Prime set up for our future guests."

This part's totally true. I figured out all the streaming platforms last night before my first check on Three. But I can't think about him and his white T-shirt and his sleep-rumpled hair right now. Not while my mom's examining me like this.

Or any other time. *I'm freshly inoculated.*

"Well, thank you, dear." My mother sends me a wry smile. "I would've known that already, if you'd called to update me. I'll admit, I was a little worried at first when we didn't hear from you. But Daddy assured me you had everything under control. You *do* have everything under control, don't you?"

"Of course I do." I force a quick scoff. Good thing *under control* is relative. "And again, I really am sorry I didn't text or call. I just got ... busy."

"Yes. With all the streaming platforms. So you said." My mother's lipsticked mouth quirks. "So what else has been going on there? Tell me everything."

Everything?

Three's warning not to mention him leapfrogs across my brain, and he's not wrong. My goal in coming here was to prove how competent I am, not to demonstrate I can't operate an oven. So I'm going to focus on the agenda I *did* promise, and eliminate the rest.

"Well, I can tell you the pictures from the contractors don't do the renovation justice," I gush. "The kitchen is a perfect blend of modern farmhouse"—minus a few *extra* reindeer—"and the property is even prettier than I remembered. Then again, the trees weren't covered in snow when we stayed here in the summertime. They're like these tall, silent sentinels surrounding the house. It's really beautiful, Mom." My throat clogs a little, as I think about all the details I'm leaving out. "Oh. And you should see Abie Lake. It's one big sheet of ice now. I'll bet you can even skate on it."

"That all sounds lovely, Sara." She peers at me, then leans in closer to the screen, her eyes roaming my face. "Are you sure *you're* all right, though?"

Whoa. My mother must know me a little better than I thought she did. "I'm great," I chirp. "Which you'll see for yourself. At the gala."

"Ah, yes." Her expression brightens. "And another birthday for you, too. I can't believe my perfect little angel's going to be twenty-nine."

"I sure am." Something twinges in my abdomen. "But I'm not so perfect, Mom."

"Well, you're there handling the evaluation so we could stay in the city," she says. "Daddy and I are just so grateful."

"Of course." I press on a weak smile. "I know how important the fundraiser is to you."

"Not as important as you are." My mother straightens on the sofa. "Did I tell you we went to Rockefeller Center last night to see the tree?"

"You didn't, but I'm glad." My parents may have their issues, but they sure do love each other. Any shred of faith I have in love is a result of their almost-forty-year marriage. "So where is Dad, anyway?" I ask. "I have a new idea for Hathaway Cooke's scholarship program. I could run it by him now."

My mom shakes her head, simultaneously *tsking*. "He went into the office about an hour ago."

"On a Sunday?"

"You know your father. He has trouble relaxing."

I smirk. "Trouble relaxing is an understatement." My dad's a founding partner who values his firm almost as much as his family. Hopefully, once I've worked there for a while, he'll feel better about taking a back seat, and trust me to continue the Hathaway legacy.

"Truth be told," my mom says, "your father probably went to work to escape me."

"Why?" I snort. "You're a complete delight."

She waves my comment away. "And *you're* being sarcastic."

"Absolutely not." My lip twitches. "So what's going on?"

"We decided to include a two-week stay at the lake house in

the gala's silent auction, and we've set our highest fundraising goal ever."

"That's great, Mom." I offer her a reassuring nod. "This place will be a perfect addition to the fundraising."

"That's what I'm hoping, but the gala's only a few days away," she points out, like I don't already feel the burden of responsibility. "And if we can't promote the property as a Platinum Stays home, the bids won't go nearly as high."

"Ah." I glance across the kitchen into the living room and dining room. "Well, everything here is gorgeous. The perfect blend of upscale and rustic. So try not to worry too much."

"Not worrying isn't my strong suit." Her face pinches. "Did you confirm the appointment with the evaluator?"

I nod. "His name is Ryan Detweiler. He's coming today at eleven."

"And don't forget, you're not allowed to be on the premises while he's there."

"Yes, Mom. I remember. He's going to let himself in when he arrives."

"He has access to the lockbox?"

"I texted the code to him and I sent a backup email too." I take a beat, meeting my mother's gaze. "Like I told you, I've got this handled, Mom."

She lets out a long sigh. "I'm sorry to be so ... particular. I'll try to relax and trust the process from now on."

"Trust *me*," I say.

"Right." She folds her hands primly. "Thank you again for taking the lead on this, Sara. Your father and I are very proud of you."

"You are?" I swallow against the lump in my throat.

"Always, dear." Her eyes soften. "You're our perfect little—"

"I know, Mom."

I square my shoulders and dredge up a smile even as a familiar wave of pressure crests in me. Each year, on my birthday, my dad insists on recounting the story of his perfect little angel to everyone at the fundraising gala. As the legend goes, he and my mom had tried for ten years to have a baby, and after more than a decade of unsuccessful attempts, they'd finally wrapped their hearts around adopting. They were about to start the process when my mom discovered she was pregnant.

With me.

So I'm a miracle baby. Their only child. The long-awaited answer to years of prayer. And for better or worse, I carry the weight of that role on my shoulders, whether they're aware of the heaviness or not.

"Call me when you have some news," my mom says. "I'll try to be patient this time. Hopefully we'll have even more to celebrate this year on Christmas Eve."

"I can't wait." I gulp down the swell of emotion in my throat. "I miss you, Mom."

"Well, you'll be home soon. And in the meantime"—she hoists a brow—"steer clear of those bears."

Chapter Twelve

Sara

Thirteen Years Ago: July

I had the best time at the 4th of July carnival today, especially on the Ferris wheel with Three. Ford kept cat-calling from the seat behind us, and now I can't stop thinking this means Three likes me.

Ford wouldn't be teasing him if he didn't, right? Still, it's probably stupid to get my hopes up. For one thing, I've only known Three a few weeks. For another, we're leaving in August. So even if I can convince my parents to come back next summer, I won't see him again for the rest of the year. I'll be stuck at a stupid all-girls school.

. . .

Speaking of which, all the girls in Abieville like Three—and I do mean ALL. And I don't blame a single one of them.

He's sweet and fun and hilarious and—let's be real—he's super-hot. So this town is full of serious female competition, and they get to live here with him year-round. So what if I put myself out there and he rejects me? Is it crazy that I already feel like that might be a little crushing?

Yes, Sara. That's crazy.

Anyway, I guess it doesn't matter what Three thinks about me or if he ends up with some other girl, because—as my dad's always reminding me—I've got big plans after high school, which means this thing I'm feeling for Three can't go anywhere beyond friendship. Still, friends aren't nothing. Friends can be great.

And I have a really good one here in Abieville.

Chapter Thirteen

Three

"What are you doing out here?" Sara calls to me from the porch. Guess she's finally done talking to her mother. Meanwhile, I've been wearing a path in the snow between the house and the row of trees separating the property from the lake. My insides are in knots, and my dumb brain's broken. I keep playing Sarah's protest on a loop.

I want this all over with as much as you do, Mom.

So, yeah. Okay. Sara and I were never meant to be together. This isn't new news. It's a ten-year-old fact. But I don't have to like that fact.

Truth is, I hate it.

"Get in the house, mister." Sara's tone is stern, but she bites back a smile, and the cinching in my gut automatically loosens. Man, I wish she didn't have that effect on me. She's standing in the open doorway wearing thin pajamas and pink fuzzy slippers. They're adorable. *She's* adorable. But I can't think this woman's adorable. Not when she's got one foot out the door.

Literally.

"Are you coming inside, or what?" Sara crosses her arms.

"Yeah. Nope, thanks."

"I'm the boss of you, remember? We've still got a couple hours to kill before the evaluation, and you need to rest."

"Not interested." I resume my pacing like a caged animal. A caged animal who happens to be out in the open in the Adirondacks.

"Stop!" she commands, and I freeze in my tracks, turning to face her again. She crosses the porch, hands hitting her hips. "Just come inside, and I'll open up a jigsaw puzzle. There's one that's all candy canes. Like, literally every piece is just red and white stripes."

"Sounds like a blast for a guy with a concussion." I toss her an eye roll to be sure she catches the sarcasm.

"Right. No puzzles." She tips her chin like she's weighing her options. "The den is stocked with games. We could play chess."

"Chess?" A guffaw puffs out of me.

"What? Too cool for you?" She approaches the porch railing, one eyebrow quirked slyly. "I'll have you know I *was* the president of our elementary school's team. We were called the Chess Nuts."

"Clever."

"Thanks." A grin crisscrosses her face. "The name was my idea. And for the record, my skills are a little rusty. So who knows? You *might* even beat me."

"Unlikely."

"Because of the concussion?"

I cock my head. "Because I've never played chess." She's not wrong, though. My brain definitely feels ... off. But at this point, I can't tell if that's due to my head injury or to being with Sara. Or both.

"How about checkers?" she persists. "It's not as cool as chess, but everyone knows how to play checkers. Even people with concussions."

I reach up and adjust my beanie, making sure the lump on my temple isn't visible. "You go on without me. I'll be all right."

"But I can't play alone." Her smile falters. "And you're not allowed to be unsupervised."

"Then supervise me out here." I nod to indicate the stretch of snow leading down to the lake. "We could go for a run. My skills are a little rusty, so who knows? You *might* even beat me."

"Sorry." Sara tips her chin. "I only run when I'm being chased."

"All right." I arch a brow. "Then let me chase you."

She shivers, and I find myself hoping her reaction's less about being cold and more about ... me. I know I shouldn't entertain these thoughts, but I'm only human. A human who once loved Sara Hathaway with his whole stupid heart and his un-concussed head.

"We can't run," she says. "You could slip and fall and make everything worse." She wraps her arms around her middle. "There must be *something* we could do that's low risk. But *not* puzzles or chess." Sara sighs, and a pang of sympathy starts clanking around my chest. She's just trying to entertain me. I don't have to make things any harder on her than they already are. "Do you want to build a snowman?"

She huffs out a laugh. "So you're quoting *Frozen* now?"

"Nah." I shake my head. "I'm not that cold."

"No, I meant the movie. *Frozen.*"

"Never heard of it."

Of course I've heard of it. I have a sister. Does Sara really believe I don't know about Elsa and Anna?

"Wow." She widens her eyes, bewildered. "Your brain really does have some big gaps."

I hitch my shoulders. "I guess so."

"Either way, it's freezing out here, and you know I'm always cold."

A fresh tremor racks her body, and my stomach plummets. Yeah. I actually do know that about Sara. I remember a lot of things I tried hard to forget. Like that first night at the beach bonfire when I gave her my sweatshirt to keep warm. The thing smelled like her for the rest of the summer.

How about her tears when you broke her heart?

Yeah. I can't forget those either.

"Three. Please." She blows a strand of hair off her face, and I fight the urge to rush over and tuck it behind her ear. I used to kiss her there, along that soft curved shell.

Man, you are in soooo much trouble.

"Just go inside out of the cold," I say, stuffing my gloved hands into my pockets. "Don't worry about me."

"I have to worry, though. You're my responsibility."

"Yeah." I grunt. "And whose fault is that?"

"Okay, fine!" she blurts. "You win. We can build a snowman. But I'll need to put on more layers if we're staying outside."

"We don't have to—"

"No." She throws up her hands. "This is what you wanted, Three. And your wish is my command." She points at a tree stump covered with an inch of snow. "Just sit there so I know you're safe while I'm gone."

"But—"

"I'll be right back."

Before I can offer up any further protest, she turns her back on me and heads inside. So I shuffle over to the stump, brushing off the snow to take a seat. I've never seen Sara dressed for the snow before. At least not in person. Sure, I probably caught a picture of her in the winter years ago. But until yesterday, I'd only imagined her in summer clothes. Mostly I tried not to imagine her at all.

Within minutes, though, she's bursting back out onto the porch, yanking up the zipper of a white jacket. "Phew! I feel better already!"

Her hair is loose and streaming down her shoulders, like a waterfall at midnight. Her hot pink beanie is topped with a turquoise ball. She's got a turquoise scarf wrapped around her neck. Turquoise mittens. Hot pink snow pants.

If you'd asked me five minutes ago if she could get any prettier than the girl I remember in a summer sundress and flip-flops, I would've said no way. Absolutely not.

And yet.

Sara Hathaway is way beyond pretty.

She's a grown woman now, grinning at me like she's ready for anything. My jaw must fall open, because she glances down, checking out her jacket and pants. "What?"

"Nothing." I slam my mouth shut. "It's just ... you look very ..."

She lifts her chin. "Warm?"

I nod. "Yeah. And also ..."

"Colorful?"

"I was going to say you look ..." My voice trails off as I fumble for an answer. The truth is, she looks incredibly beautiful. Not to mention fun. Like someone I could spend all day with. But besides all that, I know she's also kind. Generous and smart. The woman of my dreams. But I can't tell her these things. "You look ... like cotton candy," I finally manage.

She scrunches up her face. "Ugh. No."

"What's wrong with cotton candy? It's sweet and pink and fluffy."

"Fluffy's not exactly a compliment." She lets out a string of laughter, ending on a snort. "Never mind," she says. "Forget I asked."

"Yeah. Forget I said it."

"Deal." A new dimple presses into her cheek. "Oh, wait!" She lifts a finger. "I just thought of something." She ducks into the house, returning almost immediately with one large carrot and a box of Oreos. "For the snowman's nose and eyes," she says. "I figure we can spare these."

"You take your snowman building seriously, huh?" I make a move to stand from the stump, but Sara waves me back down.

"No, you stay there." She sets the carrot and Oreos on the bottom step, then trudges out into the snow.

I pull down my brow. "You want me to just sit here and ... watch you?"

"It'll be safer." She stoops to start scooping snow into a ball, then she keeps rolling and rolling until the pile slowly takes shape.

"This is ridiculous," I call out while she's finishing up the base.

"You're concussed," she says.

"I'm not *that* bad."

"You don't remember the movie *Frozen*. And you called me cotton candy." She glances over her shoulder. "I rest my case."

Man. Sara really is a lawyer.

By the time she starts forming the middle ball for the snowman's torso, I can't take it anymore. I feel more useless than I did when I was out here pacing by myself. "I'm beginning to think a puzzle would be a better use of my time," I say. "Can I do something to help? Anything? Please?"

Sara pauses, humming out loud as she considers my offer. "Why don't you gather up a couple of sticks for the snowman's arms?"

"Sure." I shrug. "But are you sure you trust me to gather sticks? I could trip and bang my head into one of those killer trunks over here."

"Don't push your luck, or I may withdraw my consent." She tips her mouth into a smirk.

"Well, we can't have that."

"Maybe find some rocks we can use for buttons, too," she says.

"Buttons?"

"For the snowman's coat."

"What coat? He's not wearing anything."

"We're pretending," she says. "Like *The Emperor's New Clothes*. Just imagine Henry in a fully regal wardrobe."

"Who's Henry? Another *Frozen* reference?"

"Henry's our snowman." She grins at me. "He needed a name. And arms and buttons."

I push out a chuckle. "Got it."

While Sara returns to working on our snowman, I head toward a copse of trees off to the right. There are no fences around this property. Just drifts of snow, plenty of trees, and the lake behind the house. Striding over to the trees, I take a loose branch to brush away the snow around the base. After locating a trio of similarly sized rocks, I find a couple of matching branches to make a pair of arms.

By the time I return, Sara's building the snowman's head. So while she's distracted, I set down my supplies and scoop up a few small handfuls of snow, packing them one at a time into tight round spheres.

Yes. I'm gearing up for a snowball fight.

My sister, cousins, and I used to do this during snow days when we were young. We'd prep a whole arsenal, waiting for other unsuspecting kids to walk down the street. Then we'd start up a war. A harmless one, of course.

We're talking exploding snow, not actual ammunition.

The memory makes me smile. So does the fact that Sara seems unaware of my growing stockpile. I probably shouldn't let myself enjoy being with her right now, but I'll blame any poor decision-making on my head injury. Besides. I'm getting tired of feeling bad, and good times with Sara were always effortless.

Until they weren't.

As she affixes the Oreo eyes and carrot nose to Henry's head, I pluck up a snowball, and wait for her to finish. When she's finally done and takes a step back to admire her handiwork, I clear my throat.

"Ahem."

She spins around, freezing for a beat. Then her eyes widen. "What are you doing?" By way of answer, I lob a snowball that lands a full yard in front of her feet, because I'm not trying to actually hit her.

That is until she taunts me.

"That's the best you can do, Fuller?" Her tone is wry, her mouth twisted into a smirk.

I collect another snowball. "That was just my warning shot, Hathaway."

"But this isn't really fair," she says. "I can't even fight back."

"Why not?"

"You're injured. And I'd never take advantage of that."

I hoist my eyebrows. "That sounds like a *you* problem."

"Oh, I see." She offers me a wicked grin, her mittens planted on her hips. "So that's how it's gonna be?"

"Yup." My lips twitch. "That's how it's gonna be."

"Good luck, then." Sara moves around behind the snowman, slowly, bending to scoop handfuls of snow and compacting them into balls with her mittens.

"Hey. You can't use Henry as a fortress."

"Really?" She pokes her head around the corner. "Then how come I am?"

"HA!" I chuck another snowball at her, but Sara ducks back to safety. So I wait. And when she stands again with a snowball ready to throw at me, my next toss is a direct hit. It's like her beanie has a bullseye on it.

"Ack! No!" she shrieks, even as the softly packed snowball bursts into nothing but powder on contact. She drops down behind Henry again, and for a split second I worry I might've hurt her. But the giggles coming from behind our snowman suggest Sara's not wounded. She's having fun.

We're having fun together.

Sara's laughter transports me back to all those sunny summer days we spent together, and for a moment my body floods with warmth. Then I remember the pain of walking away from the purest love I've ever felt and my insides turn to ice.

You heard Sara talking to her mom earlier. She can't wait to get away from Abieville.

Away from you.

She slowly peeks out at me, and the flush of joy on her cheeks makes my jaw clamp down.

A shadow passes over her face. "What's wrong?" She leaps to her feet, scrambling toward me. "Is it your head? Are you okay?" She tears a mitten off and presses her palm to my cheek. Her touch is a shock, conducting electricity straight to my bones. Heat races through my veins, pushing my bloodstream to the boiling point.

Sara's probably touched me in the past twenty-four hours. But I can't remember. I blame the concussion. And the pain meds. The blur her proximity causes in my brain. Either way, as far as I can recall, this is our first direct skin-to-skin contact in close to a decade.

Then I hear her voice:

I want this all over with as much as you do, Mom.

I jerk away from her, rearing backward, and Sara's face collapses in an avalanche of concern.

"I'm sorry. I shouldn't have rushed at you like that," she hurries to say. "I was just scared you might've been hurt."

Her irises are saucers now, and her sweet scent hovers above us. All I want is to take her in my arms and tell her she hasn't done anything wrong. That she could never do wrong in my eyes. But comforting Sara wouldn't be good for either of us. We've already slipped into old, familiar patterns far too easily. I've got to get ahold of myself and get a wall built back up between us.

Fast.

"It's not you." I work my jaw. "The snowball thing just got me thinking about Christmas with my sister. My cousins." I say this to sever the connection with Sara, but my words are still true. I *was* thinking about my family. Trouble is, I was also happy. And happiness with Sara will only make her leaving again harder. Or make me wish she'd stay this time.

"I'm so sorry." Her eyes soften at the edges. "I can only imagine how much you're missing your family right now."

"Yeah." I hazard a glance back at the house. "I tried calling my mom, but the signal wouldn't go through. Then I tried texting her, but I got a failure-to-send warning."

Sara blinks. "That was your plan, though, right? Weren't you hoping to avoid contact?"

"I guess." Heat rises in my throat.

Sara's not wrong, but most of what I've said and done in the past twenty-four hours was under the influence of a dreadful combination: my concussion, the medication, and some straight-up denial.

"Seemed like a good idea at the time," I say. "But I was mostly trying not to think too hard about the reality of the next two weeks. Everyone gone. Me stuck here alone."

"You're not alone." Sara says this, but the echo of her words to her mother ring in my head.

You have no idea how much I wish I were home already.

I swallow hard. "I'll be fine."

"Maybe you can try later and get through to your family." Her chin trembles. It's slight, but I notice. So I take another step backward, putting even more distance between her and the wave of protectiveness overtaking me.

"Sure, maybe."

Sara blinks, like she's fighting back tears. At least I'm far enough away from her now that I can't reach out and touch her. Which is good, because that's all I want to do. And at the same time, I find myself wondering if she might've felt the connection between us too. Still, that's a dangerous question. One I shouldn't be asking myself.

"After the evaluator comes, we can go to the market." She nods, establishing a strategy. "I can get a turkey. Stuffing. Cranberry sauce. Sweet potatoes. We'll make our own Christmas dinner early."

"Won't be the same."

She draws in a stuttering breath, then she exhales. Soft and slow. I want to suck the words back in, but they're already hovering in the air above us. At the very least, I should tell her I don't actually think she's responsible. That she shouldn't be mad at herself, because I'm certainly not mad. At least not at her. I'm mostly angry with myself. For being so easily influenced by her presence.

"Sara."

"What?" She looks up at me with sadness in her eyes, and my heart's a freight train plowing straight off a cliff.

"It's not your—"

ZZT.

Her whole body leaps like she's been zapped with a cattle prod, but it's just her phone buzzing. *That's* how much I put her on edge. Slipping her phone from her pocket, she quickly checks the text.

"It's the evaluator," she groans. "He's canceling our appointment."

Chapter Fourteen

Sara

Car trouble.

That's why Ryan Detweiler postponed his visit until tomorrow. Monday morning, ten o'clock. And while I'm sure the glitch was unintentional, the man's timing couldn't be worse. We were already cutting things close trying to secure Platinum Stay's approval before the gala. Christmas Eve is only three days away. So the sooner my mom can add the lake house to the silent auction, the better.

Then there's the fact that the evaluator interrupted Three and me.

For a moment there, out in the yard, we seemed to be on the verge of enjoying ourselves—putting the past behind us and letting the present be not so bad. But in the end, a few snowballs couldn't erase the fact that I ruined Three Fuller's Christmas.

I mean, sure, I'm with him for now, but as soon as this evaluation is over and he gets the all clear from the doctor, I'll be heading back to the city. And Three will be stuck in Abieville on his own.

Home alone for the holidays.

To distract him from the inevitable—and stock up on enough food to feed two people for the next few days—I drag him to the market on Main Street. All the street lamps are wrapped in garland. Jingle bells hang above every door. The midday sky is bright and sun-drenched despite the cold. Still, Three plods along beside me, one tall shadow with hunched shoulders.

His mood doesn't improve inside the shop, although the owners have done their best to turn the place into a Christmas wonderland. Thousands of paper snowflakes hang from the ceiling. Strands of red and green garland swoop over the end caps of each aisle. The bases of the fruit and vegetable bins are wrapped up like presents. It's all very fun and festive. But it's also a reminder of exactly what Three's missing.

The holidays with his family.

Ho ho ho.

As I steer our squeaky, half-full cart toward the canned goods aisle, a jubilant rendition of "We Wish You A Merry Christmas" starts playing over the sound system. The choir warbles their request for figgy pudding, and I hazard a peek at Three. "So what are *your* thoughts on figgy pudding?"

He harrumphs. "This may come as a big surprise, but I've never given much thought to figgy pudding."

"Then you're in luck." I puff out a laugh, trying not to sag under the weight of my guilt. "Because now's your chance to weigh in."

"Fine." Three shrugs, tipping his chin. "Better than fruitcake, I guess. Worse than pie."

"*Obviously* worse than pie," I squawk, pausing the cart by the relish shelves. "Pie is practically top tier, coming in just below chocolate cake."

"Disagree." Three shakes his head. "Pie is superior to cake."

"I see. So you're okay being wrong."

"Never." His mouth tugs up at one corner, and a flicker of

hope warms my chest. I want Three to be happier. But I also have to keep a tight rein on my emotions.

Focus on food, Sara.

Stomachs not hearts.

So I add a jar of olives to the cart, then collect a can of cranberry sauce, several gravy packets, and a jumbo container of mashed yams. When Three reaches out to straighten a display of stuffing boxes in danger of toppling, I ask him to grab us a box. He tosses one into the cart, and we push our way to the meat department.

The frozen turkeys on display are a little too big for two people. So while the ruddy-faced butcher tries to locate a smaller turkey in the back, I pepper Three with more Christmas-themed questions.

Distraction. Distraction. Distraction.

"Do you like marshmallows on your sweet potatoes?" I ask.

He scoffs. "Of course. I'm not a monster."

"Whipped cream or ice cream?"

"Both."

"Pumpkin pie or apple?"

"Neither," he says. "Pecan."

"Ah. Good choice. But not as good as chocolate cake."

"Incorrect," he says. "Chocolate cake is inferior to pie."

"Objection, your honor."

Three coughs out a laugh. A small one, but still. "Stop being a lawyer."

"Too late," I say. "And now I'm thinking we should hold our own trial." I nod toward the bakery across the shop. "When the butcher comes back with our turkey, we can grab a pecan pie and chocolate cake and have a dessert competition after dinner. We'll just have to swear to be impartial when we render our verdicts." I turn to meet Three's gaze again, and his eyes lock with mine.

"You don't have to do this, Sara."

I blink. "Do what?"

"Try to cheer me up."

"What if I want to?"

"What if it's not possible?"

I cross my arms. "I can be very persistent."

"Yeah. I vaguely recall that about you." His mouth curves up on one side, just enough to increase my pulse rate.

Don't stare at his lips, Sara.

Focus on something else.

Anything *but that killer almost-smile.*

"So." I gulp down the heat in my throat. "Besides snowball fights with your cousins, what other special traditions did you have as a kid?"

He drags a hand down his face, like he's considering the answer. "Are we talking about winter stuff in general? Or Christmas-specific things?"

My gaze swings to the sprigs of holly above the doors where the butcher disappeared. "Christmas, please."

"Okay." He pushes his hands into his pockets. "For one thing, my mom bakes about a billion Christmas cookies every year, but that's not really special to our family." He takes a beat. "She also keeps a pot of water with cinnamon sticks, nutmeg, and cloves simmering on the stove all season. I don't know anyone else who does that."

"Huh." I tip my chin. "Is that to eat?"

"To smell." He ducks his head, almost shyly. "That scent reminds me of Christmas every year."

"Sounds heavenly."

"Mmhmm." He presses his lips together, and I snap my focus back up to his eyes. Not that his eyes are any less tempting than his mouth.

"What else?" I ask.

"We used to do something kind of unusual, for tree trimming."

I grin at him. "Tinsel? Flocking?"

"Heh." A soft chuckle brushes his lips. "I have no idea what flocking is, and I'm pretty sure I don't *want* to know. But at our house, while my dad got the tree set up, my mom, Nella and I would sew strands of popcorn together—like with actual needles and thread—then we'd wrap them around the tree."

"Popcorn garland?"

"Yup."

"Nice." I arch a brow. "Sign me up for edible tree trimming at the Fuller House."

A slow smile sneaks onto his face. "On the day after Thanksgiving, Nella and I would cut a bunch of strips out of red and green construction paper and glue the strips into rings to make a couple of long chains. The number of rings matched however many nights there were until Christmas Eve. We'd hang our chains in our rooms, and every night before bed, we'd tear off another ring."

"Kind of like a homemade advent calendar?"

"*Exactly* like a homemade advent calendar." He pauses to work his jaw back and forth. "I've gotta say, all this nostalgic talk is really bringing me back."

Before I can ask him if that's a good thing or a bad thing, the butcher returns with a small turkey wrapped in white paper. "I found a fresh five-pounder for you." He slips the turkey into a plastic bag, and passes it over the counter to Three. "Tiny bird this year, huh?"

"Yup." Three bobs his head, placing the turkey into the cart. "Thanks, Raymond. Merry Christmas to you and Beth."

Of course Three knows the butcher and his wife by name.

Three knows everyone in Abieville.

We both fall quiet as we head to the bakery for our pecan pie and chocolate cake. I'm pretty sure Three's thinking about his dinner-for-one on actual Christmas now.

Gee, Raymond. Thanks a lot.

As we make our way to the checkout line, I push ahead of Three a few steps, then turn the cart to block his progress. "Before we go, I think we should grab a big jar of popcorn kernels from the snack section, then check the stationery aisle for construction paper, scissors, and glue. If they don't have a sundries section with sewing supplies here, we can make a pit stop at the Five and Dime for needle and thread. I'll bet they've got cheap ornaments and twinkle lights in a sales bin we can pick up there too."

"Listen, Sara." He averts his gaze. "You don't have to—"

"And *then*," I rush to add, "we'll head over the bridge to the Christmas tree farm I spotted on my way into town."

He drags a hand along the bandage at the base of his skull. "I appreciate what you're trying to do, but I'm not a kid anymore. I don't need magic and Santa Claus."

I huff out a breath. "Well, maybe I do. Need magic and Santa Claus, I mean. Come on, Three. If we're going to be stuck together for the next few days, we might as well try to have some fun. And besides. It'll be good for your brain."

He squints at me. "How do you figure?"

"Because you're going to have to teach me how to do all this stuff you were talking about." I splay my hands. "I've never made my own advent-calendar chain or strung popcorn on a tree. I've never even gotten to pick out a tree, let alone trim it. My mom always has a professional designer decorate our house for the holidays."

"But—"

"Douglas or noble?" I blurt.

"Huh?"

"Your fir trees. Noble or Douglas? Which do you prefer for Christmas?"

Our gazes meet, and Three tips his head, light flickering behind his eyes. "Wow. You really are persistent."

A grin splits my face. "That's the right answer."

Chapter Fifteen

Three

Humboldt Farms is just over the bridge, about a mile up from the docks at Abie Lake. The sprawling property isn't really so much of a farm as a few acres where Stanley Humboldt sells seasonal products he has shipped in from upstate.

Pumpkins and gourds in the fall. Christmas trees and wreaths in the winter. Fresh fruit and vegetables in the spring and summer.

This time of year, his best customers are typically tourists and a few less adventurous people living in the areas surrounding Abieville. That's because most locals go out and chop down a tree themselves—either on property they own, or on land owned by friends or family.

At this point, though, I'm not about to suggest we trudge out to my Uncle Cubby's place. We don't have a chainsaw with us, and Sara probably wouldn't let me exert that much effort anyway.

Not to mention the already-cold temperatures will keep dropping with the sun, and I'm not about to watch Sara shiver out in the woods.

Bottom line: Humboldt Farms and their pre-cut trees are our best bet under the circumstances.

As Sara drives us over the bridge, she keeps her gaze locked on the other side of the lake. At the first glimpse of red barn off to the east, she yelps.

"There!" She points toward the horizon. "That's Humboldt Farms!"

"Yes, I know where Humboldt Farms is."

She swings her focus back to the bridge. "It's just that you don't seem very excited."

"Really?" I stifle a snort. "I think I'm *just the right* amount of excited."

"Well, hopefully they'll still have some decent trees left to choose from," she chirps, ignoring my sarcasm. "What do you think we should get? Eight foot? Nine? Taller?"

I shake my head, finally surrendering to a chuckle. "I didn't measure the ceiling back at the lake house, but we're not at the Hathaway penthouse. I'd guess nine's about right. Maybe eight if you want to leave room for the star on top."

"See?" Sara shoots me a grin. "*This* is exactly why I need you."

"Hmm." I grunt, but my heart does a little zigzag in my chest. I like hearing that Sara needs me. A little too much.

No, *a lot* too much.

"Thanks for remembering to get a star by the way." She nods to indicate our haul from the Five and Dime. Bags of tinsel, white lights, ornaments, and the world's ugliest Christmas tree skirt are in the back with our groceries. Luckily, we didn't buy anything frozen, so there's just enough time to grab a tree and get back home.

Another grunt from me.

"This is all going to work out," Sara gushes, and a fresh wave of dizziness threatens my vision.

So I stare at the dashboard, trying my best to hide my brain fog from Sara. I need her to believe I'm healing. That my head's not at risk, let alone my heart. If I can just hold on a couple more days, she never has to know how much I'm beginning to dread being without her.

By the time we pull up to Humboldt Farms, Sara's officially wiggling like a puppy. "You've *got* to be kidding me," she gasps. "This is amazing! Isn't this amazing?"

My mouth goes crooked, but then I try to imagine the scene through her first-timer eyes.

Snow-dusted pine trees stretch in neat rows across from where we're parked. To the right is a beverage stand selling mulled wine and hot cocoa. Two large firepits flicker in the space between the trees and an enormous barn. The rooftop and open doors are all lit up with strands of red and green Christmas bulbs.

"I love everything about this," Sara says, almost breathless.

I nod toward the barn. "I don't want to send you into orbit, but they're probably selling gingerbread cookies and Santa hats in there. And Stanley will definitely be giving away candy canes."

"Yes, yes, and yes." She beams at me. "But first things first, we need a tree!"

She clambers out of the car and takes a shortcut to the nearest row of pines, crunching over a low snowbank at the edge of the parking lot. I follow her, hands stuffed in my pockets, watching as she ruffles the branches of each tree. She peeks around the back of them, probably searching for potential bald spots. The whole time, she's got her chin tipped, eyes in a squint, nose wrinkled in concentration.

The woman means business.

And it's adorable.

"I like this one!" She's stopped in front of an eight-foot noble fir at the edge of the third row. "What do you think?" she asks, with a little hop and clap.

I bob my head. "It's a beaut, Clark."

"Ha! I *love* that movie." Sara snort-laughs at my *Christmas Vacation* reference, her eyes shining with pure joy. She's basically a kid in a candy store right now. It's like she's never picked out a Christmas tree before.

Oh, right. I guess she hasn't.

"Hey! Mr. Fuller!" someone calls out from a few rows away. It's Sullivan Ackerman in a Santa hat, all six foot six of him, looking like Jack and his beanstalk melded into one giant teenager.

I had Sully for US history last year, and he's in my senior government class now. Good kid. Great basketball player. Talented enough to score a full ride to Ohio State next fall.

"Hey, Sully." I wave as he approaches. When he spots Sara for the first time, the kid's jaw comes unhinged.

Yeah, I get it, man. She's really something else.

He reaches up to adjust his hat, then boomerangs his focus back to me. "How ... how is ...how's your winter break going, Mr. Fuller?"

Since my bandage is hidden by the beanie, I make a snap decision not to go into any of the details. "So far, so good," I say, vaguely.

Sara lets out a barely audible yelp.

Sully nods, his gaze flicking between us, ultimately landing on me. "What can I do for you, then?"

"Oh, we're just here to get a tree." As soon as the word 'we' slips out of my mouth, I regret it. Good thing Sully's already so awkward around girls—he's probably not gonna ask about Sara. Who she is. What she means to me.

Please don't ask about Sara.

"Sure thing, Mr. Fuller." Sully nods to indicate the tree next to Sara. "Is this the one?"

"Yes!" She claps again and something stirs behind my ribs. Seeing her happy like this makes me happier than I've felt in a while. Concussion or no concussion.

"I'll just net the tree up for you and load it into your truck, then." Sully surveys the parking lot probably searching for my Chevy.

"It's the blue sedan over there today." I pull out my wallet and slip out a twenty for a tip. "Can you tie the tree to the roof?"

"'Course." I pass Sully the money while Sara hands over the keys. He ducks his head, throat blotching up. "Thanks, Mr. Fuller. Ma'am." He stuffs the bill into his pocket, then yanks the tag off the tree so I can take it to the cashier to pay. "Won't take me long."

"No rush," I say. In fact, I've got nothing but time to kill for the next couple days. And then another couple weeks before everyone's back from Hawaii. Just in time for me to go back to work again.

Vacation over.

"I've gotta grab a tree stand too," I tell Sully, careful not to use *we* this time.

"Mr. Humboldt's got some in the barn."

"Is he selling cookies tonight?"

"You bet." A grin spreads across his face. "We've got a charity thing going on in there, too." Sully cuts his gaze to Sara. "But only if you want to participate, ma'am."

"Call me Sara," she says. "And we *do* want to participate. Don't we, Three?" Sara turns and aims her hundred-watt smile on me. "'Tis the season after all!"

Without waiting for a response, she takes my hand, dragging me past one of the firepits and the beverage stand, right into the barn. As usual, the cashier station is on one side of the room along with the Christmas tree stands and a display of fresh wreaths made from pinecones and spruce. There's also a rack of Santa hats for sale, and as we pass it, Sara snatches two.

Against the opposite wall is a temporary archway set up on a low stage. The arch is decked out with white lights, holly, and bunches of mistletoe tied in red ribbon. Carver Townsend, one of Abieville's deputies, is standing on one side of the arch holding a Polaroid camera. Behind him is a cork board with a bunch of instant pictures already pinned to it.

When he spots us, his eyes immediately lock on Sara, and my guts twist as he appraises her from across the room. Not that I've got any right to be possessive of Sara. It's just that Carver and my sister are neighbors, and she's had a crush on him forever. If Nella knew Carver was gawking at Sara right now, she'd not only be hurt, she'd—

"Three!" Sara sucks in a breath, and I turn to face her. Her eyes go wide. "Did you see the sign?"

Uhhh, sorry. I've been too busy watching Carver stare at you. "What sign?"

"It's for the charity Sully talked about," she hisses. "We've *got* to get out of here."

Chapter Sixteen

*

**

**KISSES
FOR KIDS!**

**Buy a sprig of mistletoe for $10,
and your money will go to support
the Christmas Kringle Fund for Children!**

**Take a picture smooching under the arch,
and Humboldt Farms will match your donation!
Thanks
For
Your
Kiss!**

Chapter Seventeen

Sara

Kisses for Kids?

I gape at the sign like my eyeballs are magic laser beams that will morph the words into something else. ANYTHING ELSE. But they don't. I'm in a nightmare, and I can't wake up.

To be clear, I'd do a lot for kids. Just about whatever anybody asked me to.

Toys for Tots? I'm all in. Caroling at a children's hospital? Sign me up. But kissing Three Fuller? In public? And being photographed while we're doing it?

No. No way.

The cork board hanging on the wall behind the arch is already half full of Polaroids of couples kissing. My cheeks heat up, and I can practically feel my pulse leaping into warp speed. I'm barely in control of my emotions after spending less than two days with Three Fuller. Feeling his lips on mine again—even for charity—might blow my heart right out of my body and straight through the roof.

Now a sandy-haired man carrying a Polaroid camera is

striding toward us. He's wearing a Santa hat, and he reminds me of a Hemsworth brother, which is probably why he looks familiar. Either way, his face is screwed up like he's confused.

Yep. That makes two of us, buddy.

When Santa Hemsworth reaches us, he sticks his free hand out to shake Three's. "Hey, man. Aren't you supposed to be on a cruise right now? At least that's what Nella said. She asked me to keep an eye on her place while she's gone."

"Yeah." Three releases Santa Hemsworth's grip and pushes both his hands into his pockets. "Last-minute change of plans," he grumbles.

"It's all my fault," I blurt before I can stop myself. My adrenaline's kicked into overdrive and my pulse is racing. "Nella *is* on a cruise, and so is everyone else, but I attacked Three with a fire extinguisher, and he couldn't travel because of the concussion."

"Excuse me?" Santa Hemsworth blinks. "You ... attacked him?"

"Congratulations." Three lifts a brow. "You just confessed to Deputy Townsend."

"Oops." I grimace at the deputy, and my cheeks flame up even hotter than they already were. "Hello, sir. It was just one big accident. I promise. Please don't arrest me."

"Don't worry." He bobs his head, a slow smile spreading across his face. "Your secret's safe with me .... umm ...I don't believe I caught your name."

"Sara," I rush to say. "Sara Hathaway. Nice to meet you."

"Carver Townsend." He shakes my hand, and his smile gets wider. "You know what? I think we actually met a long time ago. At a summer bonfire." His gaze flicks to Three. "Your sister was there too, right?"

Three harrumphs. "I'm sure she was."

Ahhh, yes. Carver Townsend. *Now* I remember why he looks familiar. Nella used to crush on this guy. Hard. I wonder if anything ever happened between them. They'd make a really cute couple.

"Carver lives next door to Nella now," Three adds. And if I'm not mistaken, he moves an inch closer to me.

"Yeah." Carver offers another head bob. "Nella and I are good friends."

A beat of awkward silence stretches between us all until Three nods to indicate the mistletoe arch. "So I see you got roped into being the photographer for this thing, huh?"

"Nah, I volunteered." Carver shifts his weight, shoulders hitching. "Anything for the kids, right?"

"Sure. Of course." Three inclines his head toward the cork board. "But what's the deal with the pictures?"

"It was Stanley's brilliant idea. He seems to think more people will participate if they can get their pics up there on the wall, showing everyone else they donated. I figure people aren't supposed to give to charity for the credit, but the farm's matching all donations. So I can't give him too hard a time for it, right?"

"Right," I interject, gulping hard.

Carver's focus bounces between Three and me. "So. Are you two here ... together?"

"NO!" we both announce at the same time.

"Whoa!" Carver chuckles, lifting his palms in apology. "Sorry for the assumption."

"I mean, we are both *here*," I rush to say. "Together. But we aren't *together* together."

I glance at Three and catch the tic of his jaw. "I haven't been in Abieville for almost a decade," I continue. "I'm only back now because my mom and dad just finished renovating a home they bought on the lake."

Something flits behind Carver's eyes, and one corner of his mouth tugs up. "The old farmhouse across the bridge? Peabody's place?"

"That's the one."

"So." Carver keeps his eyes locked on mine. "Does this mean we'll be enjoying your presence around Abieville more often?"

"NO!" Three and I both blurt again.

"My parents are planning to list the house as a vacation rental," I explain. "I came to town for a few days to help with the process. Temporarily."

Three grunts. "In other words, she'll be gone by Christmas."

"Ah. That's too bad." Carver flashes me a grin. "I would've liked to see more of you, Sara Hathaway."

"Well, you won't." Three's voice is gruff, and I totally get it. If I had a sister with a longtime crush on the same guy, I'd hate to see him grinning at another woman too.

"As long as you're here now..." Carver jerks his chin toward the mistletoe archway. "How about a kiss for the kids, Sara? For old time's sake?"

I gape at him. Is he seriously asking to kiss me right now? Charity or not, the man is little more than a stranger. And for all I know, Three's sister still wants him. I'd never break girl code, no matter how many years have passed since I've seen Nella. But before I can turn Carver down, Three edges right up against me, using his body as a blockade.

"Not gonna happen," he says, except it comes out more like a growl. He's even more protective of his sister than I thought. And my heart swells a little at the proof of it.

"Whoa." Carver guffaws. "I wasn't asking for Sara to kiss *me*. I was talking about you two."

"OH!" My whole upper body is officially on fire now. When I glance at Three, his teeth are clenched. But I shouldn't be surprised. He ended things between us when I was handing my heart to him on a silver platter.

Why would he want to kiss me now?

"That's okay!" I dig in my purse, hands trembling. "I'll just donate the twenty dollars."

"Thanks, Sara," Carver says. "We sure do appreciate your generosity." He nods at the cork board. "But Stanley really docs want the photo evidence up on the wall to inspire everyone else to be generous too." He hitches his shoulders. "Come on, folks.

Surely you can offer one innocent little peck between friends. It's for the kids."

"For the kids?" I squeak.

Three shifts his jaw. "Just charity," he says. "It doesn't have to mean anything."

Carver grins. "Yes, it does."

I gulp. *It does?*

"Your kiss pic means more money for the kids," he says. The next thing I know, he's corralling Three and me toward the platform. I eye Three sideways waiting for him to launch an objection, but his expression remains stony and unmoved. He probably just wants to get this over with.

It doesn't have to mean anything.

My heart pounds against my ribcage as we climb the steps to the stage. The archway is twinkling with lights and dotted by sprigs of holly and red bows. Carver arranges us directly below a good-sized bunch of mistletoe. As Three turns to face me, I swallow against the lump gathering in my throat.

"We can make this quick," Three mutters under his breath. At least he's breathing. I feel like my lungs stopped functioning the minute Carver suggested we kiss.

"Wait till I give you the signal," Carver says now, backing away, holding up the camera. "I need you both in the frame. Okay, get closer, you two. Closer. Closer." He scoffs. "Come on, man. She's not gonna bite."

Three and I inch nearer to one another until he's towering above me, and I have to tip my head to meet his gaze. His blue eyes dip to my lips, his pupils dilated like big black olives. My lashes flutter against my will.

"You all right?" he asks. His Adam's apple travels the length of his throat.

"It's for the kids," I whisper. "Just charity?"

"Yes."

"And afterward we'll never speak of this again?"

"Speak of what?"

"The kiss."

"Yeah." He releases a breath. "You might need to work on the not-speaking-about-it part."

"Okay," Carver calls out. "You're good to go! Kiss away."

Three dips his chin and I rise up on my toes, slowly moving my mouth toward his. When our lips meet, soft and warm, light pulses through me—electricity at the barest of touches. The memory of being in his arms years ago sends shockwaves through my body. It's as if no time has passed. Or eternity has come and gone.

"Hold still!" Carver says.

My knees buckle, and Three's hand go to my waist, gathering my body back in. When his lips find mine again, I melt into his arms. I'm a goner. Lost to his embrace.

"Okay, got it!" Carver calls out. "You're all done."

No.

I am done for.

Chapter Eighteen

Sara

Thirteen Years Ago: August

Three and I kissed tonight.

We were at our favorite picnic table behind Dips & Scoops sharing the same bench. We'd just finished our cones, and like always, I forgot to grab a napkin, so I had a little ice cream on the edge of my mouth, which should've been embarrassing, but I can't even care about that now because of what happened next.

He reached out to wipe my lip with his thumb. Then he licked his thumb. And I guess I was staring at him because he started inching toward me. His eyes never left mine, even when he got super-close. And right before he kissed me, he asked if I was okay.

I THINK I said yes. I might've just nodded.

Either way, everything went into slow motion on the outside, while I had a total freakout on the inside. That's why the details are hard to describe. But let me tell you, Three's kiss was even better than I'd imagined. He was warm and steady and careful, and he paused to look me in the eye, like he was checking in to be sure I was all right, so I lunged at his mouth like some kind of lip-starved weirdo. Which maybe I am, since this was my first time kissing anyone, and all I can think about is doing it again.

I can't believe I have to leave tomorrow, and since I'll be away at St. Bernadette's all year, I won't see Three again until next June. Still, that brings me to the best part of tonight. Well, maybe the second best. Okay. Tied for first.

Are you ready?

Three asked if we could keep talking over the school year. And I said yes.

If my dad won't let me come back next summer, I'm probably going to die.

Chapter Nineteen

Three

Sara and I spend the drive back from Humboldt Farms listening to Christmas music with the volume cranked. Occasionally she sings a line or two, out loud and off key, but there's zero talking between us. Which makes sense, I guess. Back in the barn, we agreed not to speak about the kiss afterward. The thing is, being that close to Sara again is literally the only thing on my mind.

I've got nothing else to talk about.

Our past together came roaring back to me in a brilliant flash of warmth and light. The taste of her lips. How perfectly she fits in my arms. The way I felt about her back then.

The way I feel about her *now*.

So even though the ride is just a few miles, those miles feel like an eternity of contemplation.

For the kids, she suggested.

Just charity, I agreed.

These are the declarations running through my head as we return home, and Sara heads straight to the kitchen. "I'm going to unpack the groceries and try reaching my mom," she calls out. Guess we're still not talking.

So I decide to bring the tree inside, set up the stand, and wrap the branches in twinkle lights.

Sara bought too many strands by half a dozen, but the evidence of her enthusiasm couldn't be any more adorable. My heart swells with the desire to make this Christmas special for her. That is, until I remember she's only doing this so she can feel better about leaving me behind in a few days.

I'm about to stuff the extra strands of lights into a bag so we can return them, when Sara comes in and hands me a full glass of water with my next dose of antibiotics.

"I just love the scent of a real pine," she says, inhaling deeply. While I take my meds, she checks out the tree, nodding her approval. "My mom's fake trees always smell like ... plastic and ..." —she fumbles for a word—"giving up."

She puffs out a small laugh, but her statement shifts something in my chest. A decade ago, I spent a whole lot of time being jealous of the Hathaways. But now I wouldn't trade an authentic hometown holiday with my family for that kind of artificial perfection.

"I'm sure your mother's trees are ... majestic," I say, before draining the rest of the water.

"Oh, they are." Sara shrugs. "Thanks to the professional team The Queen pays to make every branch a masterpiece."

"Heh." I arch a brow. "Must be nice."

"In its own way," Sara says.

As she takes back the empty glass, it occurs to me we're officially talking again. I also notice she's not blushing or stammering anymore. For better or worse, she seems to have gotten over our kiss under the mistletoe pretty quickly. I guess she must've really meant it when she said there was nothing more for us to discuss. So if ignoring what happened at Humboldt Farms is this easy for her, I can continue to pretend it never happened too. In fact, I'm *glad* this is so easy for her.

Never happened.

Done and done.

"Speaking of your mom, how's she handling the news about the evaluator postponing until tomorrow?"

Sara blows out a breath. "She wasn't thrilled, but I promised her I still have everything handled." She bunches up her brow. "I did *not* tell her we're setting up a Christmas tree in the living room, because she'd probably just send her designer out to take over."

I let out a low chuckle, nodding to indicate the tree. "Well our eight-footer may not end up on any magazine cover, but at least we get to decorate it ourselves."

"My first time ever," Sara says, a smile dancing across her face. So, yeah. I'll do this one small thing for her this year, then get on with the rest of my life without her.

As she moves toward the bag of Five and Dime ornaments, I throw up a hand. "Hold on. I just need to clean up a little first, if you don't mind. I like the smell of pine trees as much as the next guy, but I've got sap all over me."

"You've got sap, and I've got good news." She nods in the direction of the guest bathroom. "It's been twenty-four hours, so I'm officially clearing you for a shower."

"No more baths?"

"Not if you keep the bandage on to minimize the water on your stitches. We can put on a dry one after."

"It's a Christmas miracle," I say. Or more likely, it's because Sara doesn't know how off-balance I've been feeling. I probably should've copped to the brain fog, or to the roll of nausea in my gut. But I don't want Sara to think these symptoms have anything to do with our kiss. No, as far as I'm concerned, these lingering side effects will remain my little secret. They're just a result of yesterday's accident. After all, this isn't my first rodeo.

Or concussion.

So I take my time enjoying every minute of my first post-injury shower. The spray of hot water feels amazing, but I'm careful not to get my head wet. I don't want to lose future show-ering privileges. Afterward, I reapply a fresh bandage, slip on some jeans, and a navy blue henley. Then I head for the kitchen like a hound dog being led by the scent of something absolutely delicious.

Not the pine tree.

Rounding the corner, I come upon Sara at the stove. She's changed into a pair of forest-green leggings and a soft white sweater. Her new Santa hat's pulled over her glossy hair. Christmas music's spilling from a portable speaker across the room, more specifically a classic rendition of "Silver Bells."

This song reminds me of cross-country skiing with my Uncle Phil, so it's always been one of my favorites. But I can't tell who's singing this version. It might be Bing Crosby. Or Frank Sinatra. One of those old-time crooners. It's smooth and nostalgic and stirs something deep in my gut.

Happiness.

That's what this is.

Sara must sense someone behind her because she spins around and drops the ladle. "Oh!" Her hand flies to her collarbone.

"Sorry." My shoulders slump. "Didn't mean to scare you."

"You're forgiven. At least I didn't throw a fire extinguisher at you." She stoops to grab the ladle. While she rinses it in the sink, I take a couple big appreciative sniffs, like the hound dog that I am.

"What smells so good?"

"Cinnamon sticks, nutmeg, and whole cloves." She tips her chin at the smaller of the two pots on the stove. "Just like your mom does." But when her eyes light up and her mouth curves into a smile, she looks *absolutely nothing* like my mom.

"I grabbed the spices as a surprise while you were getting the construction paper and glue," she says. "And you're right. This combination really does make the whole place smell like Christmas."

"Hmm." I nod at her, slowly. Threads of steam curl up toward the exhaust fan. "What else am I smelling?" Something rumbles in the larger pot, and the lid bubbles up as I move closer to the stove. "Is that popcorn?"

"Yup." Her smile spreads even wider. "This batch is almost ready for us to make some Fuller family garland. So why don't you wait for me in the living room?" She turns off the heat, jiggling the handle of the pot. A final few kernels *pop-pop-pop*. But instead of leaving, I watch her, mesmerized. After a long stretch of seconds, she turns back to me. "Go on. I'll meet you in five minutes."

She reaches a palm up and gently presses my chest, prompting me into the other room. I'm sure the gesture's innocent, but my throat goes dry and my pulse accelerates. So I make my escape to the living room, hoping to distract myself by stacking logs and getting a blaze going in the fireplace.

It seemed like a good idea at the time.

But soon enough, the leaping flames bring me back to those summer bonfires with Sara. We'd hunker down on the sand, my arm wrapped around her, safe and warm. She'd drape her legs across my lap. Eyes sparkling. Laughter on her lips.

Keep it together, Three. By Christmas, Sara will be gone.

As if my thoughts conjure her from the kitchen, Sara appears over my shoulder, setting a stack of napkins and an enormous bowl of popcorn on the coffee table. The scent of cinnamon, nutmeg and cloves clings to her. Like all the sweet spices of Christmas just took on a human form.

"I made enough popcorn to eat *and* to sew," she chirps, dropping onto the couch beside me. Her leg brushes mine, and heat shoots straight up my spine. I might as well be a chestnut roasting on an open fire.

"Are you ready?" She pulls a velvet pouch from the pocket of her cardigan.

"What's that?"

"Our sewing supplies," she says. "I got these at the Five and Dime." From the pouch she plucks two spools—one with green thread, the other red. There's a needle stuck through the center of both. "I've never actually threaded a needle, though," she admits.

"No Home Ec for you at prep school?"

"Hardly." She coughs out a weak laugh. "And it's not like my mom showed me how to sew. She wasn't exactly into darning old socks or replacing lost shirt buttons."

I reach for the red spool. "I can teach you."

Sara hikes her brow. "Well, aren't you Mr. Confident."

I try to ignore the warmth spreading up my throat. "There are plenty of things I'm not good at, believe me." *Like controlling my feelings around you, for example.* "But this is my family tradition, so I've done this once or twice. Or a couple dozen times. And I teach teenagers, remember? Surely I can teach you."

"Hey, now." Sara sneaks out a tiny snort.

"No offense." With a chuckle, I unravel at least a yard of thread, then I guide one end of it slowly through the eye of the needle. Finally something else to focus on other than Sara.

"See?" I say. "Easy."

"Okay, my turn." She draws her bottom lip up under her teeth in a move so tempting, I'm surprised I don't groan.

So much for keeping it together.

She slides the needle free from the green spool, unwinds a long stretch of thread, and cuts it. After pinching the length of thread between her thumb and forefinger, she takes a stab at getting the tip through the eye. She misses completely. "Hmph. This feels like trying to push lasagna noodles through a strainer."

"That's because your thread's split at the top. It's not going to fit in the eye like that."

She squints down at the thread. "I guess it does look a little ... thick. So what do I do?"

"You have to lick the thread."

She eyes me sideways. "Excuse me?"

"Like this." I stick my own thread into my mouth to demonstrate. "This joins the two split ends. Now it's just one point. Easier to get through."

"I see." Sara takes her thread and puts it between her lips. Then she clamps down, sliding the rest of the strand out of her mouth. A flash of pink tongue peeks through her teeth, and she holds up the thread, presenting it to me for inspection. "Did I do that right?"

Whoa. I bite my cheek to stifle another groan.

"Yeah, you did," I choke out, but my voice is obviously husky. So I clear my throat, gathering myself. "Now try again."

With her gaze laser-beamed on the needle, Sara slides her green thread straight through the eye. "I did it!" she cheers. She tosses a look of triumph my way, but by now my jaw's come completely unhinged. In fact, I'm pretty sure saliva's about to dribble down my chin.

Sara looks up and meets my gaze. Her dark eyes sparkle like two hot coals, and her cheeks flush pink. "Now what?"

Great.

How am I supposed to teach Sara anything else when my heart feels like it's just been shocked by a defibrillator?

Tearing my focus away from her lips, I grab a piece of popcorn from the bowl. I might as well have tree trunks for fingers, but I can't let Sara know how much her closeness still affects me. So feigning a nonchalance I don't feel, I push the threaded needle through the puff of popcorn a little too enthusiastically and pierce the pad of my pointer finger.

"Ouch!" Dropping the popcorn, I shove my finger in my mouth. A whiff of salt and copper hits my nose. When I pull out my finger, it's still throbbing. So I whip my hand around like I do after I get stung by a bee.

"Stop!" Sara commands. "You're going to make it worse." She reaches for my hand to examine my finger. When the wound blooms red with fresh droplets of blood, she presses a napkin to the spot. After a long moment, she slowly peels the napkin away to check for more bleeding. "Does it hurt?"

"I'll be all right," I croak, already embarrassed by my overreaction. But Sara just nods, with her gaze still settled on the pinprick.

Then she parts her lips and oh so slowly gently blows on the tip of my finger.

One long, soft stream of air.

Whoa.

Her warm breath against my wet skin ignites something inside me. And as she lifts her gaze to meet mine again, her eyes are black and achingly tender. She gulps, and the vulnerability in her expression makes me want to ... apologize.

For what? Well, I have a few ideas.

Maybe I'm sorry for busting into this house when I saw smoke instead of calling 911.

Maybe I'm sorry for letting her take care of me instead of finding someone else to do it.

Or maybe I'm just sorry for being too proud and young and stupid to be fully honest with Sara ten years ago.

I lean toward her now, waiting for her to either pull away or to make her own move. As I hold my breath, she shifts closer to me, then her gaze drops to my lips.

There's your answer, Three.

This might be the dumbest instinct I've ever been tempted to give into in my life, but when Sara exhales, the sweetness of her breath is an elixir I want to suck up and savor forever. My face inches nearer to hers, and she blinks, eyes locked on mine. Ten years without Sara in my life. Without tasting her kiss. Without her warmth and reassurance. And I'm about to end that decade of drought, when my phone starts vibrating on the table. Sara gasps and pulls away.

Great.

My sister's calling.

Chapter Twenty

Three

My insides lurch.

And not just because Nella interrupted what could've been a real kiss between Sara and me, but also because I'm about to talk to my sister without the convenient time delay of text threads and voicemail. I won't have chance to think through my responses or plan out any questions of my own. And thanks to this concussion —not to mention Sara's proximity—I'm not exactly firing on all cylinders. So it's really too bad the success or failure of this conversation could impact the mood of my entire family for the rest of their cruise.

No pressure.

Still, I swipe to answer the call. "Hey there, Smella. Long time, no talk." I force out a chuckle, then immediately kick into rambling. Of course. "The phones must be working on the ship now, huh? Although I guess you *could* be in port, too," I add. "Wait. Could you be in port already? I've kind of lost track of days."

"I'll bet," Nella says. "That sort of thing happens with a concussion."

"Heh heh heh. Yes, it does. Try to avoid them, will you?" I glance at Sara, whose face is flushed. Is she reacting to our almost-kiss? To her guilt? Maybe both.

"For the record, we're somewhere out in the middle of the ocean," Nella says. "None of us knew we had a signal until Carver called," Nella tells me. "When my phone started ringing, I almost dropped it in my mai tai."

"You talked to Carver?" I drag a hand across my bandage like I need to remind myself this is all really happening. Not a dream. At the same time, Sara rises from the couch and slowly backs away, motioning that she's going to head out onto the porch.

When I nod at her—an unspoken thank-you for the offer of privacy—she grabs her coat, slips on her boots, then dashes out the door. "So, dumb question," I say, once I'm alone again. "Obviously you talked to Carver."

Nella snorts. "That's not a question, Mr. Head Injury."

"You're right," I say. "I'll try again. Did Carver tell you who I was with?"

Nella takes a beat. "He did." Her next words come out slow and soft. "So ... Three ... I have to ask. Are you ... all right?" Her voice is full of concern without a hint of judgment. I should've known she'd focus on my well-being, not launch into warnings about Sara. Yes, my sister knows exactly how much loving Sara wrecked me, but Nella loves me too. And her compassion wins out every time.

"I'll be fine." My statement sounds gruff, even to my own ears. "You don't have to worry about me."

"But this situation." Nella lets out a sigh loud enough for me to hear. "You have to admit, it's less than ideal."

"Well, yeah." I puff out a laugh. "You're all on a cruise ship wearing leis while I'm stuck in the snow wearing gloves."

"That's not what I'm talking about," she says. After a long moment she adds, "Just tell me you're being careful."

"I always am." I swallow hard. "Some might say to a fault."

"Yes, under usual circumstances. But you've always had a weak spot when it comes to Sara."

There. Nella finally said her name.

"You're not wrong," I admit.

"But forget the fact that you became a total mush pot every summer the minute she came to town," she continues. "You also put your life on hold the whole rest of the year, waiting for her to show up for three months."

"I was a stupid kid then, Nell. I know better now, and I promise I'm being careful. I've got things under control." Even as I say this, my throat goes tight. But *under control* is subjective. And I'm not in my right mind, so yeah. I'm going with it.

"I'm glad to hear that," Nella says. "Because the last thing you need is to fall back in love with someone whose life runs completely parallel to yours."

Parallel?

I squint, even though Nella can't see my confusion. "Is parallel a bad thing?"

"Not at all." she says. "You and Sara are good people. You care about your families. You work hard and have goals and expectations. But you're also traveling entirely different paths. So while you're both heading toward your own version of success, the trajectories are still miles apart. I'm just being practical."

We fall quiet for a moment, which may sound awkward, but with Nella it's not. I love that she never feels the need to fill the silence with me. I also love that she's more comfortable speaking her mind around me than anyone else.

Which is why I have to ask.

"So you don't ... hate Sara." This comes out more like a statement than a question, and I find myself holding my breath waiting for confirmation.

"Of course I don't hate Sara. Or her parents. But I *do* hate how her parents made you feel. To be fair, though, they had no idea you'd end up overhearing their conversation. They were speaking in private, not being malicious. You were just at the wrong place at the wrong time. Or the right place," she quickly adds. "If you think things turned out for the best."

A sharp pain slices through me, and I'm suddenly right back on the porch of this same house ten years ago. Except it's summer, so all the windows are open. I hear Mr. Hathaway say something about Sara being way too involved with me. That he has to do something about it.

I freeze in place.

He goes on to say I'm just some small-town kid with zero goals beyond high school. Meanwhile Sara's about to take Stanford by storm. He's sure I'll only hold her back if we stay together, and my blood runs cold.

I don't disagree with him.

As for Mrs. Hathaway, she's shocked Sara could be so infatuated with a boy from such an unambitious family. Not a single glowing resume in the bunch. And none of us had any desire to ever leave Abieville. Didn't the Fullers want something ... more?

Listening to them talk about me—about my family—that way cracked my heart straight down the middle. I'd already been questioning my worthiness. And scared of derailing Sara's future. So hearing their confirmations out loud completely gutted me.

It guts me still.

Things only got worse when her parents went over their plan to confront Sara later that night. They were going to tell her to end things with me, and they were prepared with bribes and ultimatums if she put up a fight.

I knew how deeply Sara loved her family. That she'd only be hurt by a confrontation. And if she got angry enough, she might've rebelled. By staying with her, I'd be risking her future relationship with her parents. Not to mention, they'd be forced to spotlight all my many inadequacies. So in that moment, I decided not to let Sara find out how her mom and dad really felt about me.

No need for an argument.

In the pit of me, I already believed Sara deserved someone better than Three Fuller. So I did the only thing my stubborn ego and my broken heart could manage at the time.

I made sure Sara didn't have to choose.

"I loved her," I say, feeling both lightheaded and sick at the memory.

"So did her parents," Nella says. "You've never been a father, Three. Who knows? You might be critical or overprotective if you have kids someday too."

"Yeah." I grunt. "I'd probably be the worst."

"Stop," Nella says. "You'd be an amazing parent. You're already incredible with your students. But that's not the point."

"What is the point, then?"

"You've invested so much time and effort becoming the person you were always meant to be. You're authentically you, and I'm insanely proud of my big brother. So don't ever forget who you are, Three Fuller. And stick to that path. Be yourself. Listen to your heart. It won't steer you wrong."

My eyes begin to sting, so I blink back tears I'm not about to let fall. Man, I've been through the wringer these past two days, and my family's thousands of miles away, not to mention it's Christmastime. Of course I'm emotional.

Listen to your heart.

Be yourself.

"Enough about me," I say, clearing my clogged-up throat. "How's everyone there?"

"Do you want to hear that we're miserable without you? Or that we're getting along just fine?"

"Hmmm. I choose option two."

"Good." Nella lets out a small laugh, and I'm heartened by the change in tone.

"So Mom's really okay?"

"Of course she misses you. She can't stop saying, 'Three would just love this,' but there's so much to do and see already.

This experience is new and exciting for her and Dad. For all of us. So I just have to say ... thank you."

"For what? I didn't pay for everyone's cruise."

"No, but it was really big of you to make sure we all still went without you. That must've been hard."

"Nah. Easiest choice ever." I gulp against the returning lump in my throat, even as a swell of relief rises in me. I may be about to experience my first Christmas alone, but it sounds like the people I love are happy and safe. And they're together. That's what really matters.

"So you're not mad at me for tricking you into going on the cruise without me?" I ask to confirm. "Mom and Dad aren't, either?"

"They're the opposite of mad, Three. In fact, they're at the ship's fancy day spa right now."

"You're kidding."

"I'm not. They won a trivia match this afternoon, and the prize was some romantic massage for two. They left their cabin a little while ago wearing matching robes."

"Yeah. I did *not* need to know that." I cough out a laugh, but talking to Nella's making me feel more like me than I have in days.

Be yourself.

Listen to your heart.

Yeah. I'll try, Nell.

Chapter Twenty-One

Sara

The bell above the door to the Five and Dime jingles as I walk in for the second time today. A burst of cold night air blows in along with me. The same young clerk who was here before looks up from her *People* magazine.

"Forget something?" She stuffs the magazine behind the register. Her name tag says Cami, and she's wearing Rudolph antlers and a necklace made of blinking Christmas bulbs. "I've been too busy to restock the bins of ornaments since you and Mr. Fuller practically bought out the entire store."

Of course Cami knows Three.

Apparently he was her World History teacher two years ago, and now she's in his Government class. These are facts I discovered when she offered to give us her employee discount as we checked out.

"Oh, we have plenty of Christmas decorations," I tell her. "I'm looking for something else."

"I told you we're sold out of all our Rudolph antlers, right?"

My lip twitches. "Sadly, yes. But you wouldn't happen to still have anything for a Hawaiian-themed party would you?"

Cami wrinkles her nose. "Kind of like a luau?"

"Exactly like a luau."

"At Christmastime? I don't think so." She glances around the brightly lit shop, bursting at the scenes with all things holiday. "Why do you need luau stuff in December?"

Yeah. Good question, Cami.

The truth is, I'd been hoping to recreate a traditional Christmas for Three, but when Nella called, I realized that's not what he's actually missing. He's missing the cruise and Hawaii and being with his family. So I've been trying to celebrate the wrong holiday. Three needs something different.

Something tropical.

"I just want to surprise Mr. Fuller."

"I'm sorry." Cami frowns. "Besides the usual stuff we stock year-round, we've only got winter-themed things. What you're looking for won't be displayed again for another few months."

"I understand." I force a smile, but an ache of failure hits my stomach. At least my coming here gave Three the chance to catch up with Nella without me hovering around the house. "I knew it was a long shot," I say, turning to leave.

"Hold on." Cami steps out from behind the register. "I'll take a quick look in the back storage rooms. Who knows? We might have some leftover merchandise from last summer."

"Really?"

"It'll be the dregs, but better than nothing, right?"

I beam at her. "Thanks so much."

She shrugs. "It's for Coach Fuller. He's the best."

"Coach?"

"I'm on the basketball team." Cami bobs her head, and her Rudolph antlers slip. "He's a great coach. Great teacher. He really listens to us, you know? So if I can help out ..." Suddenly Cami's cheeks pink up, and she scurries off toward the back of the shop.

I watch her go, arms hanging at my side, and I let out a little laugh. So, Three's not only the best coach and teacher, but Cami might have a little crush on him.

While she's in the back, I check out a display of individual Christmas cards, trying to be patient. After five minutes, I start to fidget, my restlessness kicking up a notch.

This was a silly idea.

Cami's not going to find anything remotely summery lying around in the back this close to Christmas. Meanwhile, I'm stuck here and Three's at home alone with no idea where I am. He could be dizzy. Or nauseated. Or sad after talking to Nella. And I don't want him to spend even more time alone before it's absolutely necessary.

Come on, Sara. Is leaving him absolutely necessary?

He's only stuck here because of you.

You could just stay in Abieville and skip Christmas this year.

A wave of hysteria bubbles up in my throat, and I bite my tongue to keep from laughing. I can only imagine what Bristol would say if she could hear the conversation happening in my head. Even worse, my mom and dad would be devastated if I missed the Hathaway Gala. Christmas Eve. My birthday.

Impossible.

Behind me the door to the shop jingles, and a family of five enters. The parents are holding hands, and each of the kids clutches a half-eaten candy apple. They all head straight to a beverage station along the wall offering self-service fountain drinks and coffee. They're busy filling cups for themselves when Cami finally returns from the back of the store pushing a loaded cart.

"So." She grins at me. "Will this work?"

In the cart are two Hawaiian shirts—one red, one green—three hot-pink lawn flamingoes, six tiki torches, a pile of multi-colored leis, and a set of four lanterns shaped like pineapples.

"It's perfect," I tell her.

And absolutely necessary.

Back at the house, I have to make two trips to transfer all the luau supplies inside, and I temporarily pile everything next to the Christmas tree. By now, the fire's died down to a few glowing embers. Bags of ornaments and decorations crowd the floor. On the coffee table are a pair of scissors and strips of green and red construction paper.

Three must have cut those out while I was gone to use for our advent chains. His phone is beside the bowl of abandoned popcorn. But the man himself is nowhere in sight.

"Hello?" My pulse picks up. Maybe I shouldn't have left him alone so soon. He seemed pretty good all day, but we also did a lot. Maybe too much. "I'm home!" I call out louder this time.

"I'm in here!"

I cross the dining room into the kitchen, and find Three hovering over the stove, holding a spatula. On the counter is a loaf of bread, a brick of cheddar, and the butter dish.

"Grilled cheese?" I come closer, drawn by the dreamy scent of melted butter.

Three keeps his gaze on the bread sizzling in the pan. "I made one for you too."

"You didn't have to do that," I say, even as my stomach rumbles. "But it smells amazing."

"Not as fancy as the dinner you were planning, but I got hungry, and I don't know how to cook a turkey."

My eyes widen. "Your appetite's back?"

"Yeah." He shrugs. "And I figured we wouldn't have time for a big meal at this point anyway, so ..." He tips his chin to point at the cheese.

"Sandwiches are perfect."

In fact, some comfort food and a good night's sleep is probably just what we both need. Then, if Three's up to it tomorrow, we can attempt Abieville's first-ever Hawaiian Christmas luau mashup after the evaluation.

The results won't be magazine-worthy—not like the Hathaway Gala—but I'll be giving Three a little bit of everything he's missing out on because of me. Then, if all goes well, and the doctor clears him to go home on Tuesday, I can head back to the city by Christmas Eve, just like I'd always planned.

"I haven't had grilled cheese in years," I say, as my heart squeezes at the thought of leaving him alone.

"Been a while for me too." Three flips the sandwiches. "But you've been taking care of me the past two days, so I wanted to take care of you for a change."

Whoa.

Three wants to take care of me? Now my heart's not just squeezing. It's starting to melt. He glances at me, then adds more butter to the pan. "Where did you go, anyway?"

I swallow hard, not entirely sure I can speak without giving away my emotions. "That's a ... it's a ... just a little surprise," I manage. "But we should definitely eat first since you're hungry."

"Well whatever you did," he says, "thanks for giving me a chance to talk to my sister."

"Of course." I blow out a breath, grateful for the change of subject. "How is she? How's the family?"

"Nella says they miss me, but she wasn't exactly sobbing into her mai tai." He presses the sandwiches with the spatula and cheese oozes out the sides. "But honestly, I'm glad they're good. They shouldn't have to suffer because I'm not there."

"That must be a relief." I fold my arms across my middle. "I'm not sure my mom and dad would ever get over me missing Christmas. And they definitely wouldn't be okay with finding out so last minute."

"Yeah, well." His jaw ticks. "Your family *really* likes their plans."

"I'm not suggesting my mom and dad care about me more than yours do. It's just ..." My voice trails off.

"No, I get it." He lowers the heat and covers the pan. When he turns to face me, his brow's pulled down. "Christmas Eve is your birthday. And you've got that fundraiser thing every year."

"The gala."

"The gala. Right." He sets down the spatula. "That night's a double big deal for the Hathaways. Of course your mom and dad want you there."

"Yes." I let out a long, wistful sigh. "But can I tell you a secret?"

He meets my gaze, holds it for a moment. "Sure." The reply is casual, but the way he's staring at me doesn't feel so nonchalant.

"Sometimes I wish I didn't have to go at all."

"Wow." Three blinks. "Really?"

"Sometimes." My shoulders sag. "It's not so bad now, but being in the spotlight was a lot of pressure when I was young. My parents counted on me and my story to up the ante on the auction and donations."

"Huh." Three crosses his arms. "I hadn't thought of it that way."

"I'm not complaining, believe me. They have the best intentions, and I'm proud of all the money we've raised for Children's Village. As an adult, I'm honored to be a part of such a worthy cause. But when I was young, all I really wanted was a normal birthday party. With kids my age, and hot dogs and a *My Little Pony* cake, you know? Not a champagne tower and caviar."

Three tilts his head. "My Little Pony?"

"Man, I loved that show. Applejack was my favorite."

The corner of his mouth curves up. "Nella's too."

"She's got good taste." I press out a small laugh. "But the gala became less about me and more about what I could do to inspire donors. My dad always gave the same speech about how long it took him and my mom to have their miracle baby. And how important adoption and the foster care system is to creating future families. He makes me talk too, which is fine now, but was totally mortifying when I was a kid. I never knew what to say."

Three lets his arms drop. "I'll bet you did better than you think."

"Still." I let another small laugh slip out. "I hope my future kids aren't born on any holidays." I take a beat, caught off guard that I'm admitting this to anyone. "And if they are, any fundraising I do will *not* be associated with their birthdays."

Three turns away, peeking under the lid to check on sandwiches. "So. You want kids, then? Marriage? The whole nine yards?"

I shift my weight, grateful that Three's back is to me, and he can't see the flush rising on my cheeks. Because yes, I used to dream about my future husband and our imaginary kids.

The whole nine yards.

I planned the perfect wedding long before I ever came to Abieville. But then I met Three and he broke my heart, and I haven't been able to picture myself married to anybody since.

"I used to think I wanted a big family," I say softly. "But college was so demanding. Then I had a couple years of internships. Then law school. Studying for the bar. There wasn't any time for serious relationships."

"You're not in school anymore."

"No." I shrug, hoping to convince myself I've grown indifferent to all this. "But I *am* expecting Hathaway Cooke to offer me an associate position any day now." I take a beat and my stomach twinges. "At that point, I'll be putting in eighty-plus hours a week. So, I don't see myself having time for a family going forward either. At least not for a while."

Three lets out a low whistle. "Eighty-hour work weeks?"

"Eighty *plus*. And yes, it's a lot, but it's what I've always worked for. Being an attorney at Hathaway Cooke has been my goal for as long as I can remember."

"Yeah, I remember that too." Three turns to face me again. "But is that what you want?"

I open and shut my mouth wordlessly. I'm not sure anyone's ever asked me this question before.

"Sorry if that's too personal," he adds. "These are just the kinds of things I talk about with my students. We spend a lot of time working out what they see for their future. What will make them happy, not just what they *think* they should do. So." He dips his head. "Will being an associate at Hathaway Cooke make you happy?"

"Of course it will," I blurt. Any other reality would be too hard to accept.

"Good." Three turns off the burner, slides the toasted sandwiches onto plates, and cuts them in half on the diagonal. Then he plucks a couple of apples from the bowl by the sink.

"So." I clear my throat. "Is that what *you* want?"

He glances down at the fruit in his hand. "Apples? Yeah. They have tons of fiber."

"No." I swallow hard. "I meant ... do you want kids?"

"Ah. That." He brings our food over to the island. "I absolutely want kids. That's why I've got a hundred of them."

I blink. Once. Twice. "What?"

"My students. Well, technically I have a hundred and one. Like the Dalmatians." He pulls two stools out from under the counter. "You know, I went into teaching assuming the kids would learn from me, but they've taught me some of the most important lessons of my life." He takes a seat, hunching over his plate. "Sorry if that sounds corny. Or just some big cliche."

"No." I shake my head. "I think it's really sweet."

"Believe me, the kids aren't *always* sweet." A small laugh puffs out of him. "But now I know how to stop talking, so I can listen. How to hear what they're really trying to say." He takes a beat. "How to put their needs ahead of my own."

"Wow." I slide onto the stool beside him. "I'll bet you're good at that."

"I want to be," he says. "But let's just call me a work in progress."

"Well your students are lucky."

"I don't know about that." He ducks his head. "I just try to be myself. And listen to my heart. Then I hope they'll do the same."

My throat goes tight. "You must care about them a lot."

"Yeah." He averts his gaze. "I really do."

We both fall quiet, and I dig into my food like I haven't eaten in weeks. Something I thought I'd stitched up long ago is unraveling inside me. And instead of the numbness that took up space there, a hollowness spreads, waiting to be filled.

Hey, Sara. The cheese you're stuffing in your face isn't temporary putty for the gap, you know.

I take another giant bite of sandwich anyway, just as my phone buzzes in my pocket.

Good. Perfect timing for a text. I could really use the distraction.

BRISTOL

> Greetings, Sara! Consider this your daily inoculation against any coronary weakness you might be feeling. That's right. I'm here so you don't forget how badly Three Fuller hurt you. The man made you trust him, and you handed over your whole heart, which he promptly rejected, then stomped on. So do NOT go soft on me, friend. Just remember he's totally off-limits. (No matter how cute he looks.)

I eye Three sideways.

Bristol has no idea how cute he actually looks right now. Especially after that sweet confession about how much he cares about his students. A smile plays on my lips thinking about what he said.

"Is it your mom?" he asks, licking a strand of cheese from his mouth.

"Nope," I say just as a second text comes in.

BRISTOL

> Call me anytime you need extra convincing. I love you more than Three Fuller ever could.

Oof. Bristol's right, so I'll definitely have to call her later tonight, before Three and his cheese-licking cuteness completely wears me down. For now, though, I shove my phone back in my pocket. I've got a sandwich to finish scarfing.

Chapter Twenty-Two

Sara

Twelve Years Ago: June

I'm back in Abieville! Yes, that's the sound of me jumping up and down with excitement. But can you blame me? I've been looking forward to this summer since last August, and let me tell you, Three was worth the wait.

I've only been here with him for two days, but those forty-eight hours were already better than the roughly half a million minutes I missed with him this year. In fact, I may have so much fun this summer, I forget all about this journal.

We spent the first half of today tubing on the lake with Ford and Nella in their Uncle Cubby's boat. Then Three had a lifeguarding shift over at The Beachfront Inn, so we went swimming over there. This guy named Carver met us. When I realized I'd left my towel on the boat, he offered me his.

Three blew his whistle at us, just like he does whenever kids start roughhousing in the water or kicking up sand around other people. He was just kidding around, pretending to be jealous. But Nella likes Carver, so I'd never go after him even if my heart wasn't already obsessed with Three.

Oops. That's my mom calling me for dinner, but I think I'm too happy to eat. I just hope she and my dad won't be too upset when I tell them we're all meeting up at the lake for a bonfire tonight. And I hope Three and I get some alone time.

I'm already dying to kiss him. And I kind of wish he got jealous for real.

Chapter Twenty-Three

Three

I keep telling myself it's none of my business.

Like, really. Not even a little bit. I have no right to be possessive. But I sure am dying to know who just texted Sara, and if it was the same person who messaged her. Twice. She looked at her phone, and she smiled.

So now I can't stop wondering if those texts were from a man.

Is this a side effect of a concussion? Because I'm definitely fogheaded and sick to my stomach. See also: jealous.

Sure, Sara just finished telling me she's been too busy with school and internships and studying to have time for relationships. But a woman as beautiful and wonderful as Sara is—not to mention someone as generous and caring—doesn't go unnoticed. And now I'm imagining her with somebody back in the city. Maybe even *several* somebodies. If she doesn't have time to get serious, maybe she just keeps things casual and dates multiple men.

I hate that thought too.

The truth is, I haven't gotten around to asking Sara about her relationship status, mostly because I'm not sure I want to know the answer. Especially not after I saw the way Carver looked at her. At the time, I rationalized that my instinct was because Nella has a thing for Carver, and that I was just looking out for my sister. But the truth is, I didn't want Carver seeing Sara as a single woman who's available. So I put my body between them. Fast.

This has got to be some side effect of the concussion, right? I'm being totally ridiculous, not to mention unfair. I can't keep Sara away from other men forever. She deserves to be happy. To find love. And I don't want to be the guy who keeps her from that.

I *refuse* to be that guy.

I'm a grown man with a reputation for being even-tempered, hardworking, and dependable. I'm not a violent person. So how come my hands balled into fists when Sara smiled at those two back-to-back texts?

Yeah, I know. She's been out of my life for almost a decade, and whether or not she's had time for a serious relationship, she's definitely been asked out by plenty of men since then. She's kind. Smart. Hilarious. The most beautiful woman I've ever seen. Of course she's gotten attention over the years. And from more than just Carver Townsend. So I tried to follow Nella's advice. I was being myself. Listening to my heart. Making us grilled cheese. And then—

"Hey." She pokes my shoulder, and I lift my eyes from my plate. "Are you feeling all right? You're not dizzy or anything?"

"No, nothing like that."

She studies my face for a moment. "Are you sure?"

"I think I just ate too fast."

"Hmm." She bobs her head, hopefully satisfied by my answer. "Well, that sandwich was just what I needed."

I clear my throat so my gruff voice won't give me away. "If you're done, I can do the dishes."

"No way." She throws her palms up. "You cooked, I clean. Those are the rules."

"Can I at least dry while you wash?"

Her lips curve up. "Nope, thanks." There's that smile again. I hope she's not thinking about Mr. Two Texts. He didn't make Sara grilled cheese for dinner tonight. He wasn't in the kitchen with her, just being himself and listening to his heart.

Ugh.

Out of habit, I reach up to scratch my hand along the back of my neck. The bandage there is loose and probably should be replaced. This could be my out to escape and regroup for a moment, to remind myself Sara's not mine to be jealous and possessive over. "I'm gonna go get a fresh bandage," I mumble.

Before she can answer, I slip out of the kitchen, and head straight to the guest room. I need to put some distance between Sara and my feelings for her. Unfortunately, the first thing I spot is the blanket piled on the chair in the corner of the room. The same chair where Sara spent the whole night watching over me. Taking care of me. Caring *for* me.

Could she really care for me again? I wonder if that's even possible after all these years. After how badly I hurt her.

Forget the fresh bandage and distance. What I really need is some sound advice from someone I trust as much as I trust my sister.

Ford.

He'll tell me to get a grip. To get over myself and get over Sara Hathaway. So hopefully, the ship still has a working signal wherever they are on the Pacific Ocean. I'd try calling, but the guest room is just down the hall from the kitchen, and Sara's in there doing the dishes. I don't want to risk her overhearing our conversation.

So I settle on the bed to text instead. He's always got his phone glued to him, so if there's a signal, he should respond quickly. Then again, he's never been on a cruise before.

Please be there. Please be there. Please be there.

ME

> Any chance you're not stuffing your face at the all-you-can-eat buffet right now? Or bobbing for pineapple chunks in a giant mai tai?

FORD

> I'm actually warming up for the limbo contest out on the Lido deck.

A wave of relief washes over me. Ford is there and responding. He's also about to ... limbo.

ME

> Didn't mean to interrupt such vital festivities.

FORD

> The contest doesn't start for another five minutes. And anyway, you're more important. I was gonna try you earlier, but Nella called dibs after she talked to Carver.

> Speaking of which, everyone here knows Sara's the one taking care of you now. That includes your parents who just returned from a couples massages sporting rosy glows.

ME

> Yeah. Nella told me they won some spa treatment, and that's all the details I need about that. But what's the general reaction to my being here with Sara?

Bubbles ripple in the text box, then disappear.

Uh-oh. It's THAT bad?

Nella didn't mention it, but maybe they all found out Sara's the one who gave me the concussion.

FORD

Sorry. They just announced the limbo contest is moving to the Aloha deck. As for how everyone's feeling about Sara, the whole family loves her. She's awesome. And she was never the problem in your little equation.

ME

You're not helping.

FORD

With what?

ME

Keeping me from sliding farther down this slippery slope of wanting to reconnect with her. Because I've got to tell you, being this close to her again is definitely messing with my judgment.

FORD

Or maybe that concussion snapped some sense into you.

ME

Huh?

FORD

Come on, cousin. You ended things because you didn't want to interfere with the Hathaway family dynamics. And from the conversations I had with her there at the lake house and again in the ER, she doesn't sound any less attached to them than she used to be.

BUT. She also used to be awesome. And if anything, she seems more awesome now.

ME

SUPER not helpful, man.

FORD

Just being honest, because I can't be anything else with you. But maybe Sara CAN be something else.

ME

Like what?

FORD

Like more than just a heartbreak from your past. But you'll never know if you don't tell her how you really felt about her then. And how you feel about her now.

ME

Wait. Are you actually suggesting I should TRY to make something work with her?

FORD

I'm suggesting you're an adult now, so maybe you should stop acting like a kid. How you handled things ten years ago might've been understandable when you were nineteen. But now??? Dude. Grow up.

ME

Dude. That's not being honest. That's BRUTAL honesty ...

FORD

Just a bit of wisdom from the future limbo champion of the Aloha deck.

My fingers freeze, and I stare at my phone screen instead of responding. Is this text thread for real? I reached out to Ford expecting a swift kick in the teeth, or at the least a gentle reminder to stop wishing Sara and I might have potential as a couple. Instead, the man's encouraging me to share my true feelings with her.

FORD

> Speaking of limbo, I gotta go. But I do love you, brother. So good luck with Sara. Just remember to trust your gut. And maybe trust her too.

Whoa.

I stick my phone in the charger, and meet my own gaze in the mirror. Trust Sara? Trust my gut? Both feel impossible when my insides are churning. The thing is, Sara still doesn't know the reason I ended things. And telling her how I truly felt about her— why I did what I did—could make her angry. Or hurt her more. That's a risk. So is rejection. But I think it's finally time to be real. I want to be honest about our past and move forward.

The question is, will Sara?

Chapter Twenty-Four

Sara

"What the ... what?"

Three's gaping at me from the hallway, probably because I just finished displaying my haul from the Five and Dime next to the Christmas tree. Propped along the wall is a trio of pink lawn flamingoes, four purple pineapple lanterns, and six tiki torches with a collection of leis hanging from them.

"Surprise!" I chirp. "Merry Hawaiian Christmas luau!"

His gaping turns into a crooked smile. "I must admit, I did not see this coming."

I let out a breath of relief. Maybe I was only imagining that he'd seemed a little off when we were finishing dinner. "I had some help from Cami at the Five and Dime," I admit. "By the way, you didn't tell me she was on the basketball team. Maybe you can wear this to your next game." I toss him the green Hawaiian shirt, which is so big, he can slide it on directly over his long-sleeved henley.

My red one's too small to fit over my cardigan, but I have a tank top layered underneath, so I slip the sweater off, and exchange it for the Hawaiian shirt. "So what do you think?" I twirl around, modeling it for him. "Are we liking these shirts?"

"Absolutely." He chuckles, shaking his head. "But ... why?"

I glance at the bowl of popcorn, the strips of construction paper, and the bag of extra lights beside the ornaments. "I just wanted to add a little bit of island spirit to all our pre-existing yuletide decor."

He blinks, his eyes softening at the corners. "Is this because I'm missing the cruise?"

"Because you're missing your *family*." I pluck one of the leis from the tiki torch and slip it on. "Luckily plastic flowers can survive in snow, unlike real hibiscus."

"Good news." Three crosses the room, takes a lei for himself. Then he stands in front of the flamingoes, surveying their spindly legs. "Am I crazy, or are these guys dying to keep Henry company?"

"Ummm ... yes to both questions."

"And we could stick these tiki torches along the front of the house too." A grin stretches across his face, and I can't help smiling back. Three's embracing the Hawaiian Christmas spirit even more than I'd hoped. He looks down at one of the bags by the Christmas tree stand. "What about these leftover lights? The tree branches are already full, and we haven't even put the orna-ments or popcorn on. I was thinking we'd return these extra lights, but maybe we should hang them on the porch instead."

"We could do that," I say. "But the tiki torches and flamingoes will already be out there."

"Don't forget Henry."

"I'd never forget Henry." I fake a scoff. "But maybe we should spread the holiday fun inside the house." I nod in the direction of the den off the living room. I only went in there once to check the space when I arrived, but it was definitely lacking in holiday cheer. "Let's string up the extra lights in the den."

"I like the way you think." Three flashes another crescent of a smile. "You want to get started on that, while I introduce our little pink friends to Henry?"

"How are you feeling? Not dizzy at all? Light-headed?"

"I'm great after that grilled cheese."

"Okay." I wrinkle my nose. "I'm trusting you, but just be careful out there and come right back in."

While Three scoops up the flamingoes and heads out front, I take a couple of the leis, the leftover strands of lights, and a staple gun to the den. The room is freshly painted in a deep forest green. A chair rail of dark rich wood runs the length of the walls. In one corner is a large globe on a display you can spin, and I immediately hang a lei on it. Opposite the globe is a telescope with the business end aimed out the window. Another great place to hang a lei.

The rest of the space is taken up by two overstuffed armchairs, a pub table flanked by a pair of high stools, and a small leather sofa across from the old brick fireplace. Built-in bookshelves line either side of the brick. But instead of books, the shelves are filled with Adirondack knickknacks like bears holding fishing poles and stained glass art featuring mountain scenes. It's all expensive, but still rustic and kitschy.

Like my poor reindeer placemats now living in the garbage.

Dragging one of the stools over, I climb up to access the top shelves. I've got the extra strands of lights lassoed over my shoulder, and the staple gun wedged at my side. Lifting one end of the lights to the top right corner, I begin to attach the strand to the wall stapling every six inches or so. Then I climb down and nudge the stool over to begin the routine again. It's slow work, but hopefully the effect will be worth it in the end. I'm midway through the process when Three's voice rumbles from the doorway.

"Looking good, Hathaway." I peek at him over my shoulder, and find him leaning against the door jamb. My cheeks flame hot at the compliment, not to mention the fact that I'm on top of a stool, so my butt's basically at his eye level.

As if reading my thoughts, he adds, "For the record, I'm not talking about your ..."

"Oh, I know!" I cough out a laugh. "But thanks for the heads-up."

"I'm not staring at your head either." His mouth goes crooked. "Just admiring your handiwork. And you were right. This was a great idea."

My heart does a little leapfrog at this, until my inner Sara whispers in my ear again.

Don't enjoy this too much, Sara. This is all temporary.

"Need any help?" he asks.

"Nope, thanks." I hitch my shoulders. "I like doing some decorating myself for once."

"So you want me to just watch you hang those lights by yourself?"

"That's exactly what I want you to do."

He salutes me, then ambles across the room dropping onto the sofa. "I guess I'll just sit here and do what I'm told then."

I swallow hard, turning back to my task and hoping my face doesn't burst into flames. When I reach the bricked-in chimney above the fireplace, I place the last staple. I'm about to slide the stool to the other side, when I spot a wooden lever between the brick and the thick wooden mantel. Kind of like a cabinet handle.

"Huh." My brows knit together.

"Something wrong?"

"Not wrong. Just weird." I tug on the lever, and the handle moves easily at first. When I finally meet with some resistance, I pull down harder until something gives. And that's when the other side of the fireplace shudders.

With a sound like a small, creaky cough, the whole bookshelf moves inward like it's collapsing into the wall. Just a few inches. But the sliver of an opening appears.

The bookshelf is ajar.

"Whoa!" Three's already off the sofa, a little-boy-on-Christmas-morning expression on his face. "Did you know your parents have a secret door to a secret room?"

"Ha! No." I guffaw. "I'll bet my *parents* didn't even know about this space, or they probably would've turned it into a usable room during the renovation."

Three slides between the bookshelf and the ladder, pushing against the shelving with both hands. The entire wall moves inward with a long, dusty groan. He cranes his neck, peering inside. "It's a room all right. Maybe for storage or something."

I climb down the ladder. "What's in there?"

"I can't see," he says. "It's pitch black."

I creep behind him into the dark space, batting at cobwebs, resisting the urge to reach for the safety of his hand. When Three stops short, I bump into the back of him, grateful for the closeness in the dark.

Then suddenly there's a click, and the space floods with light. I blink and Three's holding on to a metal chain hanging from a naked bulb.

Moving out from behind him, I survey the now-lit room. There are stacks of boxes and a few crates, a couple of dust-covered oil paintings. Propped against one wall is a large framed mirror. A crack runs across the top, but the rest is perfectly intact. Three and I look at our reflections at the same time, our gazes finding each other in the glass.

"This is so cool," he says, his voice full of breathless wonder, then he drops to a crouch in front of a stack of unlabeled boxes. "There could be anything in here."

I swipe at a cobweb. "Those boxes don't belong to us."

"True." He nods. "But I'll bet your parents would want you to check what's inside. If the evaluator discovers something unsafe in here, he might not sign off on this as a potential listing."

"Fine." I take two steps backward. "Go ahead, Sherlock Holmes. But those boxes better not be full of skeletons."

Three peels at the strip of duct tape sealing the top of the largest box. On his knees now, he gently opens the lid, and I inch forward until I'm positioned just above him. Inside, I catch flashes of silver edges. Piles of scuffed white leather. A tangle of laces.

Three looks up at me and grins. "Ice skates."

"I used to love ice skating," I say, as he removes one pair after another. "I haven't been in years, though." In fact the last time was with Bristol the winter of our senior year. After graduation, I never felt like I had time for unproductive stuff like ... recreation. I was either working to enhance my law school applications, or studying after I got in. I'd collapse into bed at the end of each day. On weekends, I barely had enough energy to do anything besides laundry.

"This is amazing," Three breathes out as he finishes unpacking the box. "Eight matching pairs." He lines up the last set of skates on the ground beside him. "They look like they're all different sizes."

"I think the previous owner had six grandchildren, so these are probably theirs. Grandma Peabody, Grandpa Peabody, and the grandkids."

"Probably. Do you think any of them might fit us?"

"Only one way to find out." I plop onto a crate next to the now-empty box.

Three's brow quirks. "*Now* look who's excited that we came in here."

"You can say 'I told you so' if you want."

"Nah." He shakes his head. "I'll save that for later."

"How kind of you." I try on the second-to-largest pairs of skates. They're a little big for me, so I just lace them up extra tight. When I attempt to stand, Three lunges forward to help me. His touch is warm and strong—both electric and encouraging at the same time. He watches me while I take a few awkward stutter steps around the room.

"With our luck, you're going to fall and hit your head on one of those crates," he warns. "Then we'll both have concussions."

"Pessimist," I smirk, willing my ankles to stop wobbling.

"On second thought," he says, "it's pretty refreshing to see you looking this awkward."

"Awkward?" I reach up to tug at my Santa hat. "I *think* you mean adorable."

"Honestly," he tips his chin, "you remind me a little of Bambi on ice."

This gets a real laugh out of me. "Then it's a good thing I always wanted to be an animated woodland creature. And you know what?"

Step. Step. Step.

"What?"

"After the evaluator comes tomorrow, I think I'll take these babies out on the lake for a little test run."

"I believe I was promised a turkey dinner," he says.

"Oh, ye of little faith." I scoff. "I happen to be an excellent multitasker." I take a few more tentative steps back toward the entrance to the den, just as the single lightbulb flickers. "What was that?"

"The bulb's probably just loose," Three says, moving toward the light. But before he can tighten the connection, the bulb pops and sparks, then dies plunging the room into darkness.

"No!" I gasp, as the air fills with a burning electrical smell.

"Are you all right?"

"Yes, but I can't see any—ACK!"

The blade on my right skate slips, and I lose my balance, stumbling forward blindly. When I try to stop my fall by bracing myself against the bookshelf, the full weight of my body shoves the wall back into place.

We're shut inside.

Chapter Twenty-Five

Three

"I take it back." I drag a hand down my face, trying not to upset Sara. "Hanging lights in the den was clearly *not* the right move."

"Why is it so dark?" Sara yelps. "Having only one small light-bulb in here was not a very good plan." I think I hear her staggering toward me, still in her skates, and picture her falling and breaking her neck.

"Hold on. I'll come to you. Just stay still until we get those skates off of you. Otherwise you really will fall and crack your skull." I close the distance between us slowly, my arms out until I reach her. Then I take her hand to help steady her as she eases down onto a crate.

While she works on one skate, I untie the laces of the other, then I gently loosen the boot until I can safely slide it off of her foot. When my palm brushes the bare skin of her calf, goose-bumps rise along my arms.

Here I am, in a long-sleeved henley with a Hawaiian shirt layered on top, and this woman's making me shiver.

Dude. Get a grip.

"There must be a lever or handle or something on this side to get us back out of here," Sara says, once she's back in her socked feet. "Help me look."

"How? It's pitch black in here. I can't even see my hand in front of my face."

"We can just grope along the wall."

My eyes are useless, but my other senses kick in, telling me Sara's up off the crate, inching toward the moveable wall. Or at least where I think the moveable wall used to be.

So I take a few tentative steps toward the sound of her fumbling, with both my palms out protectively. When I reach the wall, I slide and pat around the edges as best I can. Sara's to the left of me as we work side by side in the blackness. But despite our best efforts, we don't come across anything remotely like a handle or a lever to release us from this room.

After a few more minutes of useless searching, Sara groans. "This is officially bad, isn't it?"

The quiver in her voice spurs me to comfort her. "It's going to be okay. We'll just have to call someone to let us out."

"Yes! Of course!" She lets out a little squeal. "You're brilliant! Who can you call?"

I pat at the pockets of my jeans. "Oh, no."

"What? Where's your phone?"

I wince. "I left it charging in the guest room. What about yours?"

"Mine's in my cardigan."

"Good."

"Which I took off in the living room."

"Oh. Yeah. Not good."

"I'm so sorry," Sara groans. "*I* did this to us."

"You were just trying to give me a memorable night." I cough out a small laugh. "Mission accomplished, by the way. Merry Hawaiian Christmas luau for the win."

"This isn't funny."

"Nobody's perfect." I shrug. "So it turns out you're human like the rest of us. Humans are allowed to make mistakes."

"But I don't want to be human!" Her words are wobbly. "I want to be … Bambi on ice."

"Well, you did a good enough impression on those skates."

"Three!" A note of panic hijacks her voice. "What if there's a time limit on how long we can breathe in here with the wall shut? We're going to suffocate, and it will be all my fault."

"I'm sure there's plenty of air," I say. "And this could've happened to anyone."

"Not true." Her protest continues in quivery bursts, punctuated by hitching breaths. "I always try too hard. And I want too much. And … and I ruin everything." She sniffles. "That's what happened with us ten years ago, right? I pushed away the one person I wanted to be closer to." She hiccups out a soft sob. "And now I've probably killed us."

"Hey, hey, hey. Please don't cry. Or exaggerate." I move toward her, but since I can't see even an inch in front of me, I whack my forehead on something hard. "Ouch!"

"Are you all right?" she gasps. "What's going on?"

"Oh, nothing. The edge of that big mirror wanted to meet my head. I'll just have matching bumps now."

"Fantastic. Now I've concussed you twice," she moans. A wooden crate creaks as she collapses on top of it, mumbling to herself. "You're so dumb, Sara. You should've made sure he was resting instead of decorating. Stop being so *reckless*, or someone's going to get *hurt*."

When her voice breaks, I want to comfort her, but I can't risk another injury in the pitch black. So I fall to my knees, crawling toward the sounds of her sniffling. When I reach her, I tug her off the crate and into my arms. "Shhh."

She buries her face against my sternum, snuffling like a puppy. "I just wanted to have some fun for once," she says as I rock her.

She's so sad and vulnerable, all I want to do is wipe her tears away. "I know you've been pushing this Christmas agenda because you feel guilty about me missing the cruise. But the truth is, I've been having more fun with you than I have in a long time. And I'm a naturally fun guy." I smile even though she can't see me. "So that's really saying something."

"You don't have to lie."

"I'm not lying. I would never—" I cut myself off. I probably shouldn't complete that sentence. Because the truth is, I haven't been totally honest with Sara. Mostly, yes. Unless you count that one time.

"So." She gulps and sniffs, catching her breath. "Where did you hit your head?"

"Here," I say, touching my brow.

She fumbles up toward me in the darkness until her fingers find my hand. Then she oh so tenderly strokes the ridges of my scalp. "Does it hurt?"

"A little."

She pulls away, rising to her knees. No more than a second later, her lips graze my temple, and she presses a gentle kiss to the spot. Her mouth is pure energy—a bolt of lightning—and a fresh shock blasts through me. In the darkness, we're not just alone. We might as well be blindfolded. There are no witnesses. Not even us.

Sara exhales—a long, soft sigh—and I reach out to cup her face. A single teardrop dribbles onto my hand, and I catch it with the tip of my finger, then bring it to my lips. Salt. Sweetness. Sara.

When I lift a thumb to smooth a strand of hair off her damp cheek, she tips her chin up, drawing in a breath. Suddenly I need to know if her mouth tastes as good as it felt on my forehead.

I've kissed Sara Hathaway many times, many years ago, but we're no longer awkward teenagers learning the ropes. We won't be kissing for charity either.

Sara's shallow breaths tell me she wants this as much as I do, but I have to be sure. I want to lock eyes with her—to see the truth there—but the darkness heightens the rest of my senses. She's cradled in my arms, holding on for dear life, and her sweet scent envelops me. The past disappears. My only focus in this moment is her.

Sliding a palm to the nape of her neck, I gather her close until her body is flush against me. Then my other hand skates along the jut of her chin, tracing a soft line down her throat and over the rise of her collarbone.

"Can I kiss you?" I rasp.

"Yes," she whimpers. "Yes."

Merry Hawaiian Christmas luau, Three.

Chapter Twenty-Six

Sara

Is this really happening?

Yes, Sara. Yes, it is.

But what does *this* mean, exactly?

It means shut up and surrender.

Well. Who am I to argue with such a commanding inner voice? I'm Sara Hathaway, the woman who's dreamed of Three Fuller's kisses for half her life. And the decade between our last real kiss and this one only stoked the heat inside me.

What happened at the Christmas tree farm doesn't count. Three was coerced by the deputy then. But no one's prompting us now, and the darkness frees me to be a little wild. A little risky.

As he lifts his hand to cup my jawline, I draw in a sharp breath and his mouth slides along my ear. My name is warm on his lips.

"Sara," he whispers.

"Please," I whisper back.

His mouth feathers across mine—a gentle hint at what's to come—and my heart leaps in my chest. His lips are both familiar and new. Testing and tested and lighting a fuse inside me. With a gasp, my mouth crashes into his, and I'm greedy and drowning in the heat of this kiss. Soon his hands are in my hair, tangled and twisting as his lips slant over mine.

In the darkness, I can't see a thing, including the potential mistake. All I know is I'm fizzing, sizzling, about to burst into—

ZZT! ZZT! ZZT!

The bulb above us pops and flickers. I'm so startled I almost fall out of Three's lap. But he wraps his arms around me, holding my body in place through the series of rapid flashes.

Light, dark, light, dark, light, dark.

When the room finally lands on light, my protective shield is officially gone.

"The light's back on!" I blurt, in an Oscar-winning performance of Captain Obvious. "We have to find a way out." But before I can lunge even two feet toward the wall, the lightbulb sputters and dies again.

"NO!"

"Are you all right?" Three asks, his breaths coming heavy.

By way of answer, I begin to stammer. "That was ... you were ... I should ... maybe we should ..."

I let my voice trail off so Three can finish the sentence, but the only thing coming from him is heavy breathing. And more heavy breathing. The spell is definitely broken.

No more kissing for me and Three.

I was just scared with a side dish of crying, and Three was trying to comfort me. Then we got a little *too* close, and the memory of that Humboldt Farms kiss we shall not speak of popped into my head—not to mention all of our kisses from ten years ago.

Three Fuller had some pretty sweet moves when he was nineteen, but the man's next-level now. He was taking his time, mouth hovering over mine, until he swept every rational thought right out of my head like a gorgeous man-broom.

So I absolutely can't let that happen again, right? At least not tonight. Not until we're out of this room and able to engage in a non-stammering, non-panting, adult conversation about what all this means.

"I think I'm going to try the lightbulb again," I say, just to have something to do. "Maybe that first attempt to tighten the connection wasn't enough. Maybe we need to *loosen* the bulb first, *then* tighten it."

Three stops his heavy breathing long enough to let out what sounds like a cough. Or a scoff. Either way, I can't just stand here doing nothing. I'm giving this a shot. So I drag a crate over beneath the spot where I estimate the dead bulb is dangling. Yes, Three was able to just stand there on his own two feet when he tried to fix the light, but I need a bit of a boost.

Climbing up onto the box, I feel around until I find the lightbulb, and accidentally bat the thing so it sways in the dark. Catching it in my hand again takes me a moment.

"Careful," Three says, as I begin to unscrew the bulb.

"Of course, I'm going to be care—" That's when the bulb slips free from the socket and out of my hand, before it crashes to the floor.

Crap.

There's a long moment of silence during which I quietly mourn the death of our only lightbulb. Then Three finally speaks. "You're wearing socks."

"Umm, yes." I nod. "But why is that relevant?"

"Because," he grits out. "There's broken glass all over the floor now."

I gulp. "You're right."

"We don't need to add bloody feet to the situation so just hold still."

"Okay, but I wasn't exactly planning to do a river dance up here on this—ACK!" I begin to slip and let out a shriek scrambling for something to grab on to. What I find is the chain for the light, and as I fall, I rip the whole thing out of the ceiling. Of course I land on Three.

He catches me with a grunt.

"I'm sorry," I say.

"I know."

He carries me away from the sad remains of our broken bulb as shattered glass crunches under his boots. His body is warm, and my arms snake around his neck. "How can you see where you're going?"

"I can't."

He adjusts his hold on me—sticking one leg out at a time, scoping out what's in front of us with his foot—then he shuffles forward. Slowly. When we've moved several yards away from the lightbulb wreckage, I say, "I think it's safe for you to put me down."

After he lowers me to the ground, I grope around for a place to sit and locate a long rectangular trunk. We each take a side.

"So." Three clears his throat. "What's the game plan now?"

"Well, we couldn't find a way out in the dark, and I just permanently murdered our only light source. Neither of us has a phone to call for help, so I'm thinking we might be stuck in here until Ryan Detweiler shows up tomorrow. He can let us out."

"Hmph. How will he get in the house?"

"He has the lockbox code," I say. "Property owners aren't supposed to be home during the evaluations, so I was planning to take you out to breakfast while he was here." At the mention of food, my stomach rumbles—traitor—and I press my hands against it. "Good thing you made that grilled cheese for us, huh? *And* you took your antibiotics. *And* you've got a fresh bandage on." I'm doing my best to find the bright side in a room that's pitch black, but my voice cracks anyway. "We should be okay overnight, right?"

"Sure." Three's quiet for a moment. "And being in the dark, resting overnight, is probably better for me than running around the yard with pink flamingoes and tiki torches anyway."

"You were *running*?"

"Exaggeration."

"Still." I groan. "I not only concussed you, I turned out to be the world's worst caretaker."

One who came awfully close to spending the rest of the night kissing you.

"You were just trying to keep me occupied."

"Right." Another groan from me. "Because I'm so boring."

He lets out a small chuckle. "I never said that."

"You didn't have to."

"Sara." He takes a beat. "The truth is, spending these past couple days with you hasn't been *all* bad."

"Oh, really?" I snort. "What was your favorite part? When I threw a fire extinguisher at your head? When your entire family left for a cruise without you? How about the time I tried to make you play chess with a concussion? Ah, right. It was *probably* the moment I locked us in this storage room, then assassinated our only lightbulb."

Three guffaws. "Well, when you put it that way ..."

"No wonder you broke up with me," I mumble under my breath. I don't intend for him to hear me say this, but he does.

"Hey. Don't do that. Please."

"No, it's all right." A long sigh escapes me. "I get it."

"You *don't*, though." His voice goes gruff. "At least not all of it, and that's on me."

"How is my cluelessness your fault?"

"Because there's some stuff we haven't talked about," he says. "Stuff about me. About us. And maybe it's time I cleared things up."

I suck in a breath. What's left for me to know? I handed him my heart. He shot me down. It was humiliating. The end.

"You want to talk about *us* right now?"

"Maybe." He blows out a gust of air. "Yeah. I do."

My pulse is whirring, and I send up a silent prayer that my voice doesn't crack. "I'm not sure this is the ideal moment for us to rehash everything that happened."

In other words, I've already gone over our breakup a million times in my head and getting over the heartbreak took years. In fact, I'm still not the same, and being back in Abieville already has me questioning my sanity.

So if Three wants to perform an autopsy on the worst night of my life, he should go ahead and do that with Ford. Or Nella. Or Kenny. His work friends. Anyone but me.

"Okay." He clears his throat. "So, when then?"

I chew my lip, considering the best answer to his question. I mean, at least it's pitch black in here. Three wouldn't be able to make out the pain in my face. But there'd also be nowhere for me to hide after we dissected the details of our one-sided breakup. And anyway, the darkness wouldn't mask the sound of my tears.

"How about *any* time we're not stuck in a small space together," I say.

Three blows out a breath. "Fair enough." But why is *he* the one sounding defeated? *I'm* the woman whose heart he broke. Still, he just wants to communicate—finally—so I kind of regret my sarcasm.

"Listen." I lean over and nudge his shoulder. "I appreciate your good intentions. But you're talking about ancient history, and I'm just not up for a deep dive into those ugly memories. Now or ever."

He bumps my shoulder back. "Message received." A beat of silence follows. "I just thought the conversation was long overdue."

"Well, *I* think we should try to make ourselves as comfortable as possible. It's going to be a long night, and I already have to pee."

Chapter Twenty-Seven

Three

Great.

So Sara doesn't want to talk about anything having to do with the two of us or our past.

Serves me right, I guess.

I got so caught up in her Christmas luau that I didn't broach the subject like I'd planned to after texting with Ford.

What can I say? She just looked so excited when I found her with the clutter of stuff she'd hoped would make the holidays more special for me. But if I'm being completely honest, that was only half the reason I didn't talk to her then.

Less than half the reason.

An eighth at most.

Most of my avoidance comes down to being afraid to tell Sara exactly how much I cared about her. How much I *still* care about her. And it's not like I suddenly got brave. I just figured the cover of darkness could provide some kind of buffer when I made my confession. She needs to know the feelings I had for her all those summers ago never truly went away. They just lay dormant, buried under years of teenage stubbornness. A young man's ego. Not to mention my determination to prove her parents wrong.

Still, I waited this long, so I won't force her to hear me out now. I can be patient. I owe Sara that much. But I'm done masking the truth, hiding from something I thought would be too difficult to confront.

When we finally get out of this room, I've got to face her in the light of day. And I have to make that happen before my follow-up appointment.

Once the doctor clears me to be on my own, Sara could decide to drop me straight off at my place with the intention of never seeing me again. So hopefully it's not too late to apologize. To be fully honest. To be the one who puts his heart on the line this time.

"So what do we do now?" Sara asks. Her Hawaiian shirt rustles beside me, and I can absolutely picture her shrug. "I wasn't expecting to sleep sitting upright all night."

"Hmm." I run a hand along the back of my neck. "I spotted some stuff at the back of the room draped in tarps before the light went out. I can collect the tarps to spread out on the floor and we can sleep there. Better than lying on bare concrete."

"Definitely better. I'll just go find my shoes and help."

As she rises, I reach for her elbow, coaxing her back down on the trunk. "Don't. You could get cut up on that broken lightbulb. Just stay here."

"And do nothing?" She scoffs. "I hate feeling useless."

"You're the farthest thing from useless. You've been taking care of me this whole time."

"Fine." She raps on the trunk. "But you can't stop me from checking in here, and in any of the other boxes I can reach without having to get up and walk around."

"Good idea," I say. "Hopefully you'll find some blankets."

"Hopefully you'll find a toilet."

I bark out a laugh, and the answering chuckle from Sara gives my insides a welcome hit of relief. Maybe I *didn't* ruin everything by suggesting we talk about our past. And prepping this place for an unexpected sleepover might be just the break we need from *that* unwelcome seriousness.

"I don't know about you," I say, hoping Sara can hear the smirk in my voice, "but I peed just before you hit me with the whole Christmas luau extravaganza. I can probably hold it all night."

"Bragger." She lets out a little snort, which is even more adorable in the dark.

"Should we start to look—"

GONG!

Sara gasps. "What was that?" She grabs my upper arm, her fingers digging into my biceps.

"Sounds like there's a grandfather clock back there."

"How come I never heard it before?"

"The bookshelves must be pretty thick. Or the room's well insulated. Maybe both. Either way, if the clock's been in here longer than a week, it must be battery operated. Big Mama has one that can last at least a year."

"But why did it only gong at us once?"

"It's probably set to chime once on the half hour."

"Every half hour?" she moans. "Ugh. Sleeping was going to be difficult enough."

"At least we'll be able to tell time."

"Well, well, well." Sara huffs out a laugh. "Look who's turned into Mr. Bright Side."

She releases my arm, and I let out a sigh, wishing she was still gripping me. Being the one Sara goes to for protection feels good. Even for a moment. Even under these less-than-ideal circumstances.

We get to work searching for any items that might make our time in here more comfortable. In the trunk we were sitting on, Sara finds an assortment of old clothing, including a coat with what feels like a faux fur hood. But only one. And it's not very big.

Under the large tarp beside the grandfather clock, I discover an old couch with one throw pillow. The cushions are saggy, the arms feel threadbare, plus a metal coil pokes up on one end, but it's actual furniture. I take a seat on the side without the busted spring and bounce a couple times. "I found a couch," I call out. "Actually it's more like a small sofa, but big enough for you to sleep on tonight."

"No way." She scoffs, and I'll just bet she's got her arms folded across her middle. "You're the one with the concussion. If you think I'm taking the couch while you get the floor, you've really lost your mind. We'll just fold up the tarps to make them thicker. I'll be just fine on the ground."

I cross my arms. "Concussion or not, I haven't stopped being a gentleman, and I'm not going to let you sleep on concrete."

"Okay." She's quiet for a moment. "Are you suggesting we try to sleep together on one small couch?"

At this, my pulse picks up. We'd have to lie very close for us both to fit. Very. Not that holding Sara all night would be torture, but kissing her will be all too tempting if she's literally in my arms. "I propose we each take one side of the couch with our heads on opposite armrests, and then stretch our legs out going in the opposite direction."

"So I get your feet in my face?" She squawks. "Nope, thanks."

I rake a hand over my head. "We're running out of options."

"All right." She exhales. "But just so we're clear, there will be no more lip action happening as long as we're stuck in here."

"Hold on." My mouth slips sideways. "Did you just say *lip action*? What exactly is *lip action*, Sara?"

"Come on. You know what I meant."

"Did you mean I might get *more* lip action when we're no longer stuck in here?"

She lets out a snort, and I hope she's smiling. "You wish, Three Fuller."

Yeah, I *do* wish, Sara Hathaway.

Too bad my birthday is in August.

Chapter Twenty-Eight

Sara

Twelve Years Ago: August

Hey, journal. Long time, no write. Lol! Like pretty much an entire summer. But I just had to record this moment because I finally gave Three his gift, and I'm pretty sure he loves it.

I waited until after he blew out the candles and made a wish. Then I pulled out the box from the leather shop. Ford labeled it a man-bracelet, Nella says it's a wrist band. Three decided to call it a cuff. By any other name, it's so sexy. On him, I mean.

Of course he has no idea I slept in the cuff every night since I bought it, and I do NOT plan to tell him that. I just wanted a little part of me to be close to something he'll hopefully wear all year long. Does that make me sound weird and creepy?

Okay, let's be honest: I don't care if I'm weird and creepy. The truth is, I'm falling for Three Fuller. Like a tree in the woods. Timber! Did anyone hear my heart crash?

The thing is, I haven't said the words out loud yet, and I'm not sure I should. Not right before I'm about to leave again. I don't want to sound desperate and clingy. So I'm just going to let the cuff do the talking for me. Silently.

Just a little reminder that I give the best birthday gifts— ha! Hopefully every time he looks at it, he'll think of me. Of course, I realize him snapping some cuff around his wrist won't be the same as us being together. But in a tiny way, a piece of me will still be connected to him when I'm gone.

Chapter Twenty-Nine

Sara

The grandfather clock gongs again, yanking me from the fog of my intermittent dozing. I crack open one sleep-crusted eye, instinctively expecting daylight, but nope. I'm still in the dark, still sharing a couch with Three, still trapped in this storage room with no escape.

I can't see a thing, so my other senses kick in, alerting me to the fact that it's not Three's feet by my face as we'd planned. It's not even his legs.

No, I'm directly on top of the man.

My first instinct is to leap up off of him, but I'm worried if I move too abruptly, he'll wake up and assume I crawled onto him on purpose. Common sense says the best way for me to handle the situation is slowly. Gently.

Don't wake the sleeping giant.

For the record, this particular giant has one arm cradling my body like I'm the little spoon, and he's the big one, except we're lying flat, not on our sides. My face is pressed into his pecs, so his

Hawaiian shirt's probably leaving button-marks on my cheek. Even worse, I'm pretty sure I drooled on him.

My mouth feels chapped and sticky, so I swallow against the dryness, and that's when the memory of Three's lips brushing mine sends butterflies swooping around my insides.

But that was earlier. Before we tried going to sleep. Once we settled on the couch, Three was nothing but chivalrous.

He insisted on lying on the side with the broken coil, so I made him take the one pathetic throw pillow to slip between his back and the cushions. Of course *his* legs stretched way past my armrest, while my legs barely reached his. When Three suggested we spread the single coat over the middle of our bodies for extra warmth, I ended up with the hood up by my face. The fur kept tickling my chin. And honestly? I was still cold.

The thing is, I'd taken my cardigan off to put on my Hawaiian shirt, and underneath the short sleeves, I only had one thin tank top. So while we were sleeping, I must've maneuvered my body around and inched my way up into Three's arms. Now the coat's draped over both of us, and he's perfectly still, except for the steady rise and fall of his rock-hard pecs.

How can he breathe with my full weight on him?

How is he sleeping through *any* of this?

I need to climb off of him soon, because I like spooning with Three a little too much. Also, I *really* have to pee now.

Like a lot.

Before I begin my slow escape from the top of Three Fuller Mountain, I allow myself to savor the altitude for a moment longer. His heart is beating—slow and steady—a peaceful throb against my cheek. I let our breathing sync up, enjoying the connection, even if I'm the only one who's aware.

Either way, this is, undoubtedly, the most comfortable pillow I've ever slept on. And while his delicious scent—all clean and piney—isn't doing me any favors in the drool department, Three's body is cloaking me in warmth and safety. I feel not just protected but cherished.

Oh, come on, Sara. Let's not get carried away.

Yes, Three and I dabbled in a bit of *lip action* last night, but he didn't want to be my long-distance boyfriend ten years ago, and he's not going to beg for a commitment now. He has a full life in Abieville. I've got a new job waiting in the city. Two different-sized spoons in two different cutlery drawers.

A small sigh slips out of me, and Three draws in a breath at the same time. My head lifts right along with the swell of his ribcage, a wave I wouldn't mind riding for a little while longer.

"Sara?"

Gah! I've been caught.

If Three is awake, he's obviously aware I'm on top of him. My best course of action is to feign ignorance, right? Play dumb. Or possum. Or both.

"Are you still sleeping?" His voice is a deep rumble in his chest, and I put on a show, faking a snuffly yawn like I'm only just stirring, even though I've already been fully conscious for several minutes.

"Hmmm," I mumble. Quite the actress, if I do say so myself. Three reaches out, drawing a finger down my cheek, and his touch is beyond soft. Tender, even. I could play dead forever if this is the kind of treatment I'd receive.

"It's nine thirty," he says.

"What?" I gasp and bolt upright, scrambling over to my original side of the couch. "How do you know?"

"I counted nine gongs the last time the grandfather clock struck. There was another gong a few minutes ago, which means it's more than half past the hour."

"But the evaluator's coming at ten," I yelp.

"I know. I didn't want to wake you, but I figured you'd want to be ready to get his attention when he gets here. We can position ourselves on the other side of the wall from the bookshelf and shout after the clock strikes ten. Let's just hope this guy is on time. And not hard of hearing."

"How long have you been awake?"

"I don't know."

"Three."

"I honestly didn't get much sleep. I kept thinking about when you asked if there was enough oxygen in the room. And I started worrying about you. Your safety."

"You said there was plenty of oxygen."

"And I'm sure there is. But you know how twisted a person's thoughts can get in the middle of the night."

"So you just stayed up?"

His silence tells me he must've been awake at whatever point I turned my body around to use him as my own personal mattress. "I don't know how you ended up underneath me," I blurt. "I must've been sleepwalking. Except I guess it was more like sleep-crawling. All over the couch. All over you. But I never would have—"

"It's okay," he interjects, cutting off my rambling. "I was the one who moved you."

My heartbeat accelerates, and I raise a hand to my flushing throat. "I don't understand."

"Your teeth were chattering, and I felt you shivering more than once. I just wanted to warm you up."

"So you pulled me on top of you?"

"I thought for sure you'd wake up, but you were sleeping like a log."

"I guess I was pretty tired after concussion watch."

"Exactly. So now we're even."

"Concussion watch 2.0," I say. "Speaking of which, how are you feeling this morning?"

"Well." He lets out a half laugh. "I can't swear I've got the best judgment right now, and some of my choices might be questionable."

Right. Like kissing me last night. Like sharing a couch with me last night. Like wanting to talk about our past last night.

Then again, I kissed the swell of his forehead first. If he's going to attach responsibility to his concussion, I'm just as much to blame.

"And of course I probably have some lingering brain fog. But all things considered, I'm feeling pretty good. That's only because someone's been taking pretty great care of me."

My shoulders hitch. "No big deal."

"I don't want to argue with you," he says, "so we'll have to agree to disagree about the size of this particular deal." He tugs on his boots. "Either way, are you just about ready to go do some yelling? I can piggyback you over to the wall since we still don't know where your shoes are."

I chew my lip for a moment, a trickle of dread creeping up my spine. "Do you really think we'll get out of here today?"

"We have to get out," he says. "If for some reason we don't get the evaluator's attention, I'll come up with another plan." He lays a palm over my hand, and his touch sends a flash of heat straight up my spine. I should probably pull away, but I don't. "I'm going to take care of you, Sara, just like you've been taking care of me. And I promise I won't let anything worse than a broken skate blade happen to you. Not now. Not ever."

When he gives my fingers a squeeze, I suck in a breath. I want to believe Three will never let anything hurt me. But what he really should've promised is that he'll never let anything happen to me *again*.

Because he already shattered my heart once.

And nothing could be worse than that.

Chapter Thirty

Three

"I thought you told me Ryan Detweiler was a guy."

"I did tell you Ryan Detweiler was a guy."

Sara and I have been pounding on the storage room wall for twenty minutes, our voices hoarse from shouting, and I'm ninety-eight percent sure the person who finally answered us is *not* a guy.

"What's going on?" a very high-pitched voice calls out. "Where are you? Are you all right?" There's banging on the bookshelf side. "I think I just broke a nail!"

Yep. Probably female. Definitely concerned.

When I imagine being in her shoes, I get it. This woman thought she was entering an empty house to judge its potential as a high-end vacation rental. Once inside, she hears screaming. Muffled screaming, but still. She comes into the den, which on the surface appears to be a deserted room, except for the cries for help coming from the other side.

Disconcerting to say the least.

"Are you Ryan Detweiler?" Sara yells, her voice cracking on

the name. Probably from a combination of too much yelling and too much exhaustion, mixed with a big dose of relief.

"How do you know my name?" the woman yells back.

"She's the homeowner," I shout, trying to help preserve Sara's voice. "We got trapped in here last night by accident."

"I promise we're friendly," Sara shouts, and my chest tightens. She's not wrong. The two of us did get a little friendly last night. And I would've gotten friendlier if Sara had been up for it.

"Also, I'm not technically the homeowner," she hollers. "I'm their daughter! Sara Hathaway? The one you've been texting with?" Her raspy words sound like nails on a chalkboard.

"You aren't supposed to be here during an evaluation," Ryan Detweiler yells. "Platinum Stays is very particular about that!"

"We didn't plan this." Sara groans, waves of frustration vibrating off of her. Under her breath she mumbles, "If this delays the approval process for the house, my mom's going to lose it."

"Ms. Detweiler?" I call to her. "If you could help get us out of here, we'd be very grateful."

"But ... how?"

"At the top corner of the bookshelf on the left, there's a lever. Just climb the stool, and tug it down—hard. The wall will open up into the room we're in."

"Is this some kind of joke?"

"No."

"Fine! But you're paying for my manicure."

This Ryan Detweiler person doesn't sound happy, but I'm more focused on Sara right now. It's still too dark for me to make out her face, but the poor thing sounds absolutely miserable. I know she's worried about disappointing her mom, so I'll do everything in my power to make sure that doesn't happen.

A minute later, the bookshelf groans open, revealing both daylight and Ryan Detweiler.

She's about our age, in a wool suit and heels with her hair slicked into a bun of strawberry blonde. She kind of reminds me of my sister, *if* Nella were a few years older and wearing a look of horror on her face.

"Thank you, thank you, thank you," Sara blurts. "I'll be right back!" She darts past the evaluator, sprinting out of the den and heading straight for the bathroom.

Ryan Detweiler's brow flies up, and she snaps her gaze to me. "Was that Sara?"

"Yeah." I manage an apologetic grimace. "She's had to go for a while, so thanks for letting us out, Ms. Detweiler."

"Call me Ryan."

"Thanks, Ryan." I glance toward the bathroom. "Anyway, things got pretty desperate last night."

Ryan sweeps her gaze around the room, surveying all the visible space from where we're standing. "So I see."

The den itself is littered with colorful leis, strands of white lights, and a staple gun. Out in the living room, remnants of popcorn garland cover the coffee table, along with strips of construction paper, scissors, glue, and tape.

Sara's sewing pouch remains on the couch. Bags from the Five and Dime sit abandoned on the floor. There are pineapple lanterns along the wall. Even the Christmas tree looks out of place, considering the lack of ornaments or a star.

I can only imagine how this scene appears: the exact opposite of what an upscale vacation rental site would offer. In fact, the interior of the Hathaway's newly renovated lake house looks nonsensical at best, and at worst, unsafe.

Ryan sniffs. "May I ask why there are pink flamingoes and tiki torches in the yard?"

"It's not what you think," I say, ruffling my bed-head hair. "Sara threw together a last-minute Hawaiian Christmas luau for me last night, and I'm sure she was planning to have everything cleaned up before you arrived this morning, but like I said, we got trapped inside that room."

"Trapped?"

"Well, we couldn't find a handle to get out."

Ryan's forehead creases. "You're telling me there's a room in this home that actually locks people inside with no means of exit?"

Oops.

Sara's parents already don't like me. I can't be the reason their house gets rejected. "There's probably a handle or a lever in there somewhere," I rush to say. "I mean, I'm sure there is. But after the lightbulb burned out, we couldn't find anything in the pitch black."

Ryan pulls down her brow even further. "So you're saying there's insufficient lighting?" She makes a note on her clipboard. I probably shouldn't tell her Sara ripped the only light right out of the ceiling.

"I know things probably look kind of bad right now." I wince. "But I grew up in and out of this house, and what the Hathaways have done to it is just—"

"Three!" Sara calls out, rushing toward us from the bathroom. "Please stop talking! Now!"

Ryan arches a brow in my direction. "Your name is ... Three?" I shrug, but I don't respond. After all, I was told to stop talking.

When Sara reaches the doorway, she converges on us panting and out of breath. "Hi there, Ms. Det—"

"Ryan. Please."

"Great!" Sara presses a grin across her face. "I'm Sara. It's so nice to finally put a face to all the texts. To be honest, I thought you were a—"

"A man, right?" she interrupts. "I know. Ryan isn't common for a woman. But my mom liked it. And since I'm not supposed to see the homeowners, I never bother warning anyone." She shifts her focus to the messy room. "But did I come at the wrong time?"

"No, no, no." Sara's eyes pop wide. "You're right on time, actually. Ten o'clock!" A nervous laugh trills out of her, and she flicks her gaze over to me. "Ryan, this is my friend, Three Fuller."

"We already met," I say. "Sort of." Bobbing my head, I reach out to shake her hand, trying to ignore the twist in my gut at being introduced as Sara's *friend*.

"Anyway." Sara pushes out a chuckle. "I'm sorry the house isn't exactly put together now…"

"Yes, your friend was just starting to explain the situation." Ryan presses her lips together. "He told me you were throwing a party when you both got stuck in that room behind the book-shelves. A room with no handle and no working light fixture, I might add."

"Well, we're not sure about the handle. And as for the light, I—"

"Ms. Hathaway, I'm afraid there's no need for me to evaluate any other part of this property. I won't be approving your home for Platinum Stays."

When Sara's face crumples, I immediately go into fix-it mode. I've got to make this better for her. "Now hold on a minute." I lift my hands as if in surrender. "I have a suggestion, if you'd be willing to hear me out."

Ryan's eyes flick to me. "I do apologize for my abruptness, Mr. Fuller, but this home is simply not up to our standards."

"I'm only asking for the chance to prove to you that it *can* be." I offer her my friendliest smile—the one my students and their parents can't say no to. "You see, underneath all these holiday extras, this home—the entire property—is elegantly appointed. The finishes and decor are new and on trend. The views of the lake are unmatched. Inside and out, this place is truly spectacular."

Ryan sniffs. "Including the flamingoes out front?"

"Heh heh heh." I force a laugh. "The flamingoes are optional. I just don't want you to make the mistake of allowing your company to miss out on a gorgeous rental home that's temporarily buried under my *friend*'s enthusiastic attempts to cheer me up."

I cut my focus to Sara who's staring at me, gape-mouthed. Sure I swooped in when she didn't ask for my help, but if I succeed, she'll hopefully forgive me. Plus erasing the look of failure on her face is all that matters now.

"The sad truth is," I continue, "I'm stuck here in town, missing out on a family vacation due to a most unfortunate injury." I tip my head, pointing first to the bandage, then at the lump.

"Oh, dear," Ryan says. "That's horrible."

"Yes," I say. "It was." Sara lets out a little yelp, but I keep my eyes lasered in on the evaluator. "I'd sure hate to think Sara's kindness to me might jeopardize the approval of this home for her, Ms. Detweiler."

"Ryan," she corrects.

"Right." Another smile from me. "So, *Ryan*, I'm guessing Sara only needs an hour or two to put this whole place right again. In the meantime, I'd be happy to show you around Abieville. As a lifelong resident, I can point out all the one-of-a-kind amenities our town has to offer future vacationers. Then, if it's all right with you, we can circle back here for you to complete your evaluation."

Sara opens her mouth. "But I—"

"You'd only need a couple hours, right?" I lift my brow, hoping she'll catch on to what I'm trying to accomplish.

"Ahem." Ryan clears her throat primly, drawing my attention back to her. "Mr. Fuller—"

"Three," I say.

"All right, Three. I'm afraid that even if these ... umm ... party supplies were cleaned up, that room behind the bookshelves would remain a problem. It's simply unsafe."

"True enough," I say. "But you haven't heard the rest of my proposal yet."

"There's more?" Sara squawks.

"Of course," I say. "If Ryan finds everything else about this place suitable, I'll make all the necessary safety adjustments myself, including an accessible handle on the inside of the room, and adequate lighting."

Sara and Ryan eye me. "You can do that?" they both ask me at the same time.

"I can, if you're willing to come back tomorrow. I have a doctor's appointment in the morning"—I pause to point at the bandage again, aiming for sympathy points—"but I'm not a man who makes promises he can't keep, and I guarantee I can have the work done by the late afternoon."

Ryan's gaze flits to Sara then back to me. "I'm sorry, but my schedule is booked solid tomorrow."

"Then make it Wednesday." I cock my brow. "Please."

"Wednesday is Christmas Eve."

"It is." I drag a hand along the back of my neck, wincing. "And since Sara graciously agreed to postpone your original appointment when you had car trouble, I'm humbly requesting you extend her the same courtesy." I let my hand drop to my chest, palm over my heart.

"Three." Sara clears her throat. "You don't have to—"

"Least I can do," I insist, cutting my gaze to her. "After all you've done for me." I'm being a friend. That's what she called me. I bob my head and smile.

"So." I swing my smile back over to Ryan. "If you're up for it, my offer stands to give you a personal tour of our town with a native Abievillian."

"Hmm." Ryan takes a moment to consider, her gaze darting between Sara and me.

"Three." Sara clears her throat. "I'm not sure being dragged around town by a stranger is in Ms. Detweiler's job description."

"Well, I hadn't thought about that," I admit, ducking shyly. "How about if our first stop is the sheriff's station? Sheriff Bender and Deputy Townsend are friends of mine, and I'd love to introduce you to our town's law enforcement. Give you a real sense of the safety here in Abieville. After that, we've got some shops and restaurants we can drive by. Over the bridge is a gorgeous inn I'd love to—"

"I'm sure she gets the idea, Three," Sara interjects. "But you're not safe to drive, remember? The concussion..."

"Oh, I haven't forgotten." I lift my chin. "And I never said I'd be the one doing the driving. So." I turn to Ryan and offer my brightest smile. "What do you say?"

Her lips part. "I say ... we can take my car."

Chapter Thirty-One

Sara

I've been stewing for precisely one hundred nineteen minutes of the two hours since Three left. I *did* just take a quick sixty-second break to chug a glass of water, which means it's been a full minute since I wondered what he's doing with Ryan Detweiler.

He wanted to show her what Abieville would offer guests from Platinum Stays, so I'm guessing he'll take her by the best shops for tourists, like Gracie's Glass Emporium, Bookishly Yours, and that old store next to the market with all the antiques and souvenirs. Flower Power is pretty cool too, especially for people into fresh arrangements and gifts. I wouldn't care too much if they stopped by Spill the Tea. But my stomach flips over imagining Three bringing Ryan to Dips & Scoops. Sure, it's not exactly ice cream season, so there's a chance he skipped that place.

But Three loves Dips & Scoops.

Well, he used to love it. Back when I thought he loved me too.

But we're not going to talk about that, remember?

Right.

Instead, I finish stowing the last of the Hawaiian Luau

supplies in the storage room behind the bookshelf, then take a moment to survey the house.

The space looks the way I assume a normal vacation home would appear during Christmastime. Since the tree still only had strands of white lights on it, I took the liberty of hanging all the ornaments myself. Three wasn't here, so I had to pull the couch over and climb on top to reach the highest branches, but I did get it done myself. I even placed the star on at the end.

I felt bad tossing the construction paper rings Three cut out into a drawer, but I figured a homemade Advent calendar wouldn't impress Platinum Stays. Honestly, I'd gotten so caught up in recreating the Fuller family traditions, I lost sight of the goal that brought me here in the first place: convincing Ryan Detweiler to approve our lake house for their listings.

Speaking of which, she could come back anytime now.

ANYTIME.

I plop on the couch in front of the Christmas tree, hoping the twinkle lights will improve my mood. No such luck. I'd been so excited to experience the kind of holiday Three grew up with, but decorating the tree alone turned out to be ... anticlimactic.

The truth is, I miss my own family.

So I decide there's no time like the present to call my mom. She's already left me multiple messages asking for updates, so I'm planning to put as positive a spin on the situation as possible, leaving out the glitch with Three and the Hawaiian Christmas luau. And the surprise storage room. And the fact that Ryan Detweiler has yet to evaluate the house.

And it's all my fault.

I take a couple of deep cleansing breaths then try to FaceTime her. The call rings and rings with no answer. Weird. I expected her to be waiting with bated breath.

I'm about to give up, when my dad's face suddenly appears on the screen. He's wearing a pinstriped suit with a red tie, and his salt and pepper hair is slicked back at the temples.

I wrinkle my nose. "Where's Mom?"

"Hello to you, too." He chuckles. "What am I, chopped liver?"

"No," I quickly backtrack. "Of course I'm happy to see you, Dad. It's just ... I called Mom's number, didn't I?"

He hoists an eyebrow. "Excellent observation, counselor. Your mother left her phone on the table so I answered it for her."

"But it's a Monday. Why aren't you at work?"

He peeks at the staircase to the second floor of their penthouse. "I surprised your mother by coming home to take her to lunch. She's been so stressed about the gala and the auction and this whole Platinum Stays situation, I wanted to give her a break. I made reservations at Gramercy Tavern. She's just getting dressed now."

My jaw drops. "You left the office in the middle of a weekday? Who are you and what have you done with my father?"

He flashes his piano-key teeth at me. "Let me fill you in on a little secret." He leans in close to his screen. "One of the perks of being the boss is getting to call all the shots. But you'll learn that soon enough."

"I see." My mouth goes crooked. "Is this your way of officially offering me that associate's position?"

Another chuckle slips out of him. "I may be a founding partner, but making that decision unilaterally wouldn't be a good look."

"Oh, I know that, Dad. I was only kidding. But the partners are making their final decisions soon, though, right?"

His smile stretches even wider. "We're meeting on Friday, as a matter of fact."

"Huh." I do a quick mental calendar-check to be sure I've got my days straight. Today is Monday. Three's follow-up appointment is tomorrow, a Tuesday. Wednesday is the gala and my birthday. Then Christmas is Thursday. "You're meeting the day after Christmas?"

"Yes, and I'm glad you'll be home by then." Another arch of his brow. "I'm anticipating an *extra* reason to celebrate this year."

Right. My job offer.

"I would've thought you'd close the office on the 26th for a three-day weekend."

"No rest for the wicked," he quips. "Or is it no rest for the *weary*?" His eyes drop into a squint. "I can never remember which one's the correct phrase. In any case, I already gave everyone the 25th off. And New Year's Day next week."

I press out a weak laugh. "That's so generous of you."

"I thought so." He straightens, tugging at his tie. "It's what's expected around here, Sara. And you'll be putting in long hours once you officially come onboard too. Not a lot of vacation time. Working on some of the lesser holidays."

"Like Arbor Day?"

"Yes." He nods, either ignoring my sarcasm or missing it completely. "That is, until you're the managing partner." He glances at the staircase again then back at me. "Then you can squeeze in a spontaneous lunch date every once in a while."

I arrange my face into a smile. My dad's expectation that I'll run Hathaway Cooke someday shouldn't come as a complete shock. After all, I've followed in his footsteps from prep school until now. Still. Working toward a goal is one thing. Having no choice in the matter is another. "I think you're getting a little ahead of yourself," I say.

"Once again, you're correct, counselor." He splays his hands, triumphant. "We'll have *many* other milestones—big and small— to celebrate before then, won't we?"

"Yes." A bead of sweat forms at my temple. Maybe two beads. "We will."

"Speaking of which, your mother told me you have some new ideas about the firm's mentorship process. I'm sure the partners would love to hear your thoughts." He pauses. "In the event that you're offered a position, of course."

"Oh, yes." More beads of sweat. "I've been meaning to talk to you about that."

My dad checks his watch. "Now's as good a time as any."

Okay. I inhale deeply, square my shoulders. Here goes nothing. "Obviously Hathaway Cooke has a long-standing scholarship and mentorship program with the Daughters of the American Revolution." I take a beat to meet my dad's gaze. "But what if we established a duplicate program with Youth Save, starting this year?"

"The non-profit?" He tips his head. "For foster kids?"

"That's the one." I swipe at my brow. "They work closely with Children's Village, but their specific mission is to get older children adopted. I've been doing some research, and the ones who are still in the system by the time they reach high school are far less likely to go to college. So I was thinking—"

"Sara." He tilts his head. "You have a good heart, and wanting to make a difference in this world is one of your greatest strengths."

"Thank you." My smile falters as I wait for the *but*.

"Of course your mother and I love Children's Village," he continues. "The Hathaway Gala is our way of personally supporting them. But *Hathaway Cooke* is a different story. We're looking to mold future associates. Our firm isn't in the business of mentoring kids who have no expectation of going to law school, let alone working for us one day."

"But that's the point, Dad." A ribbon of frustration wraps around my insides. "They *should* be able to become an attorney if they want to. They *should* have a shot at big law. Their dreams are just as important as anyone from the DAR, don't you think?"

"I *think* we'd be setting a bunch of kids up for disappointment, filling their heads with endgames that aren't realistic. At least not for most of them. You went to Stanford because that goal was achievable for you from the beginning, Sara."

No, I went to Stanford because you *went to Stanford.*

"Dad." I set my jaw. "I just think every kid deserves the chance to pursue any future they want. And if I'm going to be a part of the firm, I'd love for Hathaway Cooke to be a part of making that possible."

"*If?*"

I blink. "Well. I haven't been offered the job yet."

"Sara." My father exhales a long gust of air. "Your mother and I have made a lot of sacrifices to set you up for the best life possible, so I hope you're not forgetting your place in the Hathaway legacy."

I swallow hard. "Of course not. I just wanted to—"

"Charles?" my mother calls out. "Is that Sara on the phone?" In the corner of the screen, I see her sail down the stairs in a cashmere trench coat worthy of Gramercy Tavern. I'd originally called to update her in the first place, but a thread of anxiety unspools in my gut. She's going to ask about the evaluation. And I'm going to have to answer.

"Hi, Mom." I wave at the screen as my dad hands over the phone.

"I've been waiting to hear from you!" Her eyes go wide, and her red lips part in anticipation. "Are we approved?"

Yep. There it is.

"We should get the official sign-off on Wednesday," I chirp. *Hopefully,* I think. Bonus points for my positive spin being almost entirely the truth.

"Wednesday?" Her hand goes to her throat. "But that's Christmas Eve. The night of the gala. We're counting on the lake house to be one of our top auction items!"

"And we'll be a Platinum Stays property that morning, Mom. Plenty of time."

"But ... why Wednesday?"

"Ryan Detweiler just wants to come back to double-check everything." I take a beat. "There was a surprise we couldn't anticipate." I use the word 'we' because my mom did, but also because I'm thinking about Three and me. We sure didn't anticipate last night.

"What kind of surprise?" My mother's eyes fly open.

I lean in close, pasting a grin on my face. "Are you ready for this? I discovered a secret storage room in the den behind the bookshelves!"

She gasps. "A what?"

"A secret storage room! Isn't that cool?" Okay, I'm laying it on thick, but that's as much for her benefit as mine.

"Cool?" she squeaks.

"*Very* cool."

Even as I say this, boot steps thud up the stairs outside, and two distinct voices in two different octaves are speaking on the porch.

Three is back. And he's got Ryan Detweiler with him.

"Anyway, I've gotta go, Mom."

"I'm just worried that—"

"Everything's all right. *Better* than all right."

"Sara." She stares at me. "Are you absolutely sure?"

"Just trust me." I swallow hard.

Everything has to be all right.

Chapter Thirty-Two

Three

"Thanks for the tour."

Ryan's standing awfully close, but in her defense, this porch isn't exactly huge. So I back up until I'm practically pressed against one of the Adirondack chairs.

Am I supposed to invite her in now? I honestly have no idea. It's not like we were on a date. I was just killing a couple birds with one stone: buying Sara time to clean up any out-of-place decorations, and presenting Ryan with the very best our town has to offer future guests.

For the record, Abieville understood the assignment. And I'm not just talking about obvious stuff, like street lamps decked with garland and colored lights on every roof. She liked those things, sure. But what really impressed Ryan was something more subtle: all of Main Street smelled like Christmas.

Hot cocoa and candy canes and cinnamon.

I kept thinking, if I'd been there with Sara, I wouldn't even feel like I'm missing out on the cruise. Who needs a mai tai when Spill the Tea offers peppermint mocha with whipped cream?

Okay, a mai tai doesn't sound totally terrible.

My point is, Main Street gave us the holidays on steroids.

Afterward, Ryan and I drove across the bridge to check out the other side of the lake. The property at the Beachfront Inn isn't exactly Rockefeller Plaza, but the big tree out front of the main lobby is always grand. And Thornton Tavern was packed for lunch. People were bustling in an out in pairs and small groups.

Man, I'd love to take Sara there.

"I must admit, I was impressed," Ryan says, snapping me out of my fog. "Abieville is just the right combination of quaint and rustic. Very homey, even if it's not your home."

"I agree." I stuff my hands in my pockets. "I wouldn't want to live anywhere else." Even as I say this, though, the twinge behind my solar plexus suggests that may no longer be true.

If Sara's feeling even a fraction of the things I am, I'd be willing to at least discuss seeing where this goes. Surely the New York City public school system could use another history teacher with a penchant for lifeguard shifts, swim lessons, and girls' basketball.

A coach can dream, can't he?

"Well, I'm not surprised," Ryan says.

"Surprised by what?"

"That you love this town."

"Ah, yes. I sure do." I shift my weight, feeling ... awkward. I've been putting on a show, trying to impress Ryan for Sara's sake, but I'm still a man with a concussion who slept on a couch last night. I'm exhausted. And foggy.

And have I mentioned awkward?

"Anyway." Ryan cranes her neck, trying to see between the curtains in the front window. "You've convinced me the town itself will attract Platinum Stays guests. I just hope the Hathaway's home will meet our standards."

"Oh, it will." I tip my chin toward the yard. "Sara got the flamingoes and tiki torches put away, so I'm guessing she's ready for us."

Hold on for just a little longer. For Sara's sake. Then the show can end.

I stick my arm out like I've seen the guys do in that over-the-top Netflix series my mom and sister are obsessed with. "Shall we go through?" I offer.

Bridgerton. That's the name of the show.

Also, I'm still being awkward.

"That's not a good idea." Ryan pinches her lips.

"Oh, Sara won't mind." I drop my arm. "I'm sure she's excited for you to see the house the way she expected to have it for you in the first place."

"I'm not allowed to evaluate the property with the home-owners present."

"Yeah, I forgot about that." I duck my head. "Give me a minute, and I'll grab Sara. We can wait for you out here."

"Fine." Ryan glances at the door. "If I do most of the evaluation today, I'll only have to check the storage room on Wednesday." She puffs out a breath, shaking her head. "I still can't believe I let you talk me into driving back out here again. And on Christmas Eve, no less."

"Well." I offer her a small smile. "I'm grateful you're willing."

"You were very persuasive." Ryan examines my face for a moment. "Your friend, Sara, must be very important to you."

Friend. Right.

"She is." I clear the gravel in my throat. "The most important."

As the words come out, I realize I mean them. Deeply. Like, soul-deep. The truth is, I never got over Sara Hathaway. I don't think I ever really tried. And no, I'm not kidding myself that she shares those same sentiments. But we *have* shared space nonstop for days now. We shared a kiss yesterday. We shared a couch overnight. We woke up with our bodies tangled together this morning.

In other words, I'm already more than somebody Sara used to

go out with every summer. What I want to be now is more than the guy who broke her heart.

I can only hope that by convincing Ryan to give Sara another chance, I've also convinced Sara to see me as someone she might be able to trust again. Instead, I find her in the living room, shoulders slumped, spirit deflated.

"Hey." I glance around checking for what could've gone wrong. "Are you all right?"

"I'm okay," she says, but she's not making eye contact. "How was the tour?"

"Good." My chest is tight. I quickly survey the room, including a peek into the den and kitchen. "Looks like you were able to get things back to normal. Ryan says if we wait outside, she can evaluate the place right now. Everything but the storage room." I reach down to help Sara up, but she stands on her own, ignoring my hand. Then she heads outside, wordlessly. Uh-oh.

I wait for Ryan to move inside with her clipboard at the ready, then I turn toward Sara. "You sure you're okay?"

She drops into one of the Adirondack chairs with a sigh. "I guess I didn't *love* the fact that you begged to squire Ryan Detweiler around Abieville while I was stuck here cleaning."

I cough out a laugh. "I begged to *squire* her?"

"You know what I mean." Sara's voice is wobbly. "You flirted all over that woman like ... like a big ball of flirt."

At the risk of upsetting Sara more, I let out another small laugh. "I was just being friendly, and my friendliness worked. Ryan's inside right now, hopefully finding the house acceptable for Platinum Stays."

"So." Sara's voice is soft. Almost a whisper. "You admit it was a strategy." She lifts her chin, swallows hard.

Hold on.

Is she ... jealous?

I won't lie, my chest expands at the possibility. And I'm not proud of it—in fact I *should* be ashamed of myself—but I kind of like what this side of Sara Hathaway reveals. Even if she can't say the words out loud, the look on her face tells me she doesn't want to see me with anybody else. Which could work out well, since I don't want to see myself with anybody else either.

Even simpler, I don't want to see anyone else. Or date anyone else. Kiss anyone else. Hold anyone else but Sara in my—well, you get the picture.

"I swear I was only trying to help you," I say. "And for the record, Ryan Detweiler knows I'm not interested. At all."

Sara blinks up at me. "How?"

"How what?"

"How did she know you weren't interested *at all* after you waved your … friendliness all over her?"

I bite back a chuckle. "For the record, I behaved like a total gentleman. And she knew I wasn't interested, because the entire two hours we were together, I couldn't stop talking about you."

Sara gulps. "Me?"

"Yes."

"You talked about me for two straight hours?"

"Pretty much." I incline my head toward the chair beside hers. "May I?" When she nods, I take a seat, turning to face her. "Everywhere we went today, I had a story about you."

"Really?" Sara's cheeks pink up. "That was probably … pretty annoying for her."

"On the contrary," I say. "She told me all my anecdotes brought Abieville to life. That she could see young people, engaged couples, honeymooners, families, older folks on their anniversaries coming to this town for the quaintness. The romance. The happiness. I really sold her on the story. And the story was us."

Sara draws in a long breath. "Us?"

I meet her gaze. "Yes. I just wish … I wish there was a different ending."

"Oh."

My heart starts rattling in my chest. This is as close as I've ever gotten to admitting I made a mistake when I pushed her away. Can't get much closer without saying the actual words.

So maybe it's time I told her the whole truth.

"Sara, there's something you should know." I pause to clear the cotton in my throat. "About our last day together. That last summer ..." I let my voice trail off, fumbling for the right words, as my phone starts ringing. Volume on high.

When I don't make a move to check it, Sara's gaze flits to my pocket. "It could be your family calling from the ship," she says. "Or your doctor confirming your appointment. It could be important, Three."

My jaw shifts. "*You're* important."

"I'm also not going anywhere."

"Fine." I dig in my pocket and pull out my phone. When I see the name my chest caves in.

"So." Sara shoots a glance at the screen. "Who's calling?"

"Preston Bender."

"Who's that?"

"The sheriff."

Chapter Thirty-Three

Sara

Abieville's sheriff station is on the small side and a lacking in natural light, but it's definitely more modern on the inside than stereotypes suggest about a town this size. Instead of ancient computers and rickety chairs, the furnishings look recently updated. There's a well-appointed coffee cart in one corner, and the walls sport giant cork boards full of brightly colored fliers.

The place is mostly empty, which I'm guessing is fairly typical for a Monday afternoon. The only people in the station are the deputy, the sheriff, and a miserable Sully Ackerman.

On the drive over, Three filled me in on what he'd learned from Sheriff Bender. Apparently a witness reported Sully breaking into Abieville High, and he was already inside the building by the time Deputy Townsend caught him.

The sheriff contacted Three to see about pressing charges since he's the summer school administrator and the principal's away for Christmas. According to Three, the district has a zero-tolerance policy for illegal activity on school property, so Sully's looking at a week's suspension just for breaking in. Anything worse could mean an expulsion.

He'd lose his scholarship to OSU.

"Thanks for coming in," the sheriff says. He could be a few years older than Three, but he still looks pretty young to be in charge of an entire town's law enforcement. He's handsome in a subtle, straight-arrow kind of way, as opposed to Carver Townsend's in-your-face brand of attractiveness. Speaking of which, Carver looks up from his computer, pushes his chair back and hops to his feet.

"Sara Hathaway. Twice in two days." He tips his hat. "Lucky me."

"Yeah," Three mutters. "Not so lucky for Sully." He turns away from Carver, obviously worried about his student.

"Hey, Sully." I offer the kid a sympathetic wave. He was so helpful at Humboldt Farms, I really want to be on his side. Right now the poor thing is slumped next to the sheriff's desk in a way-too-small-for-him chair. His face is all jawline and cheek bones held together by ghost-white skin. "Are you all right?"

"Yes, Miss Hathaway." He bobs his head, then casts a pained look at Three. "Sorry, Mr. Fuller."

"I'm sure you are." Three drags two chairs over and motions for me to sit. He takes the other seat, then leans back, acting casual. He's probably hoping Sully will feel more comfortable and loosen up. "Wanna tell us what happened?"

Sheriff Bender answers for him. "An hour ago, Deputy Townsend responded to a call about a break-in at the school. He found Sully in the girl's locker room with a couple cans of spray paint."

Three blows out a breath. "Vandalism?"

The sheriff nods. "Cut and dry."

"Was anyone else with you?" Three asks Sully.

Carver jumps in to answer this time. "He was operating alone."

Three furrow his brow. "Thanks, but I was asking Sully."

"Sorry." Carver lifts his hands. "Just reporting the facts. No one else was on the scene. And it wouldn't matter anyway, because Sully immediately confessed."

"Hold on." I lean forward, my attorney side kicking in. "Did you feel coerced into making a statement?"

"I didn't intimidate him, if that's what you're suggesting." Carver arches an amused brow. "And I wasn't arresting him either, so there was no need for Miranda rights, if you were wondering about that too."

"No." I press my lips together. "I just want to be sure the boy's being fairly treated."

"Fair's my middle name." Carver smiles, then he swings his focus back to Three. "Sully told me the spray paint was part of spirit week. That he was *supposed* to be in the girls locker room to support the basketball team. That sound accurate to you?"

At this the sheriff chimes in. "I'm sure Mr. Fuller would say that damaging school property is the opposite of spirit."

Three's got his eyes trained on Sully, like he's looking for clues. "Is this true?"

"Yeah," Sully says. But he's staring down at his big hands folded in his lap. He won't make eye contact, and his response came awfully quickly. There's got to be more to this story.

"Where's the paint now?" Three asks.

"Right here," Sheriff Bender says, bringing a canvas bag over to us. "What's left of it, anyway. He already used plenty." Two metal cans clank together as he hands over the bag.

Three takes a look inside, lifts his gaze to Sully. "Red and pink?"

Sully stiffens. "Yes, sir."

"Hmm." Three rubs his chin. "If you were trying to support the basketball team, I'd expect you'd use our school colors. Black and green."

"I like red and pink," Sully grumbles.

"I do too." Three hitches his shoulders. "It is strange, though. We're in the middle of winter break right now, and the first spirit week in second semester doesn't start until midway through January."

"Tell him what you were painting," Carver says.

Sully's face gets blotchy, and he averts his eyes. "Nothing. It was dumb."

The sheriff shakes his head. "Might've been dumb, but it wasn't nothing." He turns to Three. "The kid sprayed a bunch of hearts all over one of the lockers."

"He was working on the words 'will you go' when I apprehended him," Carver interjects.

"I said it was dumb," Sully chokes. "I didn't think it would be big deal."

Will you go. Red and Pink hearts. Girl's locker room. The whole thing's starting to make sense.

"Hey, Sully." Three tilts his head. "You were gonna ask Cami Anderson to the Valentine's Day Formal, weren't you?"

His eyes pop wide, like he can't believe anyone solved the mystery. "The sheriff didn't say it was Cami's locker."

"No, he did not." Three chuckles softly. "But I've seen the way you look at that girl. You've had your eyes on her ever since my seating chart put you two in desks right next to each other."

"It was a promposal," I say, offering Sully a smile of support.

He nods, but he still looks miserable. I would too if my college scholarship was on the line. "She was supposed to find the message when we got back from winter break." He blows out a breath. "It was going to be the first clue in a two-week scavenger hunt leading to ... me."

"A prom what?" the sheriff asks.

"Ah, come on, Preston." Three pushes out an amused scoff. "What are you, a hundred years old? That's how the kids ask each other to the big dances now. They come up with these grand gestures, like baking cakes, making posters, or hijacking the intercom in the middle of morning announcements."

"Please don't tell my mom and dad," Sully blurts, and it occurs to me for the first time that Three's the adult they called here.

"Where are your parents?" I ask.

Sully grimaces. "They drove up to Rochester to bring my sister home for Christmas. She doesn't have a car up at the U, so instead of having her take the train again, they made it a family day-trip." His voice cracks on that last part. "They asked me to go with them," he adds, "but I said I had too much stuff to do."

Sheriff Bender frowns. "Stuff like vandalizing the high school?"

"All right." Three throws up a hand. "Listen, Preston. You called me down here to decide if the district wants to press charges, and as the official administrator today, I'm going to go ahead and say there's no need. We're all good."

"Really?" The sheriff scoffs. "You aren't worried about the precedent?"

"I'm not. Because Sully and I are going to repaint Cami's locker before anyone else has to find out about this." Three turns to face Sully. "Aren't we, Sullivan?"

"Yes, sir, Mr. Fuller." Sully nods so frantically, I'm afraid his head might roll right off his shoulders. "Thank you, sir."

"You're welcome." Three clears his throat. "I happen to know there's leftover paint in the custodial closet from when they redid the locker rooms a couple years back. Repainting shouldn't take too long. In fact, I figure we can go take care of that right now." He swivels to address me. "If that's all right with you, Sara."

"Of course." A slow smile breaks across my face. "I'll drive you to the school."

"Thank you too, Ms. Hathaway." Sully's hands shake as he rises to his feet. "And I'm really sorry, Sheriff Bender. Deputy Townsend." He hunches his shoulders. "I promise something like this will never happen again."

"I'm sure it won't," Three says. "But next time? Skip the

grand gesture and go with something a little more from the heart."

"Like what?" Sully asks.

"Make the girl a grilled cheese sandwich."

Chapter Thirty-Four

Sara

That sandwich comment had to be about me, right?

I've been tossing around a few other potential explanations —*any* other explanation—but Occam's Razor says the simplest solution is almost always the best one. Which is exactly why my insides feel like a china shop being decimated by a bull.

The idea that Three made me that grilled cheese as his own little promposal has my body fizzing with hope. And hope is more dangerous than a bullfight.

I need to get my poor matador heart under control.

So I'm in the hallway outside the girls' locker room taking deep, calming breaths. Meanwhile, Three and Sully are inside repainting. As it turns out, they had to address more than just the damage done to Cami's locker. Sully's aim was, shall we say, less than precise. He accidentally sprayed parts of the pink and red hearts onto the lockers on either side of hers. Since the job was going to take longer than he expected, Three insisted I stay out in the hall to avoid inhaling any fumes.

I tried telling Mr. Concussion he wouldn't be any safer breathing spray paint than I would, but he refused to subject my lungs to any paint particles. Protectiveness *and* a grilled cheese?

Cue my stomach full of butterflies.

At some point, Three and I will need to finish the conversation Sheriff Bender interrupted, but the truth is, I'm afraid to hear him out. If he claims to have real feelings for me now, can I trust him not to change his mind again? And if he's just making amends for the past, will I feel heartbroken in the friend zone?

Both options terrify me, and I hate feeling helpless like this. Not to mention useless and restless. I don't want to feel *less* when it comes to Three.

So after what feels like an eternity of waiting, I decide to call Bristol. She'll either have some good advice, or knock some sense into me. But as I pull out my phone, a new message comes in from Ryan Detweiler.

> **RYAN**
>
> I just left your house. The doors are locked.
> Try not to get stuck in the storage room again.

My heart skips a beat. Then another. What does this mean? Did we pass? Fail? Is she going to keep me in suspense until Wednesday? Before I can ask her for clarification, a follow-up text comes in.

> **RYAN**
>
> I can't complete my approval report without confirming the repairs Three guaranteed, but the rest of your house and your town tick all our boxes. Assuming the remaining issues have been addressed on time as promised, you should pass.

A squeal slips out of me, and relief floods my body. Three and I are pulling this off after almost blowing things entirely. And sure, the decision isn't totally official yet, and it's not actually *my* house or *my* town being approved. But we're so close.

I have to tell him.

Sticking my head in the doorway, I call out, "Hey! How's it going in there?"

When I get no reply, I venture a few steps into the locker room. "Hello?" I continue to creep forward until I spot Three and Sully over at the far end, side by side, facing away from me.

They're too busy peeling blue painter's tape and plastic from the edges of the lockers to notice that I'm in here now. But they must be finishing up. Three nudges Sully and Sully bumps him back, then the two of them laugh at something I can't hear.

My heart cartwheels behind my ribs, and I move even closer. When Three's face slides into profile, the angle of his jawline empties my lungs.

This man is so generous. So kind. So heartbreakingly gorgeous. *Emphasis on heartbreak.* Maybe I'm not ready to trust myself around him yet. Or ready to trust *him* again. So I'm about to sneak back out into the hallway, when Sully says, "Thanks again, Mr. Fuller. For everything." Naturally, I freeze in place like an awkward deer caught in headlights.

Bambi on ice again.

"No problem." Three shrugs, his broad shoulders hitching. "We did an okay job, I think."

"Yeah. But I'm really sorry you got dragged into this. If it weren't for you—" Sully cuts himself off, and my throat goes tight. I shouldn't be here for a personal moment like this, but the thought of being caught has me paralyzed.

Three pushes his paint goggles down off of his face, leaving them dangling around his neck. "Hey. Your heart's in the right place. And you're a good kid. That's all I know." He scoops up the tarp and shoves it in the big trashcan at the end of their row. I take the opportunity to inch backward toward the door hoping I can escape without being discovered.

In the meantime, Sully kicks the bare concrete with one giant shoe. "You don't have to say that."

"But I mean it."

Sully groans. "I just feel so stupid."

Three tips his head. "Trust me. I've been stupider."

Sully snorts. "No way."

"Way."

"Did you get in trouble too?"

"Not the kind of trouble where you end up at the sheriff's station. But, yeah. Big trouble in here." Three points at his head. "And in here." He taps his chest. "I'd do things different if I could, but I'm a history teacher." He chuckles. "I've got way too much proof that you can't change the past."

Whoa. Does Three mean us? Is he saying he wishes he could change what happened?

"Those who don't learn from the past are doomed to repeat it," Sully says. "That's what you always told us."

"You remember that, huh?"

"Yeah. You're a great teacher."

"Well you're a great student, and Cami's a great girl. Great girls like her are worth a little extra effort. Or a *lot* of extra effort."

My esophagus squeezes, and I can barely breathe. Three must be talking about me, but I don't want to hope. I can't handle another rejection. So I start inching backward toward the door praying he won't discover me.

He gathers up the paint cans and drops them into a custodial bucket. "Next time, just find a grand gesture with less vandalism and more ... romance."

Sully nods. "Like a grilled cheese sandwich?"

Three guffaws, dragging a hand along the back of his neck. "Exactly like a grilled cheese sandwich."

I suck in a breath, and Three turns, spotting me in the doorway. "Well, hello there." A smile angles across his face. "Aren't you supposed to be waiting in the hallway away from the paint fumes?"

"I was." I gulp. "I just ducked in here to check on how you two were doing." I wave my phone in the air. "And to tell you Ryan texted. The house is going to be approved."

His brows fly up. "Congratulations."

"We just have to get those repairs done. I mean *you* have to get the repairs done." I shove my phone back in my pocket. "If you still want to."

"Of course I want to." Three tips his chin. "And your timing's perfect, because we just finished up."

Sully steps to the side, acknowledging the lockers. "What do you think?"

"They look brand new." I fiddle with the zipper on my coat, trying to focus on the lockers and not on what Three was saying about the past. "I can't tell they were ever spray painted."

"Good." Sully stuffs his hands in his pockets. "Hopefully no one else ever has to know."

"Yeah, about that." Three scratches his chin. "Somebody *did* report the break in to the sheriff, and you were brought down to the station."

"But you and Ms. Hathaway were the only ones there."

"You know how small this town is." Three snorts. "Word's definitely gonna get around. So you might want to tell your parents first."

Sully cringes. "What do I say?"

"Tell them you had what *seemed* like a good idea at the time." Three nods toward the lockers. "And that you've already repaired the damage. They'll appreciate your honesty."

"What if they don't?"

"Eventually, the truth will come out. Better they hear it from you first." He bumps Sully's shoulder with a fist. "Cheer up, kid. It's almost Christmas. Your mom and dad aren't gonna kill you."

I clear my throat to get their attention. "There's another issue you're forgetting." Three and Sully both turn to me. "Cami's probably going to find out about this too. So if you really want to surprise her …"

Three blows out a breath. "Sara's right."

Sully's eyes go wide. "I gotta go."

"Your car here?" Three asks.

"Yeah." Sully starts jogging toward the hallway. "I just need a new plan!"

"Try grilled cheese," Three calls out.

Then he turns to me and smiles.

Chapter Thirty-Five

Sara

Eleven Years Ago: July

I love being in Abieville. Love, love, love! That's why I haven't written even a single word so far this summer. I'm just living in the moment, making memories, and soaking up the present while I can. June was amazing. And so far, July's been almost perfect too.

The only teeny-tiny cloud in these sunny skies is that my parents are a little worried I spend too much time with Three while we're in Abieville and too much time thinking about being with him when we aren't.

Of course they like Three—how could they not?—but my dad says it's short-sighted to leave half my brain here all year when my future is nowhere near this place. And my mom says Three's life is so different from mine, he probably has very different goals than we do.

Correction: Than I do.

Anyway, I understand their concern. They've invested so much time, energy, and money into my future. Not to mention they love me a lot. Of course they want to see me succeed. I just wish they'd trust me. I've worked way too hard to let my future plans get derailed now. I can care about my goals AND care about Three, right? I'll just have to double down the rest of the year to prove to them that I can handle both.

Because the truth is, it's not just half my brain that spends the rest of the year in Abieville. It's half my heart. And if I work hard enough, I can still achieve any goal.

Like maybe someday being Mrs. Sara Jane Fuller, Esquire.

PS: Three's still wearing his cuff.

Chapter Thirty-Six

Three

I thought Sara and I would pick up the conversation Sheriff Bender interrupted once we were finally alone again. But since we left school, she's been acting a little ... skittish. Hands fidgety, gaze darting around, barely making eye contact.

After a pit stop in the shop classroom to borrow the tools I'll need for the storage room, we lugged the equipment to the car, drove back to the lake house, and transferred everything inside. Meanwhile, whispers of my unspoken truths charged the air like electric currents.

As for Sara, she's probably just excited over the house getting approved, and I'm determined to see the rest of the process through. But that just brings us one step closer to separating again. So we've got to talk about what happened ten years ago.

To be honest, I'm nervous. Telling Sara everything could be painful, even after all this time. She might not be able to forgive me. Or her parents. Still, I'm not nineteen anymore. I've gotten better at communicating. I owe her the truth. I owe the truth to both of us.

So I follow her across the house and into the kitchen. My throat's tight, but I'm ready to go. She checks inside the oven then punches some numbers, setting the temperature to preheat.

"So about what I was starting to tell you before the whole Sully thing ..." I begin.

"Food first," Sara says, moving to the sink to wash and dry her hands.

"But—"

"Luckily a five-pound turkey only takes a couple hours, because I'm already getting hungry." She turns to face me, eyes not quite meeting mine. "I'll make dinner while you get that work done in the storage room, okay?"

"Okay." I duck my head. Sara's not ready to talk yet, which is fine. She's earned my patience. And anyway, my appetite's returned in full force. I'm hungry too.

"Will two hours be enough time for you?" She selects a large roasting pan from the cabinet, and sets it on the stovetop. "Sorry if that's a really stupid question."

"It's not." I glance at the wall clock. "I should be able to finish by then. Or at least I'll have made good progress."

"Great," she chirps, throwing open the fridge door. She pulls the turkey out and lays it in the roasting pan.

"You know, I'd be just as happy with something simple," I say. "Like spaghetti."

"We already skipped the turkey last night." She's rummaging around in the fridge again, fishing out ingredients to set on the counter. "And we have all the fixings. I'd hate to let good food go to waste. As it is, we only have tonight and tomorrow to finish the leftovers before I go home."

Home.

I bob my head. "I'll just get to work then." As I back away, a painful buzz thrums in my chest. Of course Sara is leaving Christmas Eve. It's not only her birthday, it's also the night of the Hathaway Gala. This isn't a surprise. It's something I support.

What hurts is the reminder that she'll never see *this* place as her home.

Sara's got a new job waiting for her in the city. A *career*. One she's worked for her entire life. I'm probably crazy to think there might be room for me on that path. So I head to the storage room to work out my emotions with a hammer and wrench.

All the odd jobs I've done over the years have taught me more practical skills than I could've learned in a classroom. Carpentry. Electrical. Roof repairs. Even plumbing. If only this could impress Sara's parents. But the Hathaways hire people like me, they don't marry them. They may never think I'm worthy of their daughter. And I might not think they're wrong.

Still, I won't make the same mistake I did a decade ago. The choice has to be hers this time, no matter the fallout. And she can only make the right decision if she has all the facts.

Yeah. Good luck with that, Three.

By the time Sara calls me to dinner, I've gotten the door handle upgraded and repaired the light fixture. I didn't even electrocute myself, which—the way this week's been going— would've been par for the course.

"I just need to clean up first," I call back. After testing the handle and light one last time, I quickly wash up and change into a fresh long-sleeved shirt, gray pants, and a black jacket. I'm just giving myself a pep talk, preparing to spill my guts to Sara, when I find her in the dining room.

Whoa. I'm so not worthy.

Her hair is loose, falling in glossy waves along her shoulders, and she's wearing a green dress. But not just an average green. Green like the Emerald City on *The Wizard of Oz*. The top half is fitted to her while the bottom flares out, dotted with something delicate and white, like tiny snowflakes.

"You look incredible," I blurt.

She dips into a small curtsy, peering at me from under a fringe of lashes. "You don't look so bad yourself. But the turkey's the real star of the show tonight." Her gaze flits to the table, and only then do I notice the presentation for dinner.

A rich red cloth covers the wood, with a runner down the middle. Bookending the turkey and side dishes are two complete place settings: china plates, crystal stemware, silver flatware, cloth napkins. In the center of the table, four taper candles cast a warm glow across the room

"Wow." I blow out a long breath. "You did all this in two hours?"

"It took a little longer, actually." She wrinkles her nose. "You probably just lost track of time. Speaking of which, how are the repairs going?"

"Not as impressive as all this." I nod at the table. "But the door handle works. The light works. Anyone who ends up in that storage room can see and also get out."

The edges of Sara's mouth tug up. "Mission accomplished, then."

"You should send a pic of this spread to Ryan Detweiler. Might seal the deal with Platinum Stays."

"I didn't do this for Ryan. Or for Platinum Stays." Sara smooths her hands down the front of her dress. "This is your Christmas celebration. A real one. Not a silly luau."

"I didn't think the luau was a silly idea. But this looks amazing."

She shifts her weight. Glances at the food. "Should we sit?"

I walk over to one side of the table, and pull out her chair. "After you."

"Thanks." She takes a seat, spreads the napkin in her lap, and inclines her head toward the turkey. A large knife glimmers beside the platter. "Unfortunately, I've never carved anything myself before, so ..."

"My favorite job." I smile at her. "I'd be happy to do the honors."

I carve the turkey while Sara spoons servings of potatoes and stuffing onto our plates. The scene is so domestic, my chest goes tight with longing. If this is what a future with Sara would feel like, I'd want nothing more.

"What was I thinking suggesting spaghetti?" I say. "That was a terrible idea."

Sara lets out a small laugh. "I'm glad I could convince you."

"By the way, you cooked, so I'm washing the dishes tonight." I say. "I've been told those are the rules."

"I won't argue with you. But let's actually eat before we worry about dishes."

We tuck into our meal, which is as delicious as it looks. Every few bites, I steal a glimpse at Sara. Every ten glimpses, I catch her looking at me.

After a while, she peeks through the archway that leads to kitchen. "And be sure to save room for our pie versus cake competition."

"I don't have to save room." My smile splits wider. "I've got a whole second stomach for dessert."

"Same." Another soft laugh from her. "And whatever we don't finish can be leftovers on our last night."

My smile falters and my gut constricts. Leftovers and going-away pie. Fantastic.

Sara meets my gaze across the table. "I'm just sorry you didn't get to enjoy your luau."

I gulp water from a goblet that probably costs more than my coaching stipend. "Last night didn't turn out all bad though, right?"

"No. Not all bad." Something flickers behind her eyes, but from my end of the table, I can't figure out the emotion behind it.

"You're so far away."

She dips her chin. "You can move closer. If you want."

"I do." As I take my plate and slide onto the seat beside her, a stew of emotions simmers inside me. Sara drops her focus to her plate.

"Thanks again for all you did today," she says softly. "With

Ryan. And the storage room. We're only getting approved because of you."

"Happy to help." This is what I say, but I don't want to talk about Platinum Stays or their approval. Not when Sara and I are already on borrowed time.

"I'm sure the doctor will clear you tomorrow too," she adds.

"You're probably right." The words come out gruff. "But I want to appreciate this moment first."

Sara looks over at me, the candlelight spilling across her skin. The sky in the window behind her has darkened to an inky black. She draws in a breath then exhales, studying my face for a long stretch of seconds.

"Uh-oh." I pull down my brow. "Do I have food in my teeth or something?"

She shakes her head. "No. I was just thinking."

My insides tighten. Maybe Sara's finally ready to talk. "About what?"

She glances at the table. "About the fact that I spent four summers in Abieville, and we never shared a meal like this."

"Ah. That." I half grunt, half guffaw. "The thing is, I didn't exactly have any crystal or silver or china to offer you back then. Come to think of it, I still don't."

Her gaze falls on me again, eyes softening. "For the record, I loved surviving on hot dogs, ice cream, and paper plates. All that mattered to me was being with you."

"And I didn't care what we ate or how it was served as long as we were together." I reach over to tuck a loose strand of hair behind her ear. "I just wanted to make you happy."

"You *did* make me happy."

"I wanted to be the one who made you smile."

"You did that, too."

We lock eyes. "I wanted to be worthy of you."

"You were."

My esophagus goes desert dry. "No. That's where I failed."

Chapter Thirty-Seven

Sara

"Failed?"

Three's staring at me. "Yes." His mouth shifts into a grim line.

"What are you talking about?" I pull away. "Are you saying I made you feel unworthy?" I blink at him, bewildered, and a ribbon of unease unfurls in my stomach. "Because that's definitely not how I felt. You were everything to me, and if I ever made you think otherwise ... I'm just ... I'm so sorry. I don't even know what else to say."

"Sara."

"What?" My cheeks heat up and my brain starts a rapid-fire inventory of the past. Yes, I was a prep school girl going off to an expensive college, but I sure didn't equate money with worth. And I'm pretty sure Three Fuller knew he was my whole world back then. Always.

His jaw ticks. "It wasn't you."

Another blink of bewilderment. "Then where on earth did you get the idea you were unworthy?"

His face twists into a grimace, like the words hurt him on the way out. "Partly from my own insecurity. That, I can own. And I still sometimes wonder if I'm good enough for you." He takes a beat, clears the gravel from his throat. "But it was your parents who said the actual words."

"My mom and dad?"

"I'm sorry."

"No way." I shake my head, and my spine goes stiff in defense of them. "All they ever complained about was *me*. Like my mom got annoyed when I stopped getting facials and mani-pedis with her. And my dad kept bugging me about applying for fall internships. But they absolutely *never* said a negative word about you. Ever."

Three waits several moments before responding. "Maybe not directly. Out loud." He takes another beat. "But you had to know how they felt."

"My parents liked you." My lip begins to tremble. "Because *I* liked you."

"Well, they sure didn't like me *with* you." Three's voice is gritty now, like sand pushed through a too-tight hourglass.

"That's just not true."

"Think about it, Sara." His eyes take on a tortured squint. "You were on your way to Stanford, and they were convinced I'd hold you back."

"Why are you saying this? What did they ever do to make you think they—"

"I heard them, Sara." His Adam's apple dips. "With my own ears. In their own words." I dart my eyes over to the living room couch. "They were sitting right there."

I feel like I'm at the edge of a cliff, being propelled over the edge with nothing stopping me from a swift plummet to the bottom. "You were eavesdropping?" I choke out.

"Not on purpose." Three pulls down his brow. "You were leaving the next morning, so I came over to pick you up for our last date. I had a leather cuff to give you, like mine but smaller. Kind of like a promise bracelet."

I suck in a breath, my insides doing somersaults. "You did?"

"Yeah." He averts his gaze. "I was so nervous, my hands were shaking. I had to stuff them in my pockets. When I got here, that front door was open with just the screen. So was the window. Letting in the breeze, I guess."

"I remember that day. There'd been a heatwave all week. I was packing when you texted that you were out front."

"I'd already been there for a while by then. Long enough to find out your dad thought I was ruining your future." He picks up his fork, starts tapping it against the edge of his plate. "And your mom didn't disagree."

"Whatever you heard ..." I pause for a moment, feeling sick for him, "I'm sure they didn't mean anything against you. They were probably just a little scared."

"Of me?" His eyes darken.

"No," I rush to say. "Afraid of losing me."

A sad scoff puffs across his lips. "Well, that's not what it sounded like."

"What exactly did they say?"

He releases a long, slow breath from somewhere deep inside him. Deeper than his lungs. Like it's coming from his soul. "Your dad said something like, 'Sara needs a man who'll push her to reach her potential, not some small-town kid with no goals.' Then your mom said you didn't need a man at all. That you already had your hands full with your own plans. That I'd only hold you back." He pushes his hands through his hair. "The worst part is, I didn't disagree. With either of them."

A kaleidoscope of emotions tumbles through me. If only I'd been in the room, I would've been able to defend Three. Then again, my parents never spoke this openly about him when I was around. So I had no idea, and Three didn't tell me.

"Why didn't you say something?"

He winces like my suggestion causes him real physical distress. "I'd just graduated from high school, Sara. And you know what science says about the prefrontal cortex in boys that age, right? I probably didn't reach full brain maturity until ... I don't know." He lets out a sad scoff. "A couple years ago?"

"Like Sully." I take a stuttering breath.

"Exactly like Sully."

I'm quiet for a moment, as the truth plucks at my heart-strings, like a harpist in my chest. "I was in love with you."

"Well, I didn't know that," he blurts. "Not for sure. I hoped. I wanted to believe it. But ..." His sentence dies off.

"If you just would've told me—"

"I'm telling you now," he interrupts. His voice is a husky scrape. "I was in love with you, too."

"If that's true"—my eyes burn with unshed tears—"why didn't you fight for me?"

"I couldn't." He keeps his gaze trained on me. "Not after what your dad said next."

Heat spreads through my torso, flaming up my throat, burning my cheeks. "What could've been worse?"

"He told your mom you were only using me to rebel. Biding your time with me to establish your independence." He puts *biding your time* in air quotes and my heart sinks a little lower.

"He really said I was using you?"

"Those might've been your mom's words, actually." The crease in his brow deepens. "But they both agreed you were only looking to prove you couldn't be controlled. And their theory made sense to me."

"Three."

"I know," he says. "That's a pretty tragic indictment of my confidence back then, right?" He lets out a wounded scoff. "They were going to confront you later that night—to tell you how they really felt—so I ended things first." His nostrils flare. "It was the hardest thing I've ever done, but I told myself it was the *right* thing."

"According to who?"

He averts his gaze. "You adored your mom. Your dad was your hero. You don't even want to believe me now. So I couldn't come out against them then. And I didn't want to come between you. I couldn't make you choose, Sara."

"I would've chosen you."

"Which also would've hurt you." He takes a beat, then continues slowly. "I wanted you to have the best life possible, and I wasn't the best."

"You were."

A vein pulses at his temple. "If I'd actually thought that, I would've given anything to be your man."

I let out a little yelp, then gulp down the boulder threatening an avalanche in my throat. "So you lied."

"I did."

"You made me think my first love was all in my head."

He drags a hand along the back of his neck, stopping short when he hits the bandage. "Your dad's a great lawyer, and I was working with the evidence he presented, not with what I wished were true." He swallows hard. "Your parents thought you deserved more. I agreed."

"Well, they were wrong." The corners of my eyes are wet now. "And *you* were protecting your ego."

"Maybe." His nod is almost imperceptible. "Sure. Yes. Self-preservation's a powerful motivator."

"You broke my heart."

He flinches. "I'm so sorry."

"It took me a long time to recover from losing you." *And I'm not sure I actually did.*

"Me too."

"Please don't compare us," I say. "You have no idea how much you hurt me."

Color rises in his cheeks just above the line of scruff and he runs a finger along the edge of the table. "It's hard for me to admit this, but I sometimes got embarrassed by my family back then.

Especially when I compared them to yours. Which is so stupid, and I know that now." He pauses, drawing his hand into a fist. "My folks are good people. They're hardworking. Loyal and smart. No one loves harder than they do. Just because we don't trace our roots back to the Mayflower—" He cuts himself off, then meets my gaze again. "Anyway. I couldn't stop thinking the Hathaways would always see the Fullers as ... less."

"So you broke up with me as some kind of noble means to protect your family? Does that make my parents the villains?"

"No." Three works his jaw from side to side. "I'm not trying to be the good guy here. There was a selfishness underneath everything I did. I can own that now. I was just a kid with a chip on my shoulder. And I didn't want to spend my life going down a road with you where I was always coming up short."

"You never came up short for me." I swipe at a tear cresting in my eye. "You still don't."

"Well, losing you is what stoked a fire in me to make something of myself. That pain was my fuel. Without it, I may never have ended up being Mr. Fuller at Abieville High. So I guess that's something good that came from a dark time."

"Great." A harsh cry slips out of me. "I just wish I'd known the truth."

"If you'd known, our lives would be totally different now. Would you want that?"

"I guess we'll never find out." My lip trembles, so I capture it with my teeth to stop the shake. "And now it's too late."

Three reaches for my hand, eyes boring into mine like bright blue lasers. "Is it?"

The two-word question sends my heart straight into orbit, and my mouth goes slack. "What?"

"Is it really too late for us?"

Hot tingles course through my body even as my skin breaks into chills. Is Three actually suggesting he might be open to some kind of second-chance with me? And if so, could I even trust him? The thought is terrifying. A decade ago, I took my heart out of my chest, cradled it in my palm, and handed it over to him. Then he dropped it. Right on Main Street. In the days that followed, I swore I'd never risk that kind of rejection again. And I've kept that promise to myself all this time.

But at what cost?

"Sara." He presses my fingers.

"You know what? It's been a long day." I pull my hand away, pushing back my chair, and stumbling to my feet. "Actually, it's been a long ten years." This is all too much to process, and I need a distraction to keep from losing it. As my brain clicks into practical mode, I shove all other emotions aside. "I'll be right back."

"Don't go."

Without answering him, I lurch to the kitchen to get his evening dose of antibiotics. Three may have just short-circuited my nervous system, but I'm still in charge of his health and safety. Not to mention, I still love him. And my love will always be bigger than anything else.

When I return, I hand him the pill and a glass of water like a robot on autopilot. "Here. Take this."

"Sara. Please."

Please what? my insides scream. *What more could you possibly want from me?*

Before I can ask him that, though, I have to figure out what *I* want.

"I just need to be alone right now," I say. My words are a jagged plea. "To think."

"Take all the time you need."

When his voice breaks a little on the word *need*, I almost fall to my knees and tell him the past is all water under the bridge. That we can just be together now, forever. Our own little second-chance romance, just like every Hallmark Christmas movie I've ever seen.

But I can't. Not yet.

"It's okay," he says. "I've got this." He nods to indicate the table. "The dishes. The leftovers. All of it."

My lids flutter, fighting tears. "Your appointment's in the morning. You really should get some rest."

"Nope, thanks," he says. He waits until I'm done blinking, then our eyes lock. "I told you I'd clean up tonight," he says. "And I'm never breaking my word to you again."

Chapter Thirty-Eight

Sara

Eleven Years Ago: August

I can't sleep knowing my mom's making me go back to the city with her tomorrow, two whole days earlier than we actually have to leave.

Apparently, she's tired of only being with my dad when he visits on weekends, and she just wants to be with him full-time again. Yeah, Mom. I get it.

I just want to be with Three full-time too. I'd even settle for two more days.

. . .

But surprise, surprise, Katherine Hathaway won. She's the adult, so she wins. Every time. That's why we hardly ever fight. I haven't told Three yet, but he'll probably be a good sport about it. He's so understanding. And he's all about respecting our parents.

I just don't want to end such an amazing summer on a sour note. And I hate fighting with my mom, which only makes sleeping harder.

Why can't loving people be easier?

Chapter Thirty-Nine

Sara

"Sare-Bear!" Bristol's face fills the screen and a massive smile hijacks her face. Until she gets a load of me and my poor tear-streaked cheeks. "What's wrong? Are you crying?"

"Not too much," I snuffle.

She frowns so deep I'm afraid the crease might slice her skull. "Is it Three? Do you need me to fly there tonight to beat him up? I'll totally cancel my plans."

"You can't do that." I throw myself backward on the bed, holding the phone up above my face.

"I'm not even kidding," she says. "I mean, I probably couldn't *actually* get a flight on such short notice, but I *would* blow off my date if you want to talk. In fact, I'm going to text the guy right now. We've never even gone out before, so I don't need to—"

"No, don't cancel." I sniffle and flip over onto my stomach. "Maybe just stay on the phone with me until you have to leave?"

"Of course." Bristol tips her head, and her blonde bob swings across her chin. "So what's going on? Did Three do something awful?"

I glance at the shut bedroom door. "Right now, he's in the kitchen washing all the dishes and cleaning up after dinner."

"Okaaaay." Bristol processes the information, then her frown softens. "I'm sorry, Sara, but that kind of sounds like heaven in a man."

"I know."

"So what's the problem?"

"He just shared something with me. About the past. And I don't know if it's true, or if it's just some warped version of reality that makes him feel better about what happened with us."

"Got it." Bristol nods. "So what does your gut tell you?"

I chew my lip. If I had the answer to that I probably wouldn't have spent the past five minutes crying. "A part of me wants to believe him," I say, "because that would mean he really did love me at one point. But the other part ..." My breath catches.

"Hold on." She props her phone on the vanity and pulls her stool out from under the counter. "This sounds like a long story."

"It is!" I let out a hiccup-y breath. "And your inoculation totally wore off!"

Bristol sends me a small, sympathetic smile. "There's plenty more where that came from, my friend. *If* you need it. But I'll need more details if I'm going to help you. Do you mind if I put on my makeup while we talk?"

"Of course not." I snuffle and snarf, scrambling back into a seated position at the edge of the bed. "At least one of us should look beautiful tonight."

"Stop right there with that nonsense. You're gorgeous." She peers into the screen. "In fact, you're ... oddly glowing. What's that all about?"

"That's not a glow." I puff out a weak laugh. "It's just redness from all the crying." Plucking a tissue from the box on the nightstand, I swipe at my wet cheeks then blow my nose, a sad little honk.

"Wait." Her eyes dip, surveying the rest of me. "Are you wearing your green dress right now?"

"Uh-huh." Another nod and sniffle from me.

"That's my favorite."

"Mine too," I groan.

"But why did you even have that dress in Abieville?" Bristol narrows her eyes. "Did you bring it just in case you ran into Three?"

"I just wanted to feel pretty." I lower my voice to a whisper. "And then ... and then ..." I let my sentence trail off.

"Breathe," Bristol says. "I'm right here, and I'm not going anywhere. But I think you need to start from the very beginning and tell me everything."

So I do.

While she drags a contouring stick along her cheeks, draws perfect wings across her lids, and brushes mascara over her lashes, I recount everything that's happened with Three since the concussion. She hears about Henry, our snowman. The Christmas tree farm. Getting trapped in the storage room. Ryan Detweiler. Three's grilled cheese sandwich. Sully's spray paint.

Everything.

Especially the kisses.

Telling Bristol about these moments—about the connection Three and I still share—helps to loosen the tightness in my chest. I'm almost feeling a little clearer. Until I get to tonight.

Then I picture Three's soft eyes and I hear the echo of what he thinks he overheard, and the confusion ricochets right back in again.

"So what are you thinking now?" Bristol asks, while she fills in her brows. "Do you believe he's telling the truth about your parents?"

"I believe *he* believes it." A tentative sigh skitters out of me. "And I'm just hoping my mom and dad didn't mean any of the harm they caused. But either way, I'm going to have to talk to them. If I've learned anything these past few days, it's that not sharing your feelings is a mistake."

"All right then." She slicks on a layer of lip gloss." Let's assume

Three really wants a second chance with you. Is that something you'd want, too?"

"I don't know." My heartbeat accelerates, and I lay a hand to my chest and press. "I mean, he's still the same kind, generous person I fell in love with a decade ago, except now he's a man. A man with a solid career. A man who matters to this town. A man whose goodness and worthiness I'd stack up against anyone else on this earth."

"So what's the problem?"

"His whole life is here in Abieville. His family. His school. His students."

"And?"

"And." I gulp. "I'm about to accept a full-time position at Hathaway Cooke. My dad's a founding partner. We've been planning for me to follow in his footsteps my whole life."

"Interesting." Bristol blots her lips. "You said, '*We've* been planning.'"

"It's not just my dad. I've always had the same goal."

"Okay. But is working for your dad's firm still your dream?"

I pause for a moment, considering her question. Considering my answer. "I love the law, and I love justice," I say. "I know the legal system is flawed, but I want to do my part to make it better, you know?" I tip my chin. "So yes, I want to be an attorney. And I want that for myself. I'm not just doing it for my father."

"Good answer." Bristol smiles at me. "So where does that leave Three, then? If you accept the job, you'll have to stay in the city, but that's only about three hours away. Can't you swing that?"

I swallow hard. "The distance isn't what I'm worried about."

"Then what is?"

"Three hurt me more than anyone else ever has." I shudder as the memory seeps through me. "Am I crazy to trust him again?"

"Maybe." Her shoulders hitch. "So stop worrying about him and start trusting yourself."

Chapter Forty

Three

Props to all the people who regularly do kitchen triage after enormous meals. Especially if they also happen to be operating with a concussion. Still, residual brain fog notwithstanding, I promised Sara I'd return this place to its pre-Christmas dinner spotlessness. So after she heads to her room to spend some time thinking, I spend the rest of the night up to my arms in dish soap, plastic wrap, Tupperware, and Windex.

A lot's riding on Ryan Detweiler officially approving this place on Wednesday, not to mention Sara seeing I'm a man of my word. I want to show her how much I care about her. How much I've always cared. The truth is, I've been in love with Sara Hathaway for years, but I gave her good reason to doubt me. Namely by telling her I wasn't. So once I have the dishwasher running and the refrigerator stacked with the leftovers from our dinner, I text Kenny.

I've got some proving to do.

ME

> Hey, man. You're probably in the midst of the whole nighttime-routine thing with the wife and kids, or maybe you're already in bed. So if you don't reply right now, that's cool. But I could really use your help if you've got a minute tomorrow. Preferably early in the day. But I'll take what I can get.

I don't expect a response, which is a good thing, because I don't get one. But by the time I crawl into bed, I do have most of a loose plan in place. All I need is for good old Kenny to come through for me. And if he can't, I'll just have to throw myself at Sara's feet and beg for her forgiveness.

Either way, I'm so wiped out from the physical and mental events of the past few days, I don't even realize I'm falling asleep, until I wake the next morning to the scent of coffee brewing and Sara knocking softly on the door.

"Come in," I croak, sitting up, rubbing my forehead. Thanks to Sara, I haven't missed a single dose of meds since Saturday, but I've still got a lump above my right eye that likes to say "hey" when I move too quickly.

She peeks her head in. "If you want to shower and eat something before we head to the hospital, you'd better get up. We don't want to be late."

Right. Sara doesn't want us to miss the appointment where the doc will most likely decide I'm safe to be left alone. Once he does, she'll be free to return to the city and forget everything that's happened since she returned to Abieville.

After what I told her last night, she may never want to see me again. But I'm willing to do whatever it takes to make sure that doesn't happen.

One quick shower later, I'm climbing into Sara's car, and she hands over a travel mug of coffee and a bagel she toasted up for me.

"Thanks."

"I noticed you didn't have any breakfast, and I didn't want your stomach growling in the middle of your follow-up exam."

"Fair enough."

"But I don't think the car ride to the hospital is the right time and place for us to talk."

"Fair enough."

She puffs out a breath. "Is that all you have to say to me this morning?"

"You said you weren't ready to talk. I'm just waiting for a signal from you."

"Fair enough." Sara's lip actually twitches, which has to be a good sign, doesn't it? Either way, I don't want to push my luck. So we make the trip to Northampton in silence, as per Sara's wishes. That is until my phone chimes with a text from Kenny.

KENNY

I should be able to get away when the baby goes down for a morning nap. What's up?

ME

Great. Can't talk right now, but I was hoping you could make a couple stops around town to pick up a few things for me and drop them off at my house. Should only take about a half hour. Maybe a little more. Can I call you with the specifics in a bit?

Oh. And I've got a key under the mat. Unless Ford lost it in which case you can break a window.

KENNY

Sounds easy enough. I'm in.

ME

But don't actually break my window.

KENNY

Ha. I won't. How's your head?

ME

We're about to find out. On the way to that follow-up now.

KENNY

Sara with you?

ME

Yeah. That's why I can't talk.

KENNY

Oof. Are things really going that bad?

ME

Hopefully not. But that's where you come in. I'm trying to surprise her.

KENNY

???? Okay. Now I'm really in. Just call me with the details after you see the doc. I'll help out with whatever you've got in mind, then text you back to let you know when we're ready to engage Operation Surprise Sara. #OSS

Hold on. Did Kenny seriously just make a hashtag out of my request? A wisp of a chuckle slips out of me, and warmth spreads throughout my torso. I'm finally daring to hope this holiday debacle may work out after all.

ME

You're the best, man. Thanks so much.

Sara eyes me sideways. "Everything all right over there?"

"Yeah," I say. "At least I *hope* things will be all right soon."

She shifts her focus back to the road. "Don't worry. I'm sure the doctor will clear you today."

Spoiler alert: the doctor clears me.

Time to engage Operation Surprise Sara.

Chapter Forty-One

Sara

I've been parked in the red zone outside the hospital, clenching the steering wheel for the past ten minutes. Meanwhile, Three's inside making a phone call in the waiting room. But the steering-wheel clenching isn't because Three's on the phone. I'm sure he's just trying to reach his family to tell them he no longer needs to be under twenty-four-hour watch.

That's the good news.

Also good news: Three demonstrated definite cognitive improvement during his checkup, and his stitches are healing nicely. Thanks to frequent bandage changes and all the antiseptic ointment, the doctor saw no sign of infection around either of his injuries. In fact the bump on his forehead is mostly hidden now under that mop of auburn hair. But that's where the good news ends.

Cue all the steering-wheel clenching.

The first bad news: when Three recounted our schedule over the past few days, the doctor promptly scolded us for being too active. Which was basically like scolding me. Three's the one with the concussion, after all. He's arguably not capable of making the best decisions for himself. I'm the one in charge, and I didn't do the best job I could for him.

Unacceptable.

The second piece of bad news was something we already expected thanks to Nurse Mary: Three isn't allowed to fly yet because the altitude could trigger possible cranial swelling or strokes. This means no joining his family in Hawaii for the rest of their vacation.

The final bad news we only learned today: Three still isn't safe to drive himself around. Why? Because of potential seizures or residual brain fog. Apparently the level of risk can't be determined during a quick appointment. But the doctor said Three may still be under the influence of his concussion.

This little tidbit changes everything in more than one important way.

If I leave Abieville today, Three will be stranded over Christmas without being able to drive himself anywhere. And I already didn't take good enough care of him the past few days.

Unacceptable.

Also—at the risk of continued selfishness—I can't help questioning everything Three has said and done over the past few days. With regards to me, specifically. The doctor said *still* under the influence.

I hadn't even considered the implications.

Were our kisses based on real emotion, or was his mind too blurry to know any better? Was his confession about what happened with my parents ten years ago accurate, or is he simply remembering false rationalizations?

None of the answers are reassuring.

Releasing my grip on the wheel, I glance out the window just as Three emerges from the sliding doors. There's a new bounce in his step, and he smiles as he heads toward my car. When he hops in the passenger seat, I crank the heat to fight the blast of cold air.

"Thanks for waiting," he says.

"No problem." I pull away from the curb, wishing I could channel his hopefulness.

Trust yourself, Sara.

That's what Bristol told me to do, and I was all set to follow her advice. But what if Three's suggestion that he might be open to a second chance with us was just his concussion talking?

What if we were just concussion-kissing in the storage room? *ARGH!*

"I thought you'd be happier about being off the hook," Three says. He's staring out the window at the snowbanks plowed onto the side of the road. Sunlight glints off the whiteness. It would be magical if I weren't feeling so conflicted.

"Who says I'm not happy?"

"Hmm." His mouth tips into a smirk. "The groan that just came out of you was my first clue."

Oops. I must have let that *argh* slip out loud. "I'm fine," I say. "Just tired."

"From lying awake all night thinking?"

"Something like that." I offer up a little nod, while keeping my focus on the road.

"You know, experts say the car is a perfect place to have difficult conversations, because you can just look straight ahead instead of facing the person you're with."

I tip my chin. "I've heard that too."

"So maybe we should take this chance to talk things out before you drop me off at home."

"We can." I shrug. "Except I'm not dropping you off. I'm taking you back to the lake house with me."

"Why? You heard the doctor. I'm perfectly safe to be on my own now. After Ryan Detweiler finalizes things with Platinum Stays, you'll be free to go back to the city. Home for Christmas Eve. Isn't that what you want?"

I swallow hard. I *want* to say yes, but I don't think that answer is entirely accurate anymore. And I've had enough of wondering what's true or not. "The thing is, you can't drive yet, so there's no way I'm abandoning you now. Which means I'm not going back to the city tomorrow."

"But you'll miss the Hathaway Gala."

"To be honest, I don't really mind that. What I'm *not* looking forward to is telling my parents. Talk about a difficult conversation." I cough out a sad laugh. "If only I could get them in a car so we wouldn't have to look at each other."

"Sara, no."

"No what?"

"You can't skip out on the gala." Three's voice is firm. "Or your birthday. Your mom and dad won't understand."

"I'm not skipping out." I scoff. "I'm just fulfilling an obligation. To you. And they *will* understand, because I'm going to tell them exactly why I'm staying here. Besides. If my parents didn't have respect for you ten years ago, why do you care about them now?"

"I care about you. And the fundraiser. You're the guest of honor for a cause your family's supported your entire life. It's *your* story that gets all those people donating. You're the big draw. And I don't want to be the reason Children's Village gets less money this year."

"Well, I don't see another solution," I say. "I promised Ford I'd take care of you until you could take care of yourself. So abandoning you to spend Christmas Eve and Christmas stuck at your house isn't—"

"Then I'll go with you," Three interrupts.

"What?" My eyes fly open. "Where?"

Three shifts in his seat to face me directly. "Take me to the gala."

Chapter Forty-Two

Three

Sara's jaw drops, and I can't help thinking Ford and Nella would have the same reaction. Sure, they both seemed to support me reconnecting with Sara these past few days, but going to the Hathaways' fancy fundraiser in Manhattan?

That's a whole different ballgame.

Also of note, I volunteered to jump into the lion's den, when I don't even know if Sara believes what I told her about her parents. Still, judging from the long breath she just drew in, and the tremble at her jawline, I'm guessing I'm about to find out.

"I can't take you," she says. Her voice is quiet, but edged with something rough.

"Come on." I nudge her shoulder. "I'd actually love to see the look on your mom and dad's face when I make a donation in person."

"No."

"Why? Because you're embarrassed to be seen with me?"

She frowns. "Because that would mean at least six hours in the car round trip, which can't be good for your concussion.

Not to mention, after the gala, I'd either have to drive us all the way back to Abieville in the middle of the night, or we'd be stuck staying at my parents' place. Would you really be comfortable waking up on Christmas morning with Katherine and Charles?"

I gulp, then my mouth falls open and shuts again, wordlessly. I wish I could say I'd be cool with a sleepover at the Hathaway penthouse, but I just don't know, and I won't lie to Sara.

"See?" Her shoulders slump in the wake of my silence. "I can't take you with me. And I'm not leaving you either." She takes a beat. "Not until you can safely drive yourself or until family gets back. Whichever comes first."

"Then I suppose we're at an impasse."

"We aren't. I'm staying in Abieville."

My chest goes tight, hearing those words. "You have no idea how much I'd love for you to stay. But only if you have different reasons."

She eyes me sideways. "Like what kind of reasons?"

"Like if you actually loved this town. Or if being here for the holidays meant something to you. But you only ever spent summers in Abieville, and I can't have you sticking around now—over Christmas—out of guilt."

"But I *am* guilty."

"Sara." I frown. "I came charging into that house without knocking, in a hoodie drawn so tightly over my face I might as well have been wearing a bank robber's mask. The room was smoky. You were already in a panic. Hitting me with that fire extinguisher was an instinct. It's not your fault."

She's quiet for a moment, taking this in. "Why are you defending me now?"

"Because you didn't defend yourself in the first place." I shift my gaze back out the windshield. "I let you take the blame because I think a part of me—granted, a heavily medicated and concussed part—wanted you to stick around when everyone else went on the cruise."

"No." She gapes. "You rejected my offer to stay with you at the hospital."

"The protest was pretty weak, if you recall." I smirk. "And then I threw up all over myself. Of course you weren't going to give up and abandon the pathetic vomiter in the wheelchair."

"Weren't you just nauseated from the concussion and the meds?"

"Yes. But I was also curious about who you'd become, and if I'd recognize the old Sara." I clear my throat. "Once the initial pain meds wore off, I felt so drawn to you. I kept hoping I hadn't slipped on a big pair of rose-colored nostalgia glasses."

"I felt it too," she says before I can continue. "In fact, when I first offered to stay with you, it was mostly out of guilt. But I'd be lying if I said I wasn't wondering about you too."

"Really?"

She nods. "I mean, of course I didn't want anyone in your family to miss out on their holiday because of me. But there were other options. I could've hired someone to come stay with you for a week. A home healthcare worker or something."

"Hold up." My brow arches. "Round-the-clock, in-home help isn't cheap. You have that kind of extra cash lying around? You aren't even a full-time attorney yet."

Soft laughter puffs across her lips. "Thanks for pointing that out," she says. "But you're right. I couldn't afford something like that. My parents could, though. They would've paid someone if I'd asked them."

"Ahh. Right. Of course they'd be willing to shell out any amount of money to keep Three Fuller away from their daughter."

Sara's quiet for a beat. Then she says, "That's not what I meant."

"Okay." I nod, my chest going tight. "So you gave it some thought overnight, and you've decided I'm wrong. That your parents actually liked me and the rest was all in my head."

Sara takes a quick peek in my direction. "To be honest, I don't know what to think." She cuts her eyes back to the road. "Yes, my parents are probably a bit too focused on social status ... and sure, they're overly impressed by our Mayflower heritage ... but I've never witnessed them putting down other people or intentionally criticizing anyone." She pauses to swallow. "Maybe I'm just naïve and I only see what I want to see. But don't we all do that when it comes to the ones we love?"

I clear my throat. "I guess so."

"What I *do* know is they were having a private conversation when you overheard them. So whatever they said to each other wasn't meant for your ears. Or for mine."

I blow out a breath. "And yet you're still pretty sure they would've forked over big bucks to prevent you from spending a few days with me. If you'd asked."

Sara slows as she approaches the bridge, rolling to a full stop at the deserted four-way intersection. "*You* were the one who asked me not to tell my parents I was with you." She cuts the engine, then turns to face me, a flush spreading across her cheeks. "And for the record, I never heard them speak ill of you, even after they saw how badly you broke my heart."

"Yeah." I avert my gaze. "They were probably too busy being thrilled I wasn't holding you back anymore."

"You know what? Maybe it's time to consider that you've got just as much bias against my parents as you think they have toward you."

Whoa. This shuts me up. Fast.

Balling my hands into fists, I stare out at the lake, stretching dark and frozen in front of us.

"You're right," I say, my voice gruff. "I'm sorry."

"So am I," she says. "Whether it was intentional or not, you got hurt because of me too."

"Hurt." The single syllable cracks something loose in my chest. "That's one way of putting it. Honestly, losing you felt ... closer to dying." I huff out a breath, making fun of myself. "Not to be overly dramatic."

"Are you kidding?" Sara lets out her own gust of air. "Bristol told me I could've been an extra on *The Walking Dead*."

My throat tightens like a boa constrictor's wrapped around it. "Man, I hate that."

"I didn't exactly love it."

We both fall quiet and Sara starts up the car, slowly pulling onto the bridge. We stay silent for a stretch as she drives us across the lake. Then I say, "I guess I just needed some time to grow up."

She nods. "We both did."

"Yeah." I run a hand over the top of my head, pausing on the tender swelling. "As hard as that time was, it made me pull myself together and work toward the life I have now."

Sara tips her chin. "And burying myself in work got me through the toughest years of school, internships, and tests."

"So ... are we actually saying there was an upside to what happened?"

"You know I *do* love a good silver lining." She swallows hard. "But that whole time, I never let anyone else get close to me. And I never stopped thinking about you."

When she casts her gaze my way, her dark eyes set off an avalanche of emotions tumbling along my sternum. "I couldn't forget you either. Hard as I tried."

She returns her eyes to the road. "Good."

At this point, her car is halfway across the bridge. Soon we'll be at a crossroads.

Literally.

"So what do we do now?" I ask. "About the gala? Our so-called impasse?"

"Hmm." She pauses for a moment, cocks her head. "I propose a settlement."

"Wow." I guffaw. "You really are a lawyer, aren't you?"

One corner of her mouth lifts in a half smile. "Yep. I really am."

"So what's the plan?"

"We stay at the lake house for one more night. Enjoy our leftovers and the Christmas tree. Scarf a bunch of pie and cake. Then tomorrow, once we've gotten our final approval from Ryan Detweiler, I'll drive home for the gala."

"Sounds good to me."

"But I'm going to come back first thing the next morning."

I blink. "On Christmas?"

She nods. "That way my parents will have me for my birthday and the gala, but you'll only be housebound for about ... twelve hours. Hopefully you can sleep through most of them."

"I don't know." I break into a grimace. "That's a lot of time in the car for you."

"*Maybe* I think you're worth it."

"Maybe?"

She tosses me a quick glance, her eyes bright, and my insides fizz, right along with the buzzing in my pocket. I slip my phone out and check the text.

KENNY

You're all set, buddy. #OSS

Chapter Forty-Three

Sara

"My house," Three says, looking down at his phone.

I scrunch up my nose. "What about your house?"

"Take me to my house. Please." He nods at the road ahead of us. "Once we're across the lake, stay on Bridge Street. I'll give you directions from there."

"Hold on." I scoff. "Didn't we *just* reach a settlement? I'm not dropping you off until Christmas Eve. We've got all the leftovers at the lake house. And the pie. And the tree. And have you forgotten about poor Henry?"

"I'll never forget about Henry. But ..."

"But what?"

"The clothes Ford packed for me are going to run out. I just need to grab a few things. Like socks and shirts and underwear."

"Fine." I glance at him. "I guess I can't deny a man clean boxers."

"Who says I wear boxers?" He wags his eyebrows.

"I wasn't asking."

He chuckles. "Yeah, but you definitely want to know."

Spots of heat rise in my cheeks. "Whatever you say."

"I say go past this stop sign. Then turn left."

"Hmm. So bossy."

"Hey." He arches a brow. "I gave in to your settlement, didn't I? But for the record, I still don't like the idea of you doing so much driving on back-to-back days."

"I'll survive."

"I'm also still sending a big donation along with you for you to drop off on my behalf."

This teases a soft chuckle out of me. "What am I dropping off for you? Like ... a check?"

"Maybe." His mouth quirks.

I burst out a full-on laugh. "Are you a hundred years old or something? Channeling Big Mama?"

"If you must know, yes. I, Three Fuller, have a checkbook." A grin breaks across his face. "I got an account to teach my students about old-school banking. Even the stuff they *think* they'll never need. A lot of these kids have grandparents and great-grandparents who still send birthday money via checks. So they need to know how to deal with—"

"I get the picture." I shake my head, but a smile tugs at my lips. "But I still don't know how to get to your house, so ..."

"Make a right up here. And then the next left onto Reed Street. Mine's the second house up across from the church."

Even without the precise directions, I'd probably recognize Three's craftsman, because I swear the house looks just like a Fuller. The trees out front are a little wild, bare branches stretching past the rooftop. The exterior is a light yellow. Like sunshine. A single chair sits on the porch. The trim is snow white, and the shutters are a Christmas red.

Three's place is basically happiness in a house.

As I pull into his driveway, I start to feel a bit squeamish. I don't think I'm prepared to see this grownup side of Three. Something so personal. So *him*. I'm trying to trust my emotions. To trust myself. But the inside of Three's house might be too much for me to process. I can't decide which would be worse: If there are moldy dishes in the sink and milk curdling in the fridge, or if the place is all neat and tidy and ... perfect. "I'll wait for you out here."

"It's too cold," he says. "Come on in."

"I can leave the car running. Just be quick."

"I don't want to feel rushed," he says. "My clothes may even be in the dryer. I can't remember. Just ... please."

I sigh. "Fine."

I follow him up the steps to the porch and wait as he fishes a key out from under the mat. "Now you know how to get into my house." He sends a smirk over his shoulder. "So if any of my underwear ever disappears, I'll have to report you to Sheriff Bender."

"Ha ha." I surrender to a nervous laugh as Three unlocks the door. And I'm already trembling a little as I cross the threshold behind him and a chorus of voices shouts, "Surprise!"

"Gah!" I squeal.

Three spins around, grabbing my arm to steady me, which is a good thing, because I'm about to faint. Once he's got me secured, he flashes a grin that could light up the entire town. "Happy birthday, Sara. One day early."

Peering around him, I spot Kenny blowing a noisemaker. The woman with a baby strapped to her must be his wife. In front of them are four children of varying heights, some with missing teeth, all wearing party hats, blowing horns, and waving orange streamers.

"Welcome to Operation Surprise Sara," Three says.

"Hashtag OSS," Kenny calls out.

Three puts a hand on my lower back and guides me over to the table with a sheet cake on display. It's *My Little Pony* themed, with a picture of Applejack in icing. The cups, plates, and napkins all have *My Little Pony* on them too. And at least a dozen sparkly orange helium balloons float around us.

"Three." I gasp. "How?"

"It was a team effort," Kenny chirps. I turn to him and a bright smile splits his face. "Three ordered the cake and balloons and everything else yesterday. I made the pickups and brought the stuff here while you two were at the hospital."

The woman chuckles. "I guess that makes the kids and me 'the stuff.'" She comes toward me and reaches for my hand. "I'm Madeline. Nice to meet you, Sara. And happy birthday."

"Thank you so much." I turn to Three, putting a hand to my heart, and willing my racing pulse to calm down. "I can't believe you did all this for me."

"Well, you said you always wanted a normal birthday party with balloons and cake and kids your age." He ducks his head. "Kenny's kids are a *little* young, but at one point or another, you too were three, five, seven, and nine. Just like them."

"It's perfect," I manage, but my brain's gone fizzy and light-headed. These past few days have already been overwhelming. Add two generations of Kenny to the mix, and it's all a lot to process. Still, the idea behind this is the most romantic thing anyone's ever done for me.

Yes, even the *My Little Pony* cake.

I glance around the room taking in everything—the cake, the balloons, streamers, noisemakers, party hats. In the meantime, the kids all crowd around the table begging for cake. Madeline hovers over them. "I'm going to regret letting you rugrats have so much sugar this afternoon, but you can't have a birthday without cake." She takes charge, lighting the candles, then everyone sings—at high volume and gloriously off-key.

Three moves in close and my whole body warms at his proximity. "Now close your eyes, and make a wish before you blow out the candles," he says. "But don't tell anyone what you wish for."

A giggle slips out of me. "Yes, I'm aware of the rules of blowing out candles, Three. I don't live under a rock, you know."

I shut my eyes and dig deep for the one thing I'd wish for above everything else.

I wish I could keep seeing Three Fuller after Christmas.

The kids all clap while I blow out the candles. I don't really believe in the power of a birthday wish, but still, the moment feels pretty magical in its own way. And the truth is, I'm not ready for this reconnection with Three to be over.

Hope is scary. Terrifying, even. But a birthday party—two days before Christmas—feels like the best time to have a little faith.

While Madeline cuts and serves the cake, Kenny retrieves a gallon of rocky road from the freezer and adds a scoop to each plate. Since there aren't enough chairs at Three's table, the kids just plop down on the floor and everyone digs in, chatting and laughing and going back for seconds. When Three gets a smear of frosting on his lips, all I want to do is kiss it off. But unfortunately, we're not alone.

Maybe it's not too late to change my wish.

As if on cue, Kenny tells the kids to finish up because they have to get going.

"Already?" I ask, feeling a little guilty for wishing them away, but also a little relieved and grateful.

"We just came for cake," he says. "Gotta get the baby home for a nap."

"Huh." I lift a brow. "You mean the one that's sound asleep on Madeline?"

Kenny darts his eyes to Three then back to me. "What can I say? My kids are just born ... lazy."

"Hey!" the oldest one shouts from his seat on the floor. "I'm not lazy!" Crumbs of cake spew from his mouth.

"You're right, Logan." Three chuckles. "You're not. Kenny's just too polite to admit that I asked you to come for the surprise and for cake, but I've got other plans for us after."

I swallow hard. "You do?"

His answering wink makes me blush.

As it turns out, actually getting everyone out the door takes another twenty minutes of putting away ice cream, tossing out plates, and hugging sticky faces. When Three and I come back in after walking the Monroe family out, I return to the table. More than half the sheet cake is gone now. Only half a pony left.

"Poor Applejack," I murmur.

"You *did* say Applejack was your favorite, right?"

"She used to be." I nod. "But right now, *you* are."

"So you didn't think this was all too ... juvenile?" Three wrinkles his nose. "I mean, you're used to champagne towers and caviar, and I just threw you a kid's birthday party."

My heart swells. "Considering this is the only one I've had in twenty-nine years, I couldn't have loved it more."

"Ahem." Three pulls down his brow. "Excuse me, Ms. Hathaway, but I believe you won't be twenty-nine for one more day."

"That is true."

"I intend to make the next twenty-four hours all about you."

"Oh, really?" My lip twitches. "What else did you have in mind, Mr. Fuller?"

He glances at the half-eaten cake then back at me. "My mission while you're still twenty-eight is to let you be the kid you haven't gotten to be in ... maybe forever. So we're going to do whatever YOU want to do. I'll even submit myself to a candy cane jigsaw puzzle. Or checkers. If you choose chess, you'll have to teach me ... but I'm game."

"Seriously?"

"Yep."

"Okay." I splay my hands. "I made my decision."

He chuckles. "Already?"

I flash him a smile, and my insides flutter. "Ice skating!"

"Wow." Three bobs his head. "Nice choice."

"Ever since we found that box of skates in the storage room, I've been thinking about how much I used to love to skate." I dip into a prim little curtsy.

"If ice skating is what you want, then I say, yes. Let's go. It's been a while for me too." His grin is dazzling, but a seam inside me splits straight down the middle.

On the one hand, skating with Three sounds even better than the birthday cake. But I can't forget the doctor's warning. He's already been pushing too hard. Snowball fights, Christmas tree shopping, and spray painting are one thing. But ice skating with a man who has a concussion?

"Forget it." I shake my head. "It wouldn't be safe for you. We can do something else today. How about that jigsaw puzzle?"

He scoffs. "Nope, thanks. You made your pick and I'm going to make it happen. *You'll* go skating, and I'll get to watch."

"But that's not fair to you."

"On the contrary," he says. "Bringing you joy brings *me* joy. And based on the evidence I've gathered these past few days—plus some pretty spectacular memories from ten years ago—just watching you do things is pretty satisfying all on its own." He meets my gaze, eyes locking with mine. "So what do you say, Bambi? Should we head over to the lake house and—"

I launch myself at him, and he lets out all his breath in a whoosh. Then he gathers me in, wrapping his arms all the way around my body.

Pressed against him in a big, strong bear hug, I blink back tears. This man asks nothing of me. Expects nothing from me.

He just wants me to be happy.

"Yes," I tell him. "Yes."

Chapter Forty-Four

Sara

Ten Years Ago: August

We're heading back to the city tomorrow, and I'm moving to California next week, so I really should be packing, but I can't fold T-shirts right now. My stomach's in knots, my heart's full of butterflies, and my brain is one big ball of fizz.

Three's coming over soon to take me out for our last night. Saying goodbye to him always stuffs a whole spectrum of emotions into my body.

It's the best. And the worst.

. . .

He's everything I've ever wanted in a man: kind, chivalrous, smart, not to mention the funniest person I've ever met.

The truth is I'm completely in love with Three Fuller, and I have been for a while. I'm done pretending being with him only a few months a year is enough for me. So I'm going to commit myself to him, even though we'll be long distance. I want to be his. Exclusively. More than I've ever wanted anything else.

I know it's a risk, not waiting for him to ask first, but I can see it in his eyes when he looks at me, and feel it in his touch when he holds me ...

He loves me too.

I just think neither one of us has been brave enough to say the words, because of the "expiration date" every August. And it's scary, let's be honest. Still, Three is worth all the fear. He's also worth all the hope and all the joy.

And yes, I'll be on opposite coast from him now—even farther away than when I was at St. Bernadette's—but so what? I can visit in between quarters. And I'll look for summer internships in Albany. I only hope my parents won't be too disappointed that I probably won't be coming home on breaks as often from now on. But I can't put off that conversation any longer. They need to know how I feel.

This is it. I'm about to take the bull by the horns and make my REAL dream a reality.

Wish me luck!

(One lifetime of love ... Coming up!)

Chapter Forty-Five

Three

I finish brushing snow off the other half of the fallen log we're using as a bench, and drop down beside Sara. In front of us, the lake stretches out like glass. The Hathaways' house rises behind us, sprawling across the property. As Sara begins to put on her skates, my eyes trace her every movement.

Yep. Watching Sara. Like I told her. Not too shabby.

She slips her gloves off, laying them in her lap, then she shoves her foot into the first skate. When she swipes her hair back, the smell of cinnamon and cloves wafts between us, flooding my senses.

Annnd now I'm sniffing Sara. Which is awkward, but I can't help it. In this moment, she's the most delicious thing I've ever smelled, and I've worked at a candle shop and a bakery.

Anyway, she must sense me studying her—or maybe she heard me trying to inhale her scent, hoping it might live permanently in my lungs—because she glances sideways and her lip curves up. "Are you all right?"

"Never better." I straighten my spine, acting smooth.

"Uh-oh." She chews her lip. "You're already bored, aren't you?"

"No way." I cut my eyes to her skates. "Just make sure you tie those tight. I want you to be safe, and you were a little wobbly last time."

"That's because I was walking on concrete floors. Not skating on ice." She returns to her task, her fingers working the laces. Tightening, looping, tightening. Each new stretch tugs at my heartstrings.

If I'd had one birthday wish today, it would've been to freeze time so this week wouldn't end. I love Christmas as much as the next guy, but I'd give up all future holidays to have Sara here with me. Forever.

When she leans over to deal with her other skate, her hair falls into a black drape over her shoulder, masking her profile again. So I go back to staring at her. Soaking up every detail. Possibly sniffing.

She's leaving tomorrow, and yes, she says she'll come back to Abieville on Christmas, but who knows? The doctor did clear me to be left alone. Assuming the house gets approved, she'll have no actual reason to return. Once Sara's in the city, with her parents in her ear, her dad officially offering her a job, she might decide it would be easier to stay.

And if that's what she wants, I'll have to accept it. All I care about is making her happy. And that's exactly why I'm giving her my all today. From a log, sure. But still, this is Sara's time. She's the star.

This moment isn't about fundraiser donations or bar exam results or some speech to praise the good works of Children's Village. Those things are all important, yes.

But they pale in comparison to Sara.

My gut wrenches at the thought of losing her. Again. I can't fathom another ten years—or longer—coming between us now. But I refuse to bring down the mood of this day for even a minute. So I shake it off, and press out a scoff. "You know, you're actually lucky you're skating alone out there." I lift a brow.

"Oh, really?" Sara finishes with her laces and turns to me. Her cheeks have pinked up in the chill of the air and she begins to put back on her gloves. "Why is that?"

"I have a very particular set of skills." I use my best Liam Neeson voice, and squint out at the ice, struggling not to laugh. Being around Sara makes me giddy. She's always made me giddy, I just spent a decade trying to forget that.

"What kinds of skating skills are we talking about?" Sara puffs out a little snort. "Please. Enlighten me."

"I'm so glad you asked." I throw up a gloved hand to keep track of my suggestions. "Let me count the ways. Speed. Strength. Form. Endurance. Technical prowess." When I raise my other hand as if to list another five other areas, Sara bats it away.

"I object."

"On what grounds?"

She smirks. "I'd like to argue that form and technical prowess are the same."

"Aha!" I chuckle, crossing my arms. "So you admit I'd still school you in at least *four* different skills."

Sara laughs, then tugs her beanie farther down over her ears. "You know you're awfully confident for a man who's going to be watching me from the bench. And it's not even a real bench. It's a fallen log."

With that, she pushes her body up and takes a few tentative steps forward. In front of her, the lake is mirror smooth. Dark glass in the fading daylight.

"Need any help?" I call out as she makes her way toward the ice.

"No, I've got this. Watch and learn, Liam Neeson. Watch. And. Learn."

She eases out onto the lake, using shorter strides at first. Just warming up, taking things slow. I half expected her to start showing off after my Liam Neeson bit, but she's being cautious,

251

which is a relief. Sara's always prioritized safety. Hers and everyone else's.

Baiting her was reckless.

But brain fog's making me dumb. And Sara looks so happy. Her movements appear effortless, arms arced out for balance as she glides across the ice. She lengthens her strides, sweeping out past the end of the dock. Her skates are eating up the lake as she turns right, disappearing beyond the alcove of trees.

"Where'd you go?" I yell the second as I lose sight of her. "Stay where I can see you!"

She reappears, farther out on the lake now, picking up speed, passing the dock again. But this time she heads left. "Can you see me now, Liam?" she calls out. "I'm pretty good, right?"

She spins around, skating backward, her legs and hips swaying. Her whole body moves in perfect fluidity. It's a sight to see. A white swan floating on frozen water.

"Showboater!" I holler, my hand cupped around my mouth.

"Check this out!" She turns, facing me again, then skids to a stop in a spray of ice. "That's my hockey move!"

"Very impressive."

"Glad you finally noticed," she says.

Oh, I definitely noticed.

She kicks off again, skating back toward me, chanting my *particular set of skills* at the top of her lungs: "Speed! Strength! Form! Endurance!" When she's a bit closer to shore, she attempts another skidding stop and almost loses her balance, but she recovers, coming to a halt. She's laughing now. Catching her breath. "What was that last one you claimed?" she asks. "Technical something?" She grins, her arms wide and graceful again, like a ballerina on ice.

"I think it was technical prow—"

"Wait!" she calls out, cutting me off.

"Hey." I toss her a smirk. "You're the one who asked."

"Three..." She looks down at her skates.

I tip my head. "What's up?"

"I hear a ... a ...." Her next words, aimed at her feet, come out muffled.

"A what?" I'm still laughing under my breath. "I can't hear you when you're talking to your feet."

She lifts her chin. Slowly. "The ice." Her voice is a squeaky rasp. We're both quiet for a beat, then I hear it too. A quick series of pops. Then a crackling. Her eyes go wide, and I hop up from the bench.

"Sara." Her name pushes across my lips in a low, guttural growl. "Don't move."

"Do I look like I'm moving?" she says in a panic.

"I'm coming for you. Just stay still." I glance around searching for a fallen branch or anything I can use as a potential lifeline. There's that old tire swing hanging from the big snow-covered maple tree. But even if I could reach the swing, how would I cut through the rope?

I can't. That's the answer.

The ice around Sara crackles again, and she meets my gaze, eyes frantic. "What do I do?" she moans, like an animal caught in a trap. My heart's thrashing in its cage.

We're running out of time.

"Hold on!" I rip the string out from the hood of my sweat-shirt. It's decently long, but way too thin. There's not enough substance for her cling to. Not with gloves on. Not with frozen hands.

Yanking off my gloves, then my boots, I quickly tie the shoelaces together. Then I knot one end of the hoodie string to the boot laces. The result doesn't add much length, but at least the boots are a solid mass. Better than just a hoodie string to grip, at least. Now I can inch my way out onto the ice and toss the boots to Sara. I'll wrap the hoodie string around my wrist and haul her back in with me.

Back to shore.

Back to safety.

My pulse races through my veins as I dash to the end of the

dock and clamber down the ladder. Once I reach the ice, my actions have to shift. As desperate as I am to get to Sara, I force myself to move slowly. Steady and controlled.

I ease my body out onto the ice, then lower myself to my knees, continuing until I'm sprawled flat. With my weight dispersed as evenly as possible, I can inch forward toward Sara. She's not too far from me now—thanks to the distance I covered on the dock. But terror hammers at my brain like we're still separated by a galaxy.

"I'm scared, Three." Sara whimpers, as if she's reading my mind. Her confession might as well be a thousand knives stabbing my insides.

"I know, baby," I murmur, creeping toward her on my belly. "But I've got you." My chin is up, eyes pinned to hers with a determined stare. I'd trade places with her in a nanosecond, anything to protect her first at all costs. But there are no birthday candles out here to wish on. And if I'm too hasty now—and end up plunging through the ice too—we're both doomed.

Don't even think that. You have to save her, no matter what.

Another deep groan sounds from the ice, and the kaleidoscope of cracks between Sara and me spreads. Our eyes are still locked, and when her chin quivers, my entire chest cavity might as well be crushed by a vise.

"This is it," she shrieks. "The ice is breaking!"

"No, you're okay," I assure her, even though I'm about as unsure as I've ever been in my life. "I'm coming for you, Sara. Almost there."

"Stay where you are," she chokes out. "Please."

"Not an option," I tell her, my jaw gripped in a grim clench.

"Don't risk yourself too," she begs. "Just crawl back to the dock, and call for help."

"There isn't enough time."

"You're right." Sara lets out a tiny sob, and an angry rumble comes from the depths of me.

"I won't abandon you."

Her whole body starts to tremble. This is taking too long. Wading through my blurry mind, I think about ways to help her. Things I should know.

You should've known not to let her skate on this ice in the first place.

"Now just listen to me, Sara. Focus on my voice and do what I say. I want you to lower yourself down into a squat," I instruct. "As gently as you can manage."

A squeak slips out of her. "I can't do that."

"You can. Sara, you are so strong. But you need to get your center of gravity low. Keep both your arms out in front of you. If the ice breaks, you've gotta grab the sides and hold on until I get to you. I promise I'll get to you. Even if I have to go into the water myself."

"No!" she screams. "Go back!"

"Can't do that. You're not alone. Do you hear me, Sara Hathaway? You are *not* alone. I'm not leaving you. Not now. Not ever." I'm so close. Just one more foot, and my homemade life preserver will be long enough to reach her. As gingerly as I can, I lift my hoodie string, boots dangling from the end.

"I'm going to toss this to you now," I tell her. "Catch the boot. Hold on tight. That's all you have to do."

"Okay," she sobs, hands shaking, preparing for me to throw. As the spiderweb of cracks between us expands, I heave the boot.

"Three!" she screams. The glass beneath her splits into an open mouth, and she plummets into the icy water.

Chapter Forty-Six

Sara

Ten Years Ago: October

We moved into Branner Hall more than a month ago, and Bristol still hasn't given up trying to get me to go out with her. She joked that she might as well be rooming with a zombie, but I actually feel pretty dead inside.

I've already turned down all the parties and group dates. Even the low-key hangouts on our floor. And I'm sure she means well, but the girl is relentless. She insists that meeting other students is a critical part of the freshman experience, not to mention the only way I'll ever be able to move on with my life.

. . .

I told her I'm just not ready. She said I'll never be ready until I try.

Yesterday, she put a box of Band-Aids on my desk then told me to put them all on, so we could rip them off together.

When I didn't laugh, she explained the symbolism, like I'm just too sad and pathetic to get her jokes. I'll give her that: Bristol Kane is funny, and whip-smart, and have I mentioned relentless?

She's a dog and getting me to be social is her bone. But I'm just not interested in spending time with anyone else unless it's for class. Study sessions, I'll do. But only if there's zero chance of romance.

All I care about now is getting straight A's this year. And landing the perfect summer internship. And never letting myself care about another man again.

Poor Bristol. She definitely deserves a better roommate than me.

And I sure deserved better than Three.

Chapter Forty-Seven

Sara

I've heard reports that freezing is surprisingly painless. Peaceful, even. Emily Dickinson, my favorite poet, writes about the feeling being something like a strange kind of contentment. Still as stone. Quartz, specifically. First the chill. Then the stupor. Then the letting go.

For me, plunging into Abie Lake is none of those things.

Instead of peace, there are needles. Thousands of them—no, millions—stabbing every inch of my body. A throb that steals all the air from my lungs. I gasp and gasp, but I can't catch my breath. Still, my hands instinctively scramble. Grasping. Flailing. During one desperate lunge, I snatch at Three's boot—at least I think it's a boot. And for a moment, I manage to latch on to an edge of ice, too. But my gloves are too slippery. So I kick and buck, like a fish on a line. The thing is, fish don't have skates, and they aren't wearing layers of heavy clothing intended to keep people warm. My jacket and pants are gulping up water, weighing me down.

Surrender is tempting. A swifter end to the stinging. But Three calls out for me to hold on.

"I can't lose you," he shouts. "I can't lose you!"

Over and over.

He can't lose me.

So I won't give up.

Not that a person always has a choice in the matter. Some losses are beyond anyone's control. Cruel illness. Random accidents. Old age. Nobody's fault. So I try to hold on. Really I do. But the stupor slides in anyway.

Don't let go, I hear above me.

A heart-shattering command.

Then only darkness closing in as Three hauls me from the water.

* * *

The next stretch of time is more like a twilight sleep. I don't know that I ever fully lost consciousness, but waking up fully doesn't sound appealing either. Not when the absolute numbness gives way to nonstop prickling of my skin, and I can't generate any real movements on my own. I'm a soaked rag doll. Heavy and limp. Three lays me gently by the couch, and my teeth chatter and my bones quake—a clatter of noises and sensations alerting us both to how close this call was.

The pain of it all makes me moan.

I'm so weak and chilled, I barely register heat from the fire Three rushes to build. Or the moment he peels off my sodden clothes, stripping me down to a sports bra and underwear. Before any modesty floods in, he's already wrapping me in a blanket. And when he pulls me into his arms, cradling my body to his chest, I press myself against him, absorbing the warmth of his skin.

When did he take off his jacket and shirt?

It doesn't matter. His heat is what I need. All that I want.

"You're all right, you're all right, you're all right," Three whispers into my hair, his breath a promise of life against the freeze. Over and over. "You're all right."

I try to speak, but my tongue is too thick and slow. All I manage is a sigh. His response is a quiet, "Shhh. It's okay, Sara. Just relax. You did it, my sweet girl. You did it."

I did it?

What did I do?

It doesn't matter.

You're his sweet girl.

"I've got you, Sara." His heart pounds against my cheek—a jackhammer of emotion—and he draws me even more tightly to him, like he's trying to suck me inside his body to speed up the thawing. As we rock together in the silence, he rubs my legs through the soft wool, probably trying to jumpstart my circulation. When I finally stop quivering, my limbs melted into his, Three pulls another blanket from the back of the couch and around me. Then he begins to disentangle himself, but I clutch at him, clawing to keep him close.

"No."

"Sara." He pulls away from me gently. "I need to call for help."

"Don't leave me," I groan. My lips vibrate against the sheen of his bare skin.

"But—"

"Just keep holding me." I snuggle more deeply into his embrace. "You're the one making me feel better right now. I don't need a doctor. Or an ambulance. Or anyone else. I just want to stay like this. Here. Now. With you." I try lifting my chin to look into his eyes. But I can't bend my neck enough from this angle, so I give up and drop my head back down onto his chest.

A low rumble of protest sounds in his throat. "You know, when you beaned me with that fire extinguisher, I didn't want to go to the hospital either. But you and Ford ganged up and forced me to go."

"So did Kenny." I snake an arm around his back, all the better to cling to him.

"Exactly. I was ambushed."

"And I'm not sorry about it."

As the warmth from both the fire and Three's body seeps through me, I start to imagine how different things would've been if Three hadn't gone to the hospital. The doctor wouldn't have told him he couldn't get on an airplane. He might've flown to California that same night. He could be on the cruise right now, and I'd be here alone. Not frozen, not at risk of having my heart broken again.

But there would be no popcorn strands on the Christmas tree.

There would be no Christmas tree in the first place.

No Henry out front.

No white lights along the bookshelves.

No turkey leftovers in the fridge.

No cake for my birthday.

"If you stay with me, I'll be fine," I mumble into his hot skin. "I'm just a little ... cold." My body trembles even as the words come out. "See? That shaking is just my systems bringing myself back to normal."

"Your systems?"

"Nervous. Sympathetic. Para ... para-something."

"Huh." Three rests his chin on my head and tightens his grip on me. "Even frozen, you're still presenting arguments like a lawyer."

"My particular set of skills." I try to laugh, but the sound is closer to a mouse squeaking.

Three's quiet for at least a full minute, holding me in his arms. He brushes a damp strand of hair off my face, and presses a kiss to the top of my head. "If that's what you want," he says at last. "We can just stay here. Together. For now. But you have to be okay, Sara. You just have to be okay."

"I will." I nod against him, his heartbeat a soft pulse on my cheek.

"I'm so, so sorry." His voice goes gravelly on the apology, and a pang of sympathy cuts through me. He's probably feeling just as guilty as I did after giving him a concussion.

"It's not your fault," I whisper.

But maybe it's mine.

Because I think a part of me offered to come to Abieville because I *wanted* to run into Three. A secret part buried deep down inside that packed my favorite green dress. Sure, I told myself I'd avoid him like the plague, and when Bristol questioned my wisdom, I swore I'd get in and out of town unscathed. Now here I am, lying in Three's arms, at the risk of being totally, completely ... *scathed*.

But the truth is, I feel more whole now than I ever have.

And more in love.

I meant those words a decade ago, and ten years of time hasn't snuffed the flame. My feeling simply lay dormant, waiting for this reconnection that must be meant to be. Because in all this time, no other relationship has ever come close to *us*. I thought the walls I built around my heart were to keep me safe from the potential pain of other men. But now I know what I was really doing was saving my heart for him.

"I'm going to tell my parents tomorrow," I say, slowly, the words muffled by his skin.

"About falling in the lake?"

"No." I swallow hard. "About you."

Three exhales a long gust of breath. "You think that's a good idea?"

"I need them to know everything that's happened here. Not just over these past few days, but ten years ago too. Are you okay with that?"

There's a beat of quiet. Then he says, "Am I okay with your mom and dad finding out I overheard their plans to confront you and keep us apart? And that I ended up hurting you to avoid that?

Sure. But also tell them that's why I got my act together. Got my degree. Got my career. I honestly owe them a debt of gratitude, although I didn't know it at the time."

"I'm not sure we have to go that far," I say softly. "We *both* got pretty hurt."

"But that was my choice, not theirs. And hopefully who I am now will be good enough for them."

I lift my head to press a light kiss to his chest, and goose bumps rise along his skin. "You don't have to be enough for my parents," I tell him. "Because you're enough for me."

The echo of a groan moves under his ribs. "That doesn't change our situation, though."

"We don't have to figure that out tonight."

"So." He reaches for my hand. "What should we do instead?"

I shift in his arms, and he gently tips my face up to kiss me. And despite our body heat and the warmth of the fire, we both shiver.

For a while, we stay just like that, Three cradling me in his arms while my body learns to self-regulate again. Then, even though he's the one who's supposed to be taking it easy, Three gets busy taking care of me like he's been doing it his whole life.

First, he collects dry clothes for me up in my room, then he warms us up some leftovers which we eat by the fire. After doing the dishes, he even organizes the cake and pie taste-test.

My cake wins.

But it's slightly possible he threw the competition.

Once the food's all been devoured and the dishes are washed and dried, Three makes us a nest of pillows and blankets on the floor of the living room. That's so we can watch *Home Alone* on the brand new flat-screen. Three recites almost every line, and I gleefully cheer him on. It's his favorite Christmas movie, after all. And when Kevin's mom comes home, I get a little teary-eyed.

Afterward, at my request, we make a plan to fall asleep right there in front of the Christmas tree. I've always wanted to do that, but I never could, because of the gala.

So we both try dozing in the glow of the twinkling lights, but end up talking instead—sharing stories we missed from each other's lives over the past ten years. We both have a lot of funny stories to tell with a few sad memories sprinkled in. Mostly we've been happy, which is a good thing. We just ignored the holes in our hearts and made the best of all our blessings.

Later, when the embers have all winked out, and my eyelids are thick and heavy, I'm just drifting off when I feel a sweet, soft kiss on my forehead.

"Hi," I say.

"Did I wake you?"

"I don't mind. I wasn't quite asleep yet."

"Well it's midnight now," Three whispers. "Happy Birthday, Sara Jane."

Chapter Forty-Eight

Three

So I just spent an entire night holding the woman of my dreams, and now I want to call my mom.

That's weird, right?

Yeah. Probably.

Super-weird, at least on the surface. But hear me out. These past twelve hours with Sara weren't like when we got stuck in the storage room. Or when we ended up sleeping together on that one small couch. For one thing there was no grandfather clock chiming at us every half hour. But that's not the real point.

The difference between every other moment Sara and I have been together since she returned to Abieville was the connection. What I'm feeling for her is no longer based on the great memories from years ago. And it's not about how beautiful she still is. Although—no exaggeration—she's basically a goddess in my eyes. But now that I've seen who Sara's become, I can't believe I was ever strong enough to let her walk away from me.

Scratch that. I *pushed* her away.

But as hard as that was back then—and how hard it stayed for a long time—I think we're both feeling now like that might've been the best thing for us.

The first time around, Sara and I were just having summer fun. We had days on the lake and bonfires at night. We had ice cream and the hots for each other.

(That's what my dad called it anyway. *The hots.* I gave him a lot of grief for that, but he wasn't wrong.)

Of course Sara was already smart and funny back then. And kind. Beyond gorgeous. That's an objective fact. So yes, we definitely had chemistry, and man, over those four summers, I fell hard for her. But only as hard as any kid can when he doesn't know much about himself yet.

Make no mistake. This isn't about age. Plenty of people can and do find the loves of their lives when they're young. My parents met at Abieville Elementary, and fifty years later, they're still going strong.

But for me, not fighting for Sara back then—or defending my family to the Hathaways—was strictly because I hadn't proved my worthiness to myself yet. The disapproval I gauged in her mom and dad's voice started in my own head first. I had no idea what the future held for me. I wasn't ready to stake claim to a specific career. To support a woman. To be a man.

Then there was Sara, six months younger than me, and already so clear about what she wanted. Not just to go on to become an attorney someday, but to make her parents proud. She always felt like their happiness was her responsibility. And I get why she'd believe that. Their miracle baby. Only child. She was a gift from day one, and kept on giving.

So I hope she's starting to realize she's her own person too. She can make choices that bring her happiness without worrying about her dad's legacy or whether her mom will be disappointed.

My parents never pushed me to work hard for anyone but myself. They weren't in a hurry to see me climb any ladder beyond the lifeguard stand. They always saw Abieville as a town worth building a life in. At whatever pace suits you. So they always had faith in me.

And that's exactly why I need to call my mom.

Because this morning, Ryan Detweiler approved the Hathaway's home for Platinum Stays, and ever since Sara dropped me off to head back to the city, I've been pacing the floors wanting nothing more than to be with her again.

Come on, man. You want to be with her always.

I huff out a breath, laughing at myself. Sara spent little more than an hour here for her birthday yesterday, but my house already feels empty without her. The man I am now is more committed and determined than I've ever been, but there's a gaping hole in my gut when she's gone.

No one but Sara can fill that space with the belief that we can make anything work if we want it badly enough. She had that faith ten years ago when I didn't. Now it's my turn to show her I believe in us.

Please answer. Please answer. Please answer.

"Three!" My mother's smile lights up the screen. There's an elf hat perched on her head, and a small crowd is lining up on the pool deck behind her.

"Hey, Mom." A grin takes over my face. "Am I interrupting?"

"Interrupting?" She glances over her shoulder then snaps her gaze back to me. "Oh, no. The cruise director is just about to start an ugly Christmas sweater contest."

I fake a gasp. "You didn't enter?"

"I refused on principle." She moves away from the pool deck, pushing through a swinging door into what looks to be a hallway. "I think all Christmas-themed clothes are beautiful." She tsks. "You know I always skip Aunt Elaine's ugly sweater competition."

"I do know that." I bob my head, and a wave of happiness rises in me, buoyed by the familiarity of tradition. Home. Family. "Man, I miss you guys."

"We miss you, too, Three. Very much."

"Oh, really?" I cock a brow. "Because according to Nella and

267

Ford, you all have been muddling through with mai tais and couples' massages."

"Well, in your message you basically demanded that we have a great time." She tilts her head and her elf hat almost slips off. "That is what you wanted, isn't it?"

"It is."

"So that's what we're doing." She smiles primly, readjusting her hat. "Christmas isn't the same without you, but a Hawaiian cruise isn't like any other holiday we've ever had, either. This experience is all brand new for us, so you aren't really missing our usual holiday. Those traditions live up here." She points at her head. "And here." She points at her heart.

"You're right about that."

She wags her brow. "I'm right about everything."

"Yes, you are." My eyes sting at the corners, and I think about popcorn garland on the tree, and cinnamon and nutmeg simmering on the stove. Sara tried to recreate my family's Christmas for me, but maybe I'm ready for some brand-new experiences too.

With her.

"So." My mother peers closer at me, her eyes roaming my face. "How are you holding up there? When Ford told us about what happened, I'll admit I was a little concerned. Of course he assured me you were in good hands, and I knew he wouldn't have left you if he didn't believe you were physically safe. But I wasn't so much worried about the concussion. You've had those before. I was more worried about ... Well, you know. Your being with Sara."

"We're good, Mom." A fresh smile creeps across my face. "Really good. In fact, that's kind of why I called."

"I see." Her brow lifts. "Do tell."

"The thing is, Sara and I. Well. We've ..." I pause for a beat because saying the words out loud—especially to my mom— makes everything more real. "We've ... sort of reconnected." I swallow against the dryness in my throat. "I mean we've *definitely* reconnected. And she's even more amazing than I remembered.

Which is saying a lot, because I already thought she was pretty great. But she's generous and kind. Beautiful and smart. And I'm ... I'm falling for her, Mom."

My mother lays a hand over her heart, but she doesn't say a word.

"I know from the outside, this may seem like I'm moving too fast," I continue, "but Sara and I already have four years of history, and I feel like I owe it to myself—to both of us—to try to make things work with her now."

"Ah." My mom dips her chin. "So you want to try?"

"Yes." My stomach lurches, and I can't help clenching my teeth. Is this my mother's way of saying she doesn't approve? Sara and I went through this ten years ago, and her parents' opinions came between us. But I won't let anyone else's doubt control my actions again. "You think that's a bad idea?"

My mom's gaze sweeps over me, appraising. "I'm not sure what you heard me say, Three, but I simply asked you a question. You told me you want to *try* to make things work with Sara. So now I'm wondering why you don't just *make* things work with her."

A sliver of awareness pierces my gut. I guess I have a habit of jumping to conclusions without getting clarity first. "You have a point."

"Of course I do." My mom's mouth quirks. "I'm right about everything, remember?"

"There's just one problem," I say. "I can be willing to do whatever it takes to make things work on my end, but I can't force Sara. She has to want it too."

"Obviously." My mother pauses as a pack of cruisers in sweaters and Santa hats bursts through the doors. She waves at them as they pass, then she turns her attention back to me. "So, what do you think? Does Sara want a relationship with you?"

I consider the question. "I really hurt her back then," I admit. "And I wouldn't blame her if she had trouble trusting me again. But we've been through a lot these past few days—more than I can get into right now—and I'm pretty sure she feels the same way I do."

"Which is what?"

"That I never fully got over us. In fact, I don't think I even tried."

"Well, I'm well aware of *that*, dear." My mother lets out a long sigh. "You and your sister and your long-term pining."

I cringe. "Must be hard to watch us, huh?"

"Not really." Her mouth tips up on one corner. "I've always believed the right thing will happen at the right time. For both you and Nella. And if Carver Townsend is right for your sister, I trust they'll end up together too." She breaks into a smile now. "Like you and Sara."

"Thanks, Mom." My heart swells with this reminder of her faith. "You're making it a whole lot easier for me to consider going all in on a relationship with her." I take a beat. "But she's about to accept a full-time position at her dad's law firm."

"Hathaway Cooke?"

I bite back a grimace. "Working there has been the end game she's worked for her entire life. So I can't ask her to give that up to move here, which means ..." My voice finally trails off.

"*You* might be moving."

"More than *might be*, I think."

"Aww." My mother's smile is warm. "Don't look so glum. The train can take your father and me right to the city to visit you."

"But the train takes even longer than the drive. And the drive isn't short."

"So we won't come visit you *every* day," she says. "Don't you worry about us, Three, as long as *you* feel like you could be happy someplace other than Abieville."

"I've never wanted to live anywhere else," I say. "But I don't want to live without Sara."

"Then that's all I need to hear, son." My mother grins. "Go get your girl."

Chapter Forty-Nine

Sara

I'm on Taconic State Parkway, just about halfway between Abieville and New York City, when Bristol's number pops up on my navigation screen.

"Happy birthday!" she shrieks the second I take her call. I'm surprised her voice doesn't shatter my windows. "Sara! Are you there? Can you hear me?"

"I'm pretty sure they can hear you on the moon." I chuckle to myself. "But thank you, friend."

"What's going on there?" she asks. "I tried calling you earlier, but I kept getting sent straight to your voicemail."

"Yeah." I nod, even though she can't see me. "The signal back in Abieville definitely comes and goes."

"Where are you now?"

"On my way to the gala."

"Ahh, right. Of course you are. Is it at the Windsor Club this year?"

"It's at the Windsor Club *forever*," I say on a chuckle. "Remember the time you came?"

"Are you kidding?" she squawks. "A girl doesn't forget *that* many black ties and red ballgowns in one room."

"Well, it's exactly like that, always, except the regular donors keep getting more gray hair."

"Yeah, well, I'd seriously dye mine fully silver to get my hands on more of that fancy food and free champagne." Bristol moans, like she's tasting a dish from a chef with three Michelin stars. "Plus the live band. And that spectacular Christmas tree. The silent auction. I'll never get over *not* winning that trip to Banff."

A guffaw slips out of me. "You didn't even place a bid."

"Duh. I couldn't afford to." Bristol scoffs. "Back then I could barely swing ten raffle tickets. But the whole event was beyond magical."

"It still is." My sigh is part wistful and part resigned. "You should come again sometime."

"Oooh, yes, please!" she gushes.

"Actually, I wish you could go with me tonight." I pause for a moment. "Or even better, I wish you could go *instead* of me."

"Awww, Sara." She's quiet for a stretch, probably processing the full meaning behind my statement. "I know you're not the biggest fan of being in the spotlight, and I've never had to give a speech in front of a room full of rich people, or listen to your dad tell his miracle-baby story over and over, but I've gotta admit, I'd kill to celebrate my birthday at the Windsor Club even once."

"You say that, but believe me. After experiencing twenty-eight Hathaway Galas, I think a simple at-home party might be even better."

"Lies!" she cackles.

"Nope. I'm serious. Cake, ice cream, and balloons are kind of awesome."

"Oh really?" I can practically hear the arch in her brow. "And how would you know anything about that, Ms. Hathaway?"

"Well, Ms. Kane." I take a beat, a grin spreading across my face. "I *really* need to catch you up."

Over the next half hour, I tell her all about what happened since the last time we talked. When I get to the ice skating part, she sucks in a breath. "Sara! That's insane! You could've died."

"I know," I murmur. The weight of that is still fresh in my heart. "But Three ... he saved my life."

I proceed to tell her about the rest of our night together—every sweet detail—and I end with a summary from this morning: the quick cleanup of blankets and pillows, and one last sweep of the house before Ryan Detweiler showed up.

"Did you get final approval?"

"We did," I chirp, triumphant, as a burst of relief floods my body. The fact that I automatically used the word *we* isn't lost on me either.

"Did you have to see that woman from Platinum Stays? Did she flirt with Three again?"

"To be fair, she never flirted in the first place," I say. "And he didn't either. I was just being jealous."

"Wait. YOU?" Bristol's tone shifts into exaggerated mocking. "But Sara Hathaway doesn't care about men."

"You're right." I swallow against the emotion thickening my throat. "I care about *one* man."

"Whoa." She tries to whistle, but it sounds more like a burst of high-pitched wind.

"I know. It's big, right?"

"The biggest," she says. "So what are you going to do about it, birthday girl?"

I glance at my phone to check the time remaining on my drive. "I'm going to tell my parents."

"Everything?"

"Pretty much." I shrug. "Well, I *might* leave out the details on the storage room kiss."

"Yeah. Good call."

"But they need to know I was in love with Three ten years ago, and that I never got over him. That he only broke my heart because he thought he was protecting me. I'm going to tell them he sacrificed what he wanted—me—because he knew how much *they* meant to me. And he didn't want to interfere or risk what we had. He didn't want to hurt me."

"So ... he ended up hurting you."

I blow out a long breath. "Yes."

"Hmm. I'm sensing a *but* in there."

"Yes, Three hurt me," I say. "But that was a long time ago. We're different people now, in important ways that probably couldn't have happened if we'd stayed together."

"I hate to ask, but what if your parents still don't approve of you being with Three?"

I stare out at the road, knowing that possibility grows closer with every mile. "They'll just have to get over it," I say. "I'm an adult now, and so are they. We all have to make our own choices. Follow our own paths. I can't be in charge of my mom and dad's happiness anymore."

"Atta girl!" Bristol offers me a hoot of support. "When I told you to trust yourself, you really took that to heart, huh? And I'm *really* digging this new, independent Sara. Like, truly, madly, deeply. But I'm going to play devil's advocate here for a minute, okay?"

"Okay."

"What if your dad holds the position at Hathaway Cooke over your head?" She takes a beat. "If your parents were prepared to hit you with an ultimatum last time, couldn't your dad threaten to tell the partners not to make you an associate now?"

"He could," I say, "but this time *I* have the advantage."

"How?" Bristol asks. "He's still the managing partner. And you've put a whole other decade toward your goal. Aren't you in a worse position?"

"I don't think so." My mind flashes back to all those summers I spent in Abieville, to the hope I felt, but also the uncertainty. "I know what I want in a way I didn't before," I say. "And it's not just to blindly follow in my dad's footsteps." My heart swells with the truth of the words. "Ten years ago, I put my heart on the line for Three. But I didn't know who I wanted to be yet. And I sure didn't know what love was."

"And now you do?" Bristol asks.

"Yes." I smile to myself. "And even better, so does Three."

Chapter Fifty

Three

Here's the thing: you haven't felt real, pound-your-fist frustration until the love of your life is three hours away, and in a position to —quite literally—decide NOT to come back to you. Ever. Or maybe this is a totally common occurrence in life, and *everybody's* felt this frustration.

What do I know?

Come to think of it, I'm pretty sure annoying stuff like this happens all the time in *Bridgerton*. Thanks to Nella, I've seen enough of that show to know those dudes suffer for love. And they don't get to wear joggers and a hoodie while they're doing it.

Still.

It's Christmas Eve, and Sara's probably at the Windsor Club by now. She could be talking to her parents right this minute, about her future, about us. But I can only guess what's going on, because I—probably shortsightedly—asked her not to call or text tonight.

I figured she should focus on the gala. The fundraiser part, *and* her folks. So I encouraged her not to think about me at all. I may not be a duke, but I am chivalrous.

In fact, if it weren't for this stupid concussion, I would've insisted on going to the city with her. Then I'd be there by her side, holding her hand, offering my support. No matter what.

Instead, this chivalrous guy is stuck back in Abieville feeling ... helpless. I'm dying to know what's happening. I'm dying to defend her. But I won't blow up her phone asking for updates.

I *did* almost call her dad, though.

As it turns out, a man who manages a high-profile law firm and runs an annual charity event at the Windsor is not all that hard to reach. Or maybe I was just *that* convincing when I spoke to the answering service taking calls on Christmas Eve. Either way, I had Charles Hathaway's number, and I was all set to contact him when it hit me.

If I jumped in and talked to Sara's dad first, I'd be taking away all her agency. Stealing her power before she has the chance to take control. Not to mention, I kind of need her to *want* to be with me, not end up with me because I burned some catastrophic bridge tonight, leaving her no other option.

So I'm back to pacing, but I'd rather do that over at the lake house. Which is why I'm going over there again.

What can I say? I miss Sara. I miss our Christmas tree. I miss Henry. I might even visit the flamingoes in the storage room when I get there. But don't worry. I'm not going to drive myself. I know the rules, and I don't want to poke the bear that is Sara Hathaway when she's playing nursemaid.

So I reached out to Carver Townsend instead.

He agreed to swing by, pick me up, and deliver me to the lake house. I figure it's a win-win, because I've got a few things I want to get off my chest. Might as well bum a ride at the same time.

A group of carolers just left my house after singing "Joy to the World," so I'm already at the door, watching for Carver's patrol car. When his headlights beam around the corner, I head out to meet him, my workbag in tow.

"I can't thank you enough," I say, climbing in to ride shotgun. "Seriously, man. Coming out on Christmas Eve is above and beyond. I owe you one."

"No problem." Carver checks his mirrors before making a U-turn and heading back toward Main Street. Every house and shop in town is brightly lit tonight, but the streets are mostly empty. "The sheriff's with his family," Carver says, tossing his hat into the back seat. "Makes sense I'd be the one working. I'm the only single guy at the station. For now."

"Not dating anyone? No one special in your life?"

He tips his chin. "Now those are two different questions."

"I guess you're right about that. Either way, I owe you an apology." I flash him my best *I'm sorry* look.

Carver scoffs. "What for?"

"The past couple times we saw each other, I was kinda off. Definitely not acting like myself." I suck air in through my teeth. "But it wasn't you, man. It was definitely me. Or maybe the concussion. I don't know for sure. Still, that's no excuse."

At Bridge Street, Carver hangs a right taking us to the back-road that leads to the Hathaways'. There aren't any street lights along this stretch, so he slows, scanning for deer like we all do here.

"Funny you should say that." He actually chuckles. "Because I was gonna say sorry to you for pretty obviously flirting with your girl." He pulls down his brow, but keeps his eyes on the road. "The thing is, I've got pretty terrible radar when it comes to women. And over at Humboldt's you said you and Sara were just friends. Then you were both so freaked out about the kissing wall ... I guess I believed you two weren't a thing."

"I get it." I run a hand over my head, huffing out a breath. "I was trying to believe me too."

"Anyway, as dense as I am," Carver says, "I realized about ten seconds after you two showed up at the station to help out Sully that there was something going on with you for real."

"Heh." My shoulders hitch. "I won't deny that anymore."

"Good." More chuckling from Carver. "So what's the deal, anyway?"

"It's kind of a long story." I bob my head. "We'll be at the house before I could get halfway through."

"Well, whatever's going on, I'm happy for you." He casts a quick glance my way before returning his focus to the road. "You look happy."

I am.

"I'd love to find a good woman someday too," he continues. "I'd settle down in a heartbeat."

"Really?" I arch a brow. "I'm sure the right one's just waiting around the corner."

"The thing is, I've been stuck on someone for years." He sighs. "No one else compares, to be honest. I can't stop wanting her, but I haven't been able to make anything happen with us."

"Oof. That's hard. Anyone I know?" I cock my chin, huff out a laugh. "If she lives in this town, that's a guarantee. Maybe I can help."

"Thanks." He grimaces. "But that might get awkward."

"Why?"

"She's not interested in me at all. And..." He takes a couple beats. "She's your sister."

Whoa.

"Nella?" The way all the air leaves my lungs, our car might as well have just hit a buck on the road.

"You got another sister?" Carver presses out a laugh. "If so, please introduce us. Maybe I'll have a better shot with her than Nell." He ducks his head, offering me a sad half smile. "Like I said. Bad with women."

Oh, Carver. You have no idea.

Here, I've been worried about protecting my sister's heart, while Carver—the very same man she's been dreaming about for years—actually wants her as well?

Incredible.

A rope of happiness for Nella tethers inside me. Sure, I'm her older brother, and I'm familiar with the *touch-my-sister-and-die* cliche. But that's a role better suited to the guys on *Bridgerton*, I think. I won't be dueling with Carver over Nella anytime soon.

If only she knew ...

"Listen," I start to say, but I just as quickly stop myself. Revealing my sister's true feelings to her lifelong crush is definitely not my assignment. In fact, it might be grounds for justifiable homicide.

Either way, I can be sure to drop some hints when Nella's back from her cruise.

"So." Carver glances my way, as we approach the lake house. "You got any advice for me?"

"I sure do." My mouth goes crooked. "Don't give up on her, man."

Chapter Fifty-One

Three

Home Alone is playing on the flatscreen again. The part where Kevin McAllister's about to slap that aftershave on his face. I'm on the couch at the Hathaways' polishing off the last of the pecan pie.

Just being helpful.

I'd worry about making a mess, except Mrs. Hathaway already has a regular cleaning service scheduled to come the day before the first guests arrive. Sara told her mom she'd leave the place spotless, but Katherine told *her* dust accumulates within a matter of hours. So.

Regular cleaning service it is.

Shoveling the last forkful in my mouth, I take care not to spill any crumbs on my laptop. Turns out pacing around the house wasn't as good a distraction as I'd hoped, so I decided to be productive, which means scrolling job openings for history teachers in New York City.

Not that I'd ever break my current contract. My commitment here comes first, so no matter what happens with Sara, I'll be a coach and educator at Abieville High through the rest of this school year.

Still, a lot of schools start interviewing for fall positions in the late winter or early spring. I figured before then, I should get a feel for the different salaries, and the number of years I'd be able to transfer to a new district. It's all useful information.

And a little scary.

The cost of living in Manhattan will be a rude awakening, so it's a good thing I've always been frugal. By now, I've built up a decent amount of savings, and—as we've already established—I'm not afraid to take on side gigs to pull my weight. I'm also totally okay with my wife making more money than me, for the record.

I know that sounds like I'm putting the cart before the horse, calling Sara my wife.

I haven't even told her I love her out loud yet. But that's my first order of business when she comes back from the city. Next will be finding a job. Then the cart. And the horse.

Heh.

A notification pings in the top corner of my screen. I've got a new message on my work email. I flash back to the night of my concussion, telling my parents I'd stayed back to work on grades. I guess I could make that a true story, and actually dive in now.

First things first, though, I open up my inbox. There are a few unread messages. One from our overachieving booster club president wanting to discuss our March Madness fundraiser. One from our principal wishing us a restful winter break and a happy new year.

But the two most recent emails are from the Ackermans. One from Sully, one from his parents.

I won't lie—I've been a little concerned about what Mr. and Mrs. Ackerman might have to say to me. Not that I did anything wrong by helping out their son with his little paint project. But even the best parents can get defensive when it comes to their kids. Lay blame where it doesn't belong. They could be embarrassed. Or afraid the school might decide to press charges after all. Either way, I check my gut before reading the email.

I shouldn't have worried.

From: theackermanfive@gmail.com
To: Bradford Fuller

Dear Mr. Fuller,
Our family wants to thank you for the graciousness you displayed while handling Sullivan's transgression this week. You could've chosen to make an example of Sully. Instead, you helped him repair the damage he'd caused, then offered advice along with your kindness.
Our son took your words to heart and told us everything the minute we returned from picking Lark up from school. (She says hello, by the way. And that you're still her favorite teacher. Brennan's crossing his fingers he'll be in your class too in a couple of years.)
Coach Fuller, you are a true asset to Abieville High, both in the class-room and on the basketball court. All the Ackermans are grateful to you and for you. We hope your Christmas is warm and wonderful and that your new year is full of blessings.
Sincerely,
Jeffrey and Melissa Ackerman

I'm reasonably sure Jeff and Mel won't be expecting a response from me on Christmas Eve, so I decide to skip a reply for now. I'm on winter break, after all, and technically off the clock. Still, I read through their message two more times, swallowing the lump in my throat.

There will be other students to teach, coach, and care about wherever I land. I'm sure of it. But leaving this town means saying goodbye to families like Sully Ackerman's.

It means I'll never have Brennan in my classroom, which is too bad. Lark and Sully are pretty great. Speaking of which.

From: sullivanthetotalballer@gmail.com
To: Bradford Fuller
She said yes.

That's it. But those few words tell me everything I need to know. I make a mental note to talk to Sully about maybe getting a more professional email address before college. I'm also tempted to ask if his promposal to Cami ended up involving grilled cheese.

But that can come later.

I send him my own three-word reply, then I sit back to watch Kevin talk to that old man in the church.

To: sullivanthetotalballer@gmail.com
Good for you.

Man, I love that kid. And I love my school. I love this entire town. But I love Sara Hathaway more.

Now I just have to tell her.

Chapter Fifty-Two

Sara

I totally missed the gala.

And I'm not even kidding. Thanks to my mother insisting I stick around until after Ryan Detweiler completed all the approval paperwork, I was already cutting my arrival close. Then I had to drop Three off at his place. Then a multi-car pileup— precipitated by some kind of major negligence on one of the driver's parts—shut down all lanes just outside the Lincoln Tunnel.

Oops.

The whole area was clogged with emergency responders, law enforcement, and investigators, not to mention everyone and their brother trying to get into the city for Christmas. Including me.

Fortunately, my parents didn't get too upset when I called them to explain what was holding me up.

I figured they'd understand. My mom and dad aren't monsters. They're Hathaways. And they were mostly just grateful

I wasn't a part of the accident—which everyone at the gala was talking about.

When I admitted I'd be running a little late, my parents took the news in stride. Unfortunately, *a little late* turned into me being stuck for three hours in a virtual parking lot. Now I'm rushing into the Winston Club, smoothing down my dress, and fluffing my hair for … absolutely nobody.

The only people still here—besides my mom and dad—are the caterers packing up the food, and a cleanup crew tackling all the wine spills and shoe scuffs.

My father spots me first, striding over to offer a hug. He's dashing and handsome in a pair of black tuxedo pants and his signature white dinner jacket.

"You okay, sweetheart?"

"I'm safe," I say, although my insides are in knots. I was already nervous about talking to my parents about Three. Then missing the gala threw a new wrench into the toolbox of my stomach.

"Well, that's all that really matters," he says as my mom comes floating around the corner. Her hair is in a perfect updo and her red gown swooshes behind her. Even after a long night of hostessing, the woman looks pageant ready.

Mrs. America: Sixty-Plus Division.

"Oh, Sara. I'm so glad you're all right." She hugs me too, on the opposite side of my father, then she takes a step back appraising me. "Lovely gown, dear. Is it new?"

"No." I look down at my skirt. "I wore this one last year."

"Really?" She furrows her brow. "You brought a dress with you to Abieville?"

"I have a new one at the tailor's, but I wasn't sure the alterations would be done in time, so I brought a couple of backup dresses in case I got delayed at the house longer than expected. Which, it turns out, I did."

"That's my girl," my dad says, patting me on the shoulder. "The future of Hathaway Cooke. Always prepared."

Oof. Now the knots in my stomach have knots.

"You must be starving," my mother chimes in, although I can't imagine eating a thing in this moment. "I had the caterers set aside a plate for you." She nods toward the swinging doors that lead to the kitchen. "We served filet mignon, artichoke, and parmesan fingerlings. All your favorites, for your birthday."

"Thanks, Mom. I wish I could've joined you."

My father grins at me gamely. "Well, there's always next year."

And the year after that. Forever and ever. I press on a smile. "So. How did your speech go?"

My mother pats his shoulder. "He was wonderful, as always."

"And the auction?"

She beams at me. "The Abieville getaway was one of the biggest hits of the evening," she says. "And we owe all that to you. I was a little worried when you weren't here to speak, but everything worked out."

"Now that's an understatement," my dad chimes in. "Your mother left out the part where we hit our highest fundraising numbers ever tonight. A new record. New goal to exceed next year."

"Wow, Dad." I grin at him. "That's incredible."

"And your *father* left out the part where he made a little addition to his speech this year," my mom says. "After sharing the usual story about the miracle of your arrival, he tacked on a harrowing narrative about you not being here because you were caught up in that dreadful Lincoln Tunnel debacle." She presses her lips together. "He played on everyone's sympathies with a new twist, since so many of them have heard the rest before."

"And it worked," my dad interjects.

"But you made it sound like our Sara could've been in peril." My mother shoots him a horrified look. "Our only child, Charles."

"*Could've*, Kate, not *was*." He turns and tosses me a wink. "So I may have laid the drama on a *tad* thick, but it was for the children. A worthy cause, wouldn't you agree?"

I hunch my shoulders. "Sure?"

"Now we'll be able to donate the most money Children's Village has ever received from a single event." He arches a brow. "Until next year."

My mother rolls her eyes, even as a smile tugs at her lips. "You're only competing with yourself, dear."

"That's just plain smart," he says. "It's a guaranteed win."

"Mom's not wrong," I say, nudging him. "You *are* pretty competitive."

"Mea culpa." He splays his hands, letting out a soft chuckle and not sounding the least bit guilty. "Now, if you two will excuse me, I'm off to tip the staff."

As he heads across the room, pushing through the doors into the kitchen, my mom rounds on me, her brow hitched. "You know, you're almost as competitive as he is, Sara."

I lay a hand over my collarbone in mock protest. "Moi?"

"Vous." She huffs out a laugh. "Between the two of you, I've lived the past twenty-nine years in the middle of an overachiever sandwich."

"Huh. That's a little bit like the pot calling the kettle black, isn't it?" I tease. "You pushed me to succeed almost as hard as Dad did."

"Hmm." She pulls down her brow. "You think so?"

"Of course I do!" I gape at her, surprised she might be unaware of this. "You were always super-focused on my grades and test scores and applications. You wanted me to get accepted to all the top schools too. Maybe even more than Dad and I did."

"Only because I never had a chance to," she blurts. Then she slams her lips shut.

"Mom." I take a beat to examine her face. "You never had a chance to *what*?"

She glances around the room, although there's no one else within earshot. "Believe me, Sara, I'm very happy being Mrs. Charles Hathaway. I always have been, and I always will be." She lowers her voice, and her throat begins to flush. "But my entire adult life centered around being his wife, and then your mother. I oversee our home, not our bank accounts. That's how I was raised —to be the support system of a family. A homemaker. And I wouldn't have it any other way. But maybe ..." She inclines her head closer to my ear. "*Maybe* a part of me wanted my only daughter to have ... options."

"Wow," I say a little breathless, mostly because the rest of the air is leaving my lungs. It takes me a moment to fill them back up again. "How come you've never said any of this before?"

She squares her shoulders before responding. "I suppose I didn't want to sound like I was complaining." She tips her chin. "And I'm not sure I knew exactly how I felt myself. Not until my therapist asked about me and *my* mother. Then we got onto the subject of expectations, and the next thing you know ..." She shrugs.

"You're in therapy?" I stare at my mother, wide-eyed. This, more than almost anything else in the past few days, might be the most shocking. "I mean, I think it's great. But you have a thera-pist? For real?"

"For most of this year." She offers a prim nod. "Doctor Hahn is fabulous. Didn't I tell you about her?"

"No. You most certainly did not tell me."

"Well, you really should try therapy yourself, Sara." She says this like the fact that therapy can be effective is some kind of new information. "It's done wonders for our marriage."

"I'll bet." I cough out a laugh. "Dr. Hahn sure seems to be bringing out the honesty in you."

"Now, Sara." She lays a palm on my shoulder. "I don't want you to think I haven't been perfectly content with my life. *More* than content."

"I know that."

"I *love* my life."

"I know that too, Mom."

Her eyes laser in on mine. "Do you, though?"

"Yes." I squint up at her, confused. "I just said that. I know you love your life. And I'm so glad."

"No." She meets my gaze again, her eyes softening this time. "I mean do *you* love *your* life?"

Oh. OH.

I draw in a rush of air. "Of course I do."

"Because I have to say"—she tips her chin—"you haven't seemed truly happy in a very long time. Not since ... well..." She lets her sentence die off.

"Since when?"

Her brows pinch together. "Since that last summer you and I were in Abieville."

Whoa.

"That's why I talked your father into buying the Peabodys' lake house," she goes on. "I wanted a project, and I thought the investment would be sound—you know I enjoy a good renovation—but I also have such fond memories of that place. I felt like you and I had fun there, even when Daddy had to leave during the week. Just the two of us." Her voice is quiet now, and a dull ache leaks into my heart.

"You're right, Mom. We did have fun together. And I *was* happy."

More pinching of the brow. "Until you broke up with that boy."

My stomach lurches. "Three broke up with me, Mom. You know that."

"You're right. I do." Her responding nod is tight. "And I knew you were sad back then, but you refused to talk to me about it. Then you were off to college, and you got so busy, and ... things changed. You changed. Everything changed." She sniffs, then squares her shoulders. "*We* grew apart."

"I grew up, Mom."

"Yes, you did." Her eyes scan my face, and the edges begin to shine. "And I'm so very proud of you. So is your father. In fact—" She casts a glance across the ballroom just as he emerges from the swinging doors. "He can't wait to bring you onboard at Hathaway Cooke. So don't tell him I said anything, but ... you got the job!"

Another lurch of my stomach. "Mom."

"What?" She blinks at me. "I was a big part of your journey too, you know. Why should your father be the one who always gets to share the good news?"

We both fall silent as he approaches. "Hello, beautiful girls." He breaks into a grin. "Ready to head out? I'd like to get my family home before Christmas."

My mother glances at me, then she pats at her sleek updo. "I believe it *is* Christmas, Charles."

"Is it?" He checks his watch. "Well, what do you know? You're right, Kate. It's past midnight." He turns to me, his smile faltering. "I guess we missed your entire birthday, Sara. For the first time since the day you were born."

"I'm so sorry, dear." My mother's lips curve into a frown. "We'll just have to make the gala extra-special for you next year."

"Actually"—I bob my head—"I had a pretty great birthday, anyway."

My dad cocks his head. "In Abieville?"

"Alone?" My mother blinks.

"Let's get home and get some sleep," I say. "We've got a lot to catch up on tomorrow."

Chapter Fifty-Three

Sara

"So you're saying he overheard our *entire* conversation?" My mother darts a glance from me over to my father.

It's Christmas morning, and they're seated on the Chesterfield sofa. I'm slouched in the wingback armchair closest to the tree. This might not have been the optimal time to share everything about Three, but I owe them all the facts: the good, the bad, and the concussion.

"He didn't intend to, but the window was open when he came to pick me up, so ..." I pause to take a sip of eggnog from my Cindy-Lou Who mug. My mom's clutching a mug featuring Max, from the part of the movie when the poor dog's stuck wearing homemade antlers. My dad's got the Grinch mug, but he hasn't touched a drop since I started spilling my guts about the past few days.

"And now you think *we're* to blame for what happened between you two?" My mother's hand flies to her throat.

"No. That's not what I meant at all."

My dad pulls down his brow. "I don't suppose the boy has any actual proof of the alleged interaction." His frown means business, but it's hard to take him seriously when we're all dressed in pajamas covered in cartoon reindeers.

Kind of like the kitchen linens I burned.

Talk about extra.

But our holiday traditions—even our silly matching pajamas—are just more proof of my parents' love for me. That's been a burden sometimes, and also a blessing. The hard part's being honest about both sides of the coin.

"Can you please switch off the lawyer talk, Dad?" A bundle of nerves continues to fizz behind my ribs. "I'm not accusing you of anything."

"I should hope not." He leans forward and sets his mug on the glass-topped coffee table. "I can't be expected to remember the details about something I may or may not have said more than a decade ago."

"I wasn't asking for specifics, Dad. I'm just curious." I swallow hard. This is the part that might get a little sticky. "Is Three right? Were you really *that* worried he might hold me back? Did you think my whole future was at risk?"

"Yes." My dad shifts his jaw. "Yes, and yes."

"Wow." Okay, then. At least he's not shying away from the truth. "That's awfully direct."

"I'm a direct man," he says. "And an honest one." He settles back against the couch, and crosses his slippered feet. "I may not remember my exact words, but I haven't forgotten how distracted you were back then. Far too distracted. It got worse every summer. Your mother and I weren't about to let you throw away years of prep school and private tutors—all those exclusive interviews at top universities—over some infatuation with a boy you barely knew."

I take a beat, slowly processing my father's admission. I have to give my dad credit for owning his part in this, not trying to deflect.

Still, he is wrong on one important count. "I knew him, Dad."

"Even so." He folds his arms across his chest. "The lake house was just a vacation spot for our family. A place to escape from reality, not build a future. You had concrete, hard-to-reach goals, and Abieville wasn't in the blueprints."

"It's true," my mother chimes in. "So when you and Three broke up, your father and I thought ..." She adjusts the collar of her pajama top. "That just seemed like the right thing happening at the right time."

"It was." My father grunts. "And for the record, you've built the exact life you always wanted. Every dream you've ever worked for is finally coming true."

I nod in partial agreement even as a belt of tension tightens around my chest. This all makes sense, and I can't fault my parents' logic. But there's something else I have to ask before I can move on.

"Did you ever think ..." I look down at my lap. "Did you feel like the Fullers weren't good enough for the Hathaways?"

"Not *good* enough?"

I lift my gaze to meet his.

"Absolutely not," he insists. "And I'm a little insulted by the question."

"I'm so sorry," I say, because I truly am. Three admitted this could've been a conclusion he drew from his own insecurities. And I owe my parents the same benefit of the doubt I'm giving him.

"To be fair," my mother says, "we didn't really *know* the Fullers back then. Or now, for that matter."

"Either way," my father adds, "we don't judge people by their last names."

"Although I do like a good search on an ancestry site," my mother chimes in. "Family trees are fascinating. And I can't help it if the Hathaways have a particularly rich history."

"Before you ask," my father says, "she's *not* talking about wealth, Sara. Your mother and I value a man's contributions to the world, not his wallet." He takes a beat and shoots a glance at my mom. "Or *her* wallet. Women contribute just as much as men."

"They do," I agree, and the belt of tightness around my chest loosens a notch. "And for the record, Three Fuller contributes more to the people in his life than just about anyone I've ever known." I let a hint of a smile curve my lips. "But he *also* sent a donation with me for Children's Village. You can confirm that later if you want. The check is from Bradford Fuller."

"We believe you, Sara," my mother says.

My father rubs at his chin. "The question is, do *you* believe *us?*"

"I want to believe you," I say, aiming for total honesty.

"Hmm." My dad lifts an eyebrow. "Way to hedge your bets, counselor."

"Thanks." I tip my chin. "I learned from the best."

My mother takes a sip of her eggnog, then sets her mug down. "You know, your father and I only ever wanted you to be happy, Sara."

"I know that, and I'm so grateful." I release a long sigh, thinking it would be easy to stop right here, but I'm determined to speak the whole truth and nothing but the truth right now. "What if the things that make me happy don't align with yours anymore?"

My father clears his throat. "I suppose that depends." There's an edge to his voice, like a serrated knife slicing through an agenda. "We're still your parents. And you're still our only child. So your mother and I are always going to have opinions."

"Opinions are great," I say. "*If* I ask for them. But what I could really do without from now on is all the … pressure."

"Pressure?" My mom's brow lifts. "Us?"

I stifle a guffaw. They can be so clueless sometimes.

Then again, can't we all?

"Sara." My dad steeples his fingers in his lap. "What you call pressure, your mother and I call support."

"Encouragement," she adds.

"Inspiration," he says.

"And I don't disagree with you." I tilt my head. "But I grew up with this sort of ... unspoken assumption that I'd be a carbon copy of Dad. So I never slowed down to ask myself what *I* wanted." I pause for a beat, my fingernails digging into my palms. "I applied to the same schools. Went after the same scholarships. Won the same awards." I meet my mom's gaze. "I soaked up all your positive reinforcement too. I got so caught up in the high of pleasing you, I convinced everyone I wanted to *be* you. Even myself."

"Well." My mother throws her hands in the air like she's giving up. "I had *absolutely* no idea you felt like this."

"I didn't either." My eyes soften. "I think we were *all* just operating with the evidence presented to us."

My father clears his throat. "The partners at Hathaway Cooke are about to extend you an offer tomorrow." He grips his knees. "Are you saying you don't want to accept it?"

I slide off my chair, moving around the table to kneel in front of him. "I'm saying nothing you and Mom taught me has gone to waste. Not a single lesson. But the most important one *might* be happening right now."

He exhales. "And what lesson is that?"

I hitch my shoulders. "Letting go of expectations."

A small yelp slips out of my mom, and she fumbles for my hand. Then she reaches for my father, so we're all holding hands like a little triangle of people in reindeer pajamas.

"You know, the key to all this *really* is better communication," she says. "That's what Doctor Hahn always says. We just need to CO. MMU. NI. CATE."

My father shoots me a look, then he smiles at my mom. "That's quite the revolutionary conclusion, Kate. How much does Doctor Hahn charge per session?"

I bite back a laugh. "I know this has been a lot to take in. Just, please." I squeeze my parents' hands. "Try to keep an open mind, okay?"

Even as I say this, I realize I need to give them at least as much grace and patience as I'm asking for Three and me. Still, in time, I hope they'll understand why I fell for him.

Twice.

Over breakfast, I tell them all the ways Three and I have taken care of each other these past few days. How he treats his family and friends, not to mention all the people of Abieville. As I go on, a wave of warmth crests in me—a fresh swell of love for Three Fuller. A man as wonderful as he is thinks I'm worthy. He makes me feel precious just as I am. Protected. And cherished.

The feeling is entirely mutual.

More than anything, I want to rush to his side and spill out every emotion crowding my heart. I want to tell him my future won't be complete without him. That I love him with my whole soul. But he's hours away, and I'm with my mom and dad asking them to trust me. So for now, I say all this to my parents.

The ones who loved me first.

Chapter Fifty-Four

Three

"Merry Christmas."

I'm vaguely aware of Sara's lips brushing mine, and the smell of something sweet hovering in the air. "Carol of the Bells" hums in the background. Obviously, I'm dreaming. So I groan, shifting on the couch and willing myself to stay asleep.

"Three."

"Noooo," I mumble. "I don't want to wake up."

"Merry Christmas," the soft voice says again.

Wait. What?

I bolt upright so quickly, I almost bonk Sara's head.

Just what we need. Another concussion.

"Wait. Are you real?" I croak, rubbing at my sleep-crusted eyes. I must've drifted off when Kevin McAllister was dealing with the Wet Bandits for the second time.

"I am."

"I thought I was dreaming."

Sara's perched beside me on the couch in yet another pair of

Christmas pajamas, this set with a reindeer print, including Rudolf with a big red nose. On the coffee table next to my laptop is a plate of frosted cookies she must've brought from home—gingerbread, sugar, snickerdoodle—all covered in plastic wrap.

"Nope. Not dreaming." She reaches out to stroke my messy bedhead. "But if you really want to sleep more ..."

"I don't," I blurt, lurching forward to gather her into my arms. She smells like fresh shampoo and clean laundry. I never want to let her go again. Eventually, though, Sara detaches herself from my barnacle grip, leaning back just far enough to gift me with the best smile of my life.

"Hi," she says.

"Hi." I grin back at her. "When did you get here?"

"Just now."

"Did you knock?"

"I let myself in."

"And you put the Pandora Christmas station on?"

"I did."

"What time is it?"

"You're sure full of questions this morning." Her mouth twitches. "But for the record, it's almost one o'clock."

"Seriously?" I do a quick calculation, but my brain's still sleep-drunk. "That means I've been out for—like—a lot of hours."

"I tried calling you late last night," she says, "and again first thing this morning, but you didn't answer. Either time."

I glance at my phone stuck between my laptop and the plate of cookies. "I must've been pretty dead to the world not to hear."

"Well. You've had a busy week." Her shoulders pitch up. "But I did get your text last night that you were over here, watching *Home Alone*."

"Oh, there were multiple viewings." I roll my neck around to stretch out the stiffness. "Kevin McAllister and I rocked around the Christmas tree more than once. He's quite the prankster."

"He sure is." Sara lets out a chuckle, eyes sparkling at me. "Anyway, I would've been here sooner, but I had a celebratory breakfast with my mom and dad, then raced here as fast as possible."

"You raced here?" I screw my face up in a mock scolding. "*That* doesn't sound safe."

Sara's mouth angles sideways. "Your honor, I'd like to rephrase. What I *meant* to say is, the drive back to Abieville was executed slowly and safely."

Your honor. Right.

"So, did your dad give you the job, then?" My body tenses waiting for the answer. "Is that the reason for the celebratory breakfast?"

Sara glances at our tree, twinkling by the window. On the other side of the glass, a marshmallow world sits bathed in white. "The breakfast was about Christmas," she says. "And my birthday. Plus the best night of fundraising the Hathaway Gala's ever had."

"That's amazing!" I nod, genuinely happy for her. "And really great for Children's Village."

"It is," she agrees. "Also ... I *did* get the job at Hathaway Cooke."

I meet her gaze and my pulse picks up. This new position means I'll either be moving to the city, or spending a whole lot of time apart from her now. "Congratulations, Sara." I muster up a slow smile. "You deserve this."

"I'd like to rephrase." She shakes her head. "What I meant to say is, the *partners* will be extending me an official offer tomorrow, but my dad let the news slip."

"That's still huge," I say, reaching for her hand. "You've been working toward this goal for as long as I've known you."

She quirks a brow. "Longer."

"Well, I have some news too," I tell her, squeezing her hand. "I've been doing a little research." I nod to indicate my laptop. "And you might be surprised to learn how many high school history teachers are needed in your neck of the woods."

"That doesn't surprise me in the slightest." She shrugs. "Teachers are incredibly important. And one high school history teacher, in particular, is incredibly important *to me.*"

"I sure hope you're talking about yours truly."

Sara ducks her head, feigning shyness. "You know I am, Mr. Fuller."

"Good." A grin creeps across my face. "Then I assume you won't object if I apply for teaching jobs out your way for next school year?"

"I do, in fact object," she says.

My smile wavers. "Wait. Are we still joking around?"

"I'm not." She lifts her shoulders. "I don't want you to apply to teaching positions in the city."

Whoa.

My gut twinges, and I pull my hand away, struggling to absorb what she's saying. I didn't see this coming, and I want to respect her wishes, but I also need to be honest about how I feel. "Okay, I get it. You probably think I'm moving too fast." I gulp down the boulder threatening to block my throat. "But I'm going to plead my case now, because I didn't fight for you ten years ago. Back then, I told you I wasn't looking for something serious. I said I had no interest in a long-distance relationship. I claimed I didn't feel the same way about you as you felt about me. But I wasn't telling the truth. I *did* want those things. And I *still* want them. Well, everything except the long-distance part. The truth is, Sara Hathaway, I just want to be near you ... forever ... no matter what. And if that means me moving to the city, then I'll move to the city. Please."

She blinks at me, and her lips part. "Three."

"In other words, I'm not just applying for a new teaching job. I'm applying to be your man." I reach for her hands again, holding them both in mine. "In case I haven't made that abundantly clear."

She offers up a small laugh. "Oh, you're being the *most* abundant right now. But I still don't want you to move to the city."

I stare at her, bewildered. "But ... why?"

"Because *I* don't want to live there. And I'm going to turn down the position at Hathaway Cooke."

"Wait, what?" My jaw drops.

"I'd like to rephrase," she says. "I *do* want to be an attorney. That part hasn't changed. But when I imagine my vision for an ideal future, an eighty-hour work week just isn't a part of the picture."

"Eighty-*plus*."

"Ah." A smirk tugs at her lips. "So you *were* paying attention."

I quirk a brow. "Abundantly."

"Anyway, I've been doing some thinking ..." She takes the tip of her finger and touches it to my forehead, slowly drawing a gentle line downward, along my nose, over my lips, across my chin, all the way to my chest, where she lays a palm directly over my heart, which—I'm pretty sure—is about to pound right through my ribcage.

"Thinking about what?"

She meets my gaze. "What if I moved *here*, set up my own office in Abieville, and worked independently for myself?"

Cue my chest cavity exploding.

"I could take on cases that really matter to me," she continues. "Family law, not corporate. I'd like to specialize in adoption and foster care, but also do wills, trusts, estate planning." She tilts her head, and her eyes are shining so much brighter than they ever did when she talked about Hathaway Cooke. "What do you think?"

"I think you're brilliant," I blurt, and I mean it. Still, a rope of unease is coiling around my middle. "What about your parents, though?" I swallow hard, forcing myself to hold her gaze. "Do they know about any of this?"

She nods. "I already told them everything."

"Wow." I blow out a long gust of air. "I wish I could've been with you when you did."

"Me too." She gives my hands another squeeze.

"So." I take a beat. "How did they react when you told them?"

"Actually—" She pauses for a breath. "They want to talk to you."

Chapter Fifty-Five

Three

Plot twist: Sara's mom and dad have been parked in the driveway this entire time waiting to be invited in. To a house they own.

Apparently, once Sara explained what went down with us ten years ago—plus our last few days together, not to mention her plans to relocate to Abieville—the Hathaways insisted on coming here to have a face-to-face conversation with me.

Gulp.

As a side note: their driver has the day off, so Mr. Hathaway actually drove his family here himself in their town car. For three hours. On Christmas.

Big gulp.

I hear a car door slam out front, and my heart starts thrashing. Or, more accurately, my heart starts thrashing even *more*, because my engines started running pretty hot the moment Sara said she wanted to move here.

For the record, I'm no longer worried about the Hathaways saying something negative about me. Even if they did, I'm not that same kid with a chip on his shoulder I was back then. Much as I'd like to gain Sara's parents' approval, their opinions can't sway what I know to be true about myself anymore. And anyway, I have to believe Sara wouldn't bring her parents down here if they were going to thoroughly object to us.

Either way, if we're going to have a future together, we'd better believe in each other beyond a shadow of a doubt.

She flashes me a quick smile as she pushes through the door just ahead of her parents. They're both sporting winter-white pants and turtleneck sweaters that look a tad on the itchy side. As if this moment isn't awkward enough, I'm still wearing the joggers and hoodie I had on when I fell asleep last night. I stand to meet them, extending a hand. Sara's dad reaches me first.

"Merry Christmas, sir." I immediately regret the opening line, but my greeting is nothing if not accurate.

"Hello, Three." His grip is firm, maybe a little extra firm, which makes sense under the circumstances.

I nod at Sara's mom, my eyes bouncing between her and her firm-handed husband. "It's good to see you again, Mrs. Hathaway."

"Please." She offers me a tentative smile. "We're all adults. Call us Kate and Charles."

"I will." This is what I say, but I've already decided I *might* try not to use their names today. Or ever. "Thanks for coming all the way out here." I glance out the window. "Quite the drive."

"Sure." Charles surveys the room, like he's seeing it for the first time since the renovation. Then again, he probably is. "I used to make the same trip back and forth every weekend over the summers we stayed here."

I duck my head. "I guess you did."

"Anyway, we're glad to get the chance to catch up with you," Katherine pipes up. "And the place looks wonderful."

Sara offers to give them a tour, including a stop by the storage room. I stay behind, building a fire in the fireplace, and soaking up the surreal pivot this day has taken. When the three of them return to the living room, Sara joins me over by the mantel, reaching for my hand. She gives my fingers a quick press, and I immediately feel more at ease. That's the effect she has on me in less than a week.

Well. Less than a week, plus four summers.

"Should we have a seat?" Katherine suggests. She and Charles each take opposite sides of the couch, and Sara moves over to sit between them. While the Hathaways are creating their own little coed triumvirate, I take the lone armchair.

I miss Sara's hand already.

"If you don't mind"—Charles tugs at the neck of his sweater —"Katherine and I would like to clear something up with you right away." I nod in wordless agreement, and he darts quick peeks sideways at his wife and daughter. "Sara shared with us what you overheard here—many years ago—and I'll be honest with you, Three, I don't remember that conversation."

Right.

I'm not surprised the details aren't burned into Charles Hathaway's brain. After all, he got his way that day. Within hours, Sara and I were over, which is exactly what the man wanted. Mission accomplished.

"But while the specifics may have escaped me," he adds, "I *do* recall my general sentiments at the time. And I was not in favor of you and Sara pursuing a serious relationship."

Another nod from me. "Yes, I figured that out."

"I'd like to claim you misheard me," he continues, "but that wouldn't necessarily be true. I probably did say exactly what you remember. And if I sounded judgmental, or my words knocked you down, I'm sorry."

"Thank you, sir."

"I didn't come here to make excuses." He casts a quick glance at Sara, then his eyes swing back to me. "But if you have a daughter someday, maybe you'll understand where I was coming from." He lays both palms on his knees and leans forward. "We spent our summers here in Abieville, but as time went by, Katherine and I felt like we were losing Sara the other nine months of the year. We were afraid her focus in college would be compromised. That she'd end up sacrificing her goals. So we thought—"

"Dad," Sara interrupts. "We've already discussed this. Three and I did. Then I talked to you and Mom. So there's no need to rehash what you said and your reasons for it all over again. That's not why you came here."

"You're right." His jaw shifts. "In any case, I'd like to hear from you, Three. This is all a lot to take in, you know. Sara came back to Abieville on a family errand completely unrelated to you. And yet, you two ended up reconnecting. Unexpectedly."

"Well, I might've had *some* idea I'd see him," Sara quips. "And I'm a grownup, Dad. I don't need anyone else to understand us but us."

"Grownup or not," Katherine says, turning to face Sara, "you're still our baby." Her voice cracks, and she flicks her gaze over to me. "All Charles and I care about—all we've ever cared about—is our daughter's happiness."

I clear the jagged edge in my throat. "Then I'm glad to report, we have the same goal."

"That's obvious, just seeing the two of you together." Katherine's eyes glimmer with unshed tears. "Sara's never looked so happy."

Charles grunts. "So you'll take care of her." The words are a statement, not a question, which I hope means he already believes this. Still, I want to do my part to remove any lingering doubts. It's time to plead my case.

"I'm a hard worker, sir, and I make a good, honest living." My bones feel tight in my torso, but I carry on. "I intend to do whatever it takes to provide for your daughter. Always."

"Same," Sara pipes up. "I mean, I want to provide for us, too."

My gaze sweeps over to her, and the warmth of her smile is a blanket on my insides. "How about we take care of each other?"

She lifts her palm and lays it on her chest just over her heart. "Deal."

When I do the same, mirroring her, Sara sucks in a breath and points across the table. "The cuff."

I glance down to the sleeve of my shirt now riding up my forearm. "Oh. This. Yes." Around my wrist is the same leather cuff Sara gave me for my birthday years ago. "I still have yours too." I nod to indicate the only present under the tree. "And I guess I just ruined the surprise."

"You kept them both? All this time?" Her questions are breathless but full of joy.

My lip curves up on one side. "I told you I never got over you."

Sara hops up, squeezing between her mother's legs and the coffee table. At the same time, I slowly rise from the chair. So when she leaps into my arms, I'm ready to catch her.

I'll always catch Sara.

She wraps her legs around my middle, and plants the sweetest kiss on my mouth.

"I'd like to rephrase." I grin at her. "I never stopped loving you."

Chapter Fifty-Six

Sara's Voicemail: December 31st

From Bristol: Happy New Year's Eve! What are you and your gorgeous man up to tonight? Besides being ridiculously adorable, I mean? Ugh. I'm so jealous of you two. Actually, no. Forget I said that. I'm not ready to settle down yet. I AM, however, ready to be a maid of honor. I know it's early, so no pressure if you won't be asking me for another year or so. But I do look good in pink and I will say yes in case you're wondering.

From The Queen: Sorry we missed your call. Daddy and I were on a no-phones date. Our plan was to finish dinner and beat the crowds to be back home well before the ball drops, which I'm pleased to say we accomplished. But I did want to tell you I've been doing a bit of research, and you'll never guess what I discovered: The name Fuller is listed on the Mayflower manifest, which means our forefathers and Three's could've been on the boat together. How delightful is that? Anyway, kisses. And Happy New Year, dear.

. . .

From Dad: Hello, Sara. I had a talk with the partners this week, and they'd like to pursue that project you mentioned—the possible mentorship/scholarship program between Hathaway Cooke and the kids at Youth Save. We decided we could maintain our current program with the DAR and add the new one you proposed. But we're hoping you'd be willing to take the lead on that as an independent contractor. Call me to discuss the details if you're interested. But no work talk until Monday. I'm taking the whole weekend off.

Nella: Hi, Sara! We're docked in Hawaii, so I hope this message goes through. I don't know if Three mentioned this to you, but I got my real estate license last year, and I'd love to help you find office space either in Abieville or somewhere nearby if you're up for it. Pro bono, of course, as the lawyers say. We can chat when I get back from the cruise. Speaking of which, can you keep a secret? Text or call me if you get this.

* * *

"Best New Year's Day ever," Three says, pulling me down onto the couch. We just finished dinner and we're at his place now since the lake house is officially a Platinum Stays home.

The first renters arrive tomorrow morning, on January 2nd. My mom is beyond pleased with herself.

When the cleaning crew came to detail the place, I suggested we move our Christmas tree over to Three's house. That turned out to be an unrealistic pipe dream, though. The popcorn garland wasn't exactly fresh, and too many needles were falling off. Plus we didn't have a truck.

But Three and I *did* build our own snowman in his front yard this week. Make that a snow-woman. Her name is Henrietta.

She's got Oreo eyes and a carrot nose too. She and her boyfriend, Henry, are currently negotiating a long-distance relationship.

"Best *week* ever." I drop a kiss on Three's nose, then I snuggle even closer to him, my cheek burrowing into his chest.

"I won't argue with that." His arms wrap around me, and I've never felt so warm and safe and secure. Like a hibernating bear.

"You want to watch a movie?" I peek up at the clock to check the time. The TV below it is still playing Christmas music. I'd begged to keep the holiday station on for one more day, and Three happily agreed.

He shakes his head now, placing his fingers under my chin. Then he gently tips my face up to meet his. "I have a better idea."

As his lips find mine, I shut my eyes surrendering to the sweetness. His kiss is tender at first and completely perfect—after all, we've been practicing for days—but I want more. Wiggling free from his embrace, I flip around and climb onto his lap. Then I position myself so my head hovers over his, and I'm gazing down into his eyes. "Hi, there."

"Hi." A low moan rumbles in the back of his throat, and he sits up too, while keeping one arm around my back, strong and steady. Like it's meant to be there forever. With his free hand, he reaches up to brush my hair from my face. Then he slides his palm to the nape of my neck, drawing my face down slowly.

The anticipation is agony.

When our mouths finally meet, just the barest of grazes, he breathes into me. "I love this."

Another brush of our lips. "Me too."

"Wait. I'd like to rephrase," he says. "I love *you*, Sara Hathaway." As his lips slide to my throat, emotions surge up from deep inside me, crowding my ribs. "I've always loved you," he murmurs against my skin. "And I always will."

"I love you, too," I whisper. "So much." When my voice catches, he pulls away, and we lock eyes.

"If you'll let me," he says, "I'll keep loving you a little bit more every single day for the rest of our lives."

Tears well in my eyes, and I nod and sniffle, raining kisses all over his forehead. I only pause when I reach the point of impact with the fire extinguisher. The spot's still bruised, but it's definitely healing. I press my lips there, gently, to honor the moment that brought us together again.

As the song changes to "I'll Be Home for Christmas," we both break into smiles. Minutes later, we're still holding each other when footsteps and voices sound outside.

"Huh." Three glances at the entryway. "It's a week late for carolers."

I climb off his lap just in time for the handle to rattle. Then Mr. and Mrs. Fuller throw open the door. They both bustle inside, with Nella close on their heels. For several seconds, Three's completely silent, frozen and gaping at his family.

"Surprise!" I squeal. After another stunned beat, Three leaps up from the couch. Then the Fullers converge in the middle of the room. A massive group hug of maximum love. Eventually, Three's mom peers over her shoulder at me.

"Don't just stand there acting like you didn't know this was coming, Sara." She grins. "Get on over here and join the Original Fuller House hug."

"Yes, ma'am!" I come to Three's side and he wraps an arm around me, pulling me close.

His father bobs his head. "Nice to see you again, Sara."

"Welcome back!" Nella hoots.

Three sweeps his gaze around the room, taking in the cluster of Fullers and me. "I have no idea what's happening," he chokes. His eyes are wet, and his voice goes gravelly.

"The cruise was wonderful on the way to Hawaii," his mom says. "And we all loved being on the island. But we missed the holidays with you, dear. We'd seen enough of the ocean already, and the rest of the family understood why we wanted to fly back early."

His father clears his throat. "Plus I wasn't sure you'd remember to check my pipes, son. No offense."

"None taken." Three shakes his head, a bewildered chuckle slipping out. "So did you all just *Home Alone* me?"

Nella chirps, "We sure did."

I break into a laugh of pure joy. "And you make a pretty cute Kevin McCallister."

Epilogue

ONE YEAR LATER

Three

I'm pacing around outside yet another door—waiting for Sara—again. Except this time, my heart's so packed with happiness, I feel like all four chambers are about to burst. The thing is, Sara's bladder felt the same way. That's why she's in the bathroom now with Nella and Bristol.

They're helping her pee.

Apparently that's hard to do in a wedding dress.

The brand-new Mrs. Fuller and I have been married just long enough to take pictures outside the church, then caravan over to the reception along with the rest of the wedding party. Doing the math, that means we took our vows about an hour ago, but I *feel* like I've loved this woman forever.

It took us a decade, but everything worked out. Sara and I are right where we're supposed to be.

Minus the bathroom wall.

In the lobby, enormous double doors open, sending a gust of wintery air toward the registration desk. The entrance is dripping with colored lights. Christmas music spills across the way. I'm in the hall that separates the rest of the inn from the Tavern. Our guests are already inside the main room waiting for us to start the reception.

According to the seating chart my bride labored over, our groomsmen—Mac, Brady, and Kenny—are at Table Two with their wives. Ford was with them, last time I checked, with an empty chair reserved for Bristol beside him. She's the maid of honor. Ford's my best man. They've been eyeing each other since she got to Abieville.

Not that it matters, but Sara and I approve.

"There you are!" My mother slips through the Tavern door and joins me in the hallway. "Where's my beautiful daughter-in-law?" She picks a bit of dust off my coat and adjusts the red rose in my lapel. "Everybody's waiting for the DJ to introduce the happy couple."

Everybody.

Man, I love the that word. I love the people. Almost as much as I adore my bride.

"We'll be in soon. Sara just needed a minute." I nod at the bathroom, and bite back a laugh at the thought of a single wedding dress requiring three people to navigate. "How are things going at Table One?"

"Oh, just lovely." My mother's smile is warm, if a little on the crooked side. "The Hathaways have been telling everyone the Christmas tree here at the inn rivals the one in Rockefeller Plaza."

I cock a brow. "They actually said that?"

"They did." My mother shrugs. "I think they *might* be exaggerating. But they do mean well."

"Yeah, they do," I say. And I really believe that.

"Katherine also filled us in on the many, *many* preparations for this year's big Hathaway Gala." My mom smooths her hands down her floor-length dress. "She also said this would be perfect for the occasion."

"She's right, Mom. You look beautiful."

"Well." She presses a hand to her cheek. "Thank you, but

today's not about me. And the gala isn't either. Speaking of which, I'm glad they pushed the date until after your honeymoon."

"Yeah. Me too." I bob my head. "There's talk about moving the event permanently, so Christmas Eve and Sara's birthday can be separate from the fundraiser, but that's a big ship to steer in a new direction."

"Either way, it's a wonderful cause, and we'll be thrilled to attend." Her nose twitches. "Well, *I'll* be thrilled. Your father's not so sure he wants to put on a tux again."

This pulls a laugh out of me. "Tell Dad he's gotta get some use out of that thing until Nella and Carver finally get their act together and get married."

My mother squawks, then lowers her voice. "From your lips to God's ears."

Just then, the bathroom door flies open, and Nella and Bristol scurry out into the hall. They've got their hair up in matching twists, and their satin dresses shine.

"Everything all right in there, ladies?" I peek over their heads as the door slowly shuts behind them. "With the dress ... and ... the rest of it?"

"Sara's coming," Nella says. "She just has to reapply her lipstick."

"Yeah." Bristol snorts. "*Someone* keeps kissing it off."

We all chuckle at this, but the way Bristol and Ford have been getting along, I get the feeling she might be losing some lipstick herself tonight.

I'll never tell.

"Oh!" My mother flutters her hands in my direction. "That reminds me. I'm supposed to let you know the florist hung some mistletoe over the dance floor. Everyone's expecting you to kiss during the first song."

"Thanks for the heads-up." I wag my eyebrows. "I'll be sure to warn Sara."

"Want us to wait for you two before we go in?" Nella asks.

"Nah. You all go ahead," I say. "I want to be alone with my wife for a moment."

They disappear into the Tavern at the same time Sara floats out into the hallway. She's a vision in white—all silk and seed pearls and smiles—plus the leather cuff that matches the one I never take off. I may never get over the sight of her. Or the fact that we finally belong to each other.

"Hey there, *husband*." She draws the word out like she's savoring it. "Sorry about that little pit stop."

I tug her into my arms. "And I'm sorry about your lipstick."

"What about my lipstick?"

"I'm *about* to mess it up."

"Wait!" She throws a hand up between us and presses her palm against my chest, but she can't stop laughing and her eyes are all lit up.

So I pull her even closer. "I think we've waited long enough."

"Be gentle with me," she whispers.

I cup her chin lifting her face to mine. "Your wish is my command." Then, with all the love in my bursting heart, I tenderly kiss the bride.

Her lips are sweetness and spice. Fire and ice. Sara's every color on the spectrum. And since I already know there's mistletoe above the dance floor, I want this kiss to be just for us.

When we finally break away to catch our breath, I couldn't care less that my mouth is smeared with some shade of lipstick called *apple* or *chimney* or *cherry Chapstick*.

"Hold on." Sara studies my face, then draws her thumb across my lips, but her gentle touch accomplishes less cleaning of lipstick and more ... caressing of my mouth. "I adore this mess," she tells me softly.

A low groan sounds in the back of my throat. "If we don't get into that reception now," I tell her, "I may just throw you over my shoulder and take you home."

Heat flickers behind her eyes. "I may not mind."

"Don't tempt me, wife," I growl.

"Hmm." Her lips slip into a mock pout. "My parents *did* pay a lot to rent this place out, though."

"They did."

She draws her lip under her teeth. "And I suppose you're worth the wait."

"So are you." The words come out gruff, choked with emotion. Quite frankly, I'd wait for this woman forever.

So I slide my hand into hers, and together we head into the reception to greet our guests. When we enter, the DJ's playing some old classic love song. I think it's Frank Sinatra. As soon as he spots us, he plucks up his microphone. "Friends and family of the bride and groom," he announces. "Please help me give a big round of applause for the newly minted Mr. and Mrs. Fuller!"

The crowd goes wild, hooting and hollering, and clapping their brains out. But instead of moving directly onto the dance floor, I lead Sara over to the DJ platform and reach for the microphone myself. The DJ grins and passes it to me, lowering the music. I take a deep breath, and survey the room full of beaming faces. Our wedding guests. Everyone I care about on earth gathered in one place.

For us.

"Hello, there!" I boom into the mic, then I yank it away and lower my voice to avoid any screeching feedback. "Today I stand before you as the happiest man who's ever lived." My voice cracks a little, and I shift my weight. "That's thanks in part to all of you, but especially thanks to her." I clutch Sara's hand and hold it up high, grinning like a total fool. "Ladies and gentlemen." I turn and bow to her. "My wife."

Everybody cheers, and the DJ starts playing, "All I Want For Christmas is You."

Truer words never belted out, Mariah.

I don't want anything but Sara.

As I guide her onto the dance floor, I've never felt more complete. More hopeful. More at home. And when we launch into the choreography she talked me into learning, I don't even care that I've never looked more ridiculous. I've also never been more in love.

Midway through the song, a low murmur starts among the guests, eventually building to a chant.

"Mistletoe! Mistletoe! Mistletoe!"

Of course.

How could I forget we're dancing directly under the mistletoe? And apparently the crowd demands I do something about it. So I glance at Sara and a bright smile breaks across her face. She stops mid-step, twirling toward me until she lands securely my arms.

"Hi, husband," she chirps.

"Hello there, wife." With one palm planted firmly at her back, I drop her into a dip. Then I drop a kiss onto the sweetest lips in history.

This moment is everything I ever dreamed of, and barely hoped someday would come true. I started life out with a pretty full heart.

Then Sara Hathaway made it fuller.

The End.

**Want more of Sara and Three's happily ever after?
Grab their bonus epilogue at Juliechristianson.com!**

Let's have some fun!

Also by Julie Christianson

The Abieville Love Stories Series:

That Time I Kissed My Brother's Best Friend

That Time I Kissed The Groomsman Grump

That Time I Kissed My Beachfront Boss

That Time We Kissed Under the Mistletoe

The Apple Valley Love Stories Series:

The Mostly Real McCoy: A Sweet Romantic Comedy (Apple Valley Love Stories Book 1)

My Own Best Enemy: A Sweet Romantic Comedy (Apple Valley Love Stories Book 2)

Pretending I Love Lucy: A Sweet Romantic Comedy (Apple Valley Love Stories Book 3)

The Even Odder Couple: A Sweet Romantic Comedy (Apple Valley Love Stories Book 4)

Jill Came Tumbling: A Sweet Romantic Comedy (An Apple Valley Love Story Novella)

The Sweater Weather Series

Faking the Fall: A Fake-Dating Celebrity RomCom

A Note from Julie

This book is only a reality after a series of stops and starts. I began writing *That Time We Kissed Under the Mistletoe* two years ago —in 2022—with just the seed of the opening chapter running through my mind. I liked the premise, but I started to worry that a series starting with a holiday plot line might be somewhat limiting.

Also, full disclosure, I was a little sad about having completed the Apple Valley Love Stories series. I just wasn't ready to dive head-first into my next one. (Also I'm terrible at strategy.)

Instead, I took my novella *My Red, White & Blue Christmas* and turned it into *That Time I Kissed My Brother's Best Friend* to release in November of that year. Did you notice that this places a holiday book at the beginning of the series? Yeah. Me too.

See also: Not good at strategy. Still, I love Kasey and Beau's mashup of the 4th of July and Christmas, so I'm cool with the way things turned out.

At that point, though, I felt like I couldn't write *Under the Mistletoe* and have TWO holiday books back to back, let alone release a Christmas romcom in the spring, so I wrote *That Time I Kissed the Groomsman Grump*. I love that book so much. I have zero regrets. Natalie and Brady will forever be one of my favorite couples.

But you'd think it would finally be *Under the Mistletoe*'s time to shine over the Christmas of 2023, right?

Yep. Me, too. But the bulk of my focus last fall was taken up by the Sweater Weather series, one of the highlights of my author career. Still no regrets. And although I started working on *Under the Mistletoe* again after *Faking the Fall*, I felt too rushed. I didn't want to dash off a story I didn't love just for the sake of publishing a Christmas book in December.

So I decided to push *Under the Mistletoe* one more year, and I wrote *That Time I Kissed My Beachfront Boss*. Getting to include Hadley and Link from *Faking the Fall* in Olivia and Hudson's story was a real treat, and I adore that book with my whole heart.

Totally worth the reshuffle. Which brings us to 2024. FINALLY.

Working on *Under the Mistletoe* for the third time was … daunting. By then, I'd released three other books in the series. As an author, I'd changed. The characters had developed. The town had evolved. My heart had grown three sizes for the people of Abieville. (Especially for my MMC, Three.)

I wanted *Under the Mistletoe* to not only be a great Christmas story, but also a great romcom that could stand alone outside of the rest of the holidays. I was ready to make this the best book I'd ever written. (NO PRESSURE, JULIE!)

TLDR:
I don't think I've ever worked harder on a project than this one.
I love Christmas, and I love my readers.
I hope this brings you comfort and joy all year long.

XO,
Julie

#noregrets

Acknowledgments

First, I'm going back to the beginning to thank my mom and dad (again) for being the best parents any human's ever had in the history of ever. My sister, Nancy, and I are just the luckiest to have Jim and Diane Christianson as our role models and constant cheerleaders.

Side note: I call the four of us Original Christianson, the inspiration for Three Fuller's family text thread. (The love is real, for their fictional family and ours.)

Next up: my incredible husband and wonderful kids. There aren't enough good words to express my devotion to these three, how supported I feel, how beyond grateful I am to be Bill's wife and the mother of Jack and Karly. See also: my fur babies, Scout and Zoe, who keep mama company all day, every day. Thank you, sweet girls.

Leah, Kortney, and Christina: Thank you for always lifting me up, making me laugh, and having my back. I love you ladies hard. (Sorry if that sounds a little dirty - ha!)

Kiki, Jenny, Melanie, Patty, Carina, and Courtney: Your friendship and the Sweater Weather collaboration has been a dream come true. Thank you for letting me be a part of something so magical. There's no other way to describe it.

Brittany: I can't wait for our Texas adventure to begin, and you *might* even get me into a yoga class someday. Here's to future heart-to-heart talks on the beach. (You're a gem.)

Jennie: I owe my career to you, plain and simple. I'll cherish you forever, friend. (*Bisous!*)

To the WST, Charlene, Kim, Laurel, Rina, and Shauna: For ten years, we've shared our hearts with each other, our dreams, our hopes and fears ... and I am so thankful to have this group in my life.

Jo and Ranee: You talk me off cliffs, point out plot gaps, make suggestions, and encourage me to keep working until I've got the best story I'm capable of writing. From my very first book until this one, thank you, thank you.

Theresa at Marginalia Editing: Your proofreading skills are amazing. (Any remaining errors are my own!)

To Shaela at Blue Water Books: Your covers were the first, best investment I made in my author career.

Karen: Your brain is my last line of content-defense and making sure my "California doesn't show" lol! I love having you for a bonus sister. PS: I picked Ohio State over UNC for you.

To my dear, sweet, hard-working, steadfast, committed, loyal Bookstagram friends: Your love and support are a constant source of inspiration, and I only keep writing these stories for you. At some point during each scene, I pause to think about pleasing YOU.

What will make you grin? Laugh? Get a little teary-eyed? Burst with joy? So thank you from the bottom of my heart for being my reason.

Every single one of you.

About the Author

Julie Christianson is a former high school English teacher and current romcom addict living in the suburbs of Los Angeles.

A lapsed marathon runner, Julie loves her hilarious family, her two crazy rescue dogs, and cracking up at her own jokes. Her goal is to write stories that make you laugh out loud, fall in love, and live happily ever after.

Learn more about her books at juliechristianson.com.

Made in the USA
Columbia, SC
02 October 2024

42958354R00202

MY HOLLY JOLLY CHRISTMAS JUST WENT UP IN SMOKE. LITERALLY...

Playing nursemaid to Bradford "Three" Fuller is the last thing I need for Christmas.

But for the next few days, I'm stuck in charge of my ex's sparkling eyes, his ridiculous abs, and his (mostly) accidental kisses.

I don't have a choice.

You see, Three's only hurt because of me. And not like he hurt me a decade ago. Like... I literally concussed the man with a fire extinguisher.

Still, a make-or-break mission for my parents is what brought me back to the small town where he crushed my tender heart in the first place.

And if I screw up, I risk my mother's approval plus the job at my father's law firm I've worked for my entire life.

So I sure hope Santa stuffs my stocking full of self-control. And a defibrillator.

Because my heart just may be broken by this second chance with Three...

ISBN 9798339213482

9 798339 213482

9000

JULIECHRISTIANSON.COM